Feminism and the Family in England

For Eugénie

Feminism and the Family in England 1880–1939

Carol Dyhouse

Basil Blackwell

Basil Blackwell Ltd
108 Cowley Road, Oxford, OX4 1JF, UK

Basil Blackwell Inc.
432 Park Avenue South, Suite 1503
New York, NY 10016, USA

British Library Cataloguing in Publication Data

Dyhouse, Carol, *1948–*
    Feminism and the family in England
    1880–1939
    1. England. Families. Role of women, 1880–1993
    I. Title
    306.8'5'0942

    ISBN 0–631–16735–8
    ISBN 0–631–16736–6 PBK

Library of Congress Cataloging in Publication Data

Dyhouse, Carol, 1948–
    Feminism and the family in England, 1880–1939/Carol Dyhouse.
       p.   cm.
    Includes index.
    ISBN 0–631–16735–8: – ISBN 0–631–16736–6 (pbk.):
    1. Family – England – History – 19th century. 2. Family – England
    – History – 20th century. 3. Marriage – England – History – 19th
    century. 4. Marriage – England – History – 20th century.
    5. Feminism and literature – England – History – 19th century.
    6. Feminism and literature – England – History – 20th century.
    I. Title.
    HQ615.D94   1989
    305.4'2'0942 – dc19

Typeset in 11 on 12 pt Baskerville
by Setrite.
Printed in Great Britain by T. J Press, Padstow

Contents

Introduction

This book is concerned with feminist thinking about the family during the period between about 1880 and 1939. Rather surprisingly, this is not yet an area which has been explored in detail. The literature on the history of feminism in late-nineteenth- and early-twentieth-century England has traditionally tended to concentrate on education and the suffrage movement. We have recently seen the publication of important new work on sexuality and prostitution (by Judith Walkowitz, Jeffrey Weeks and others) − work which is clearly of relevance to the study of both feminism and contemporary ideas about family life.[1] Writing on the history of feminism has also broadened its scope to explore feminism as a social movement and to look more carefully at its ideology. Texts such as Olive Banks's *Becoming a Feminist: The Social Origins of First Wave Feminism* (1986)[2] and Les Garner's *Stepping Stones to Women's Liberty: Feminist Ideas in the Women's Suffrage Movement 1900−1918* (1984)[3] contain much that relates to our theme, as does the collection of essays edited by Jane Lewis, *Labour and Love: Women's Experience*

[1] See, for instance, Judith R. Walkowitz, *Prostitution and Victorian Society: Women, Class and the State* (Cambridge University Press, London 1980); Walkowitz, 'Male vice and feminist virtue: feminism and the politics of prostitution in nineteenth century Britain', *History Workshop Journal* (Spring 1982); Jeffrey Weeks, *Sex, Politics and Society: The Regulation of Sexuality since 1800* (Longman, London and New York, 1981).

[2] Olive Banks, *Becoming a Feminist: The Social Origins of 'First Wave' Feminism* (Wheatsheaf, Brighton, 1986). See also the same author's *Faces of Feminism: A Study of Feminism as a Social Movement* (Martin Robertson, Oxford, 1981).

[3] Les Garner, *Stepping Stones to Women's Liberty: Feminist Ideas in the Women's Suffrage Movement 1900−1918* (Heinemann, London, 1984). See also David Rubenstein, *Before the Suffragettes: Women's Emancipation in the 1890s* (Harvester, Brighton, 1986).

2	*Introduction*

of Home and Family 1850—1940 (1986).[4] But none of these texts
has chosen to address feminism's involvement with the family
as its central concern.

It is interesting to note that two studies which appeared
slightly earlier than these seem to have made an important
impact on the literature dealing with the history of feminism.
These texts, Olive and J. A. Banks's *Feminism and Family Planning
in Victorian England* (1964)[5] and Constance Rover's *Love, Morals
and the Feminists* (1970),[6] both emphasized the conservatism of
feminists on issues concerning the family and sexuality. Olive
and J. A. Banks's contention that feminists played little part in
advancing the campaign for birth control has subsequently
been challenged, most notably by Angus McLaren, whose important study of *Birth Control in Nineteenth Century England* appeared
in 1978.[7] Rover's study had itself drawn heavily on the Banks's
interpretation of late-Victorian feminism as having shied away
from the socially explosive issue of family limitation in the last
quarter of the century. At least up until the First World War,
alleged Rover, 'The charge against the main groups of feminists . . . is that they supposed the rigid code of Victorian morality
rather than claiming for women emotional and sexual freedom
as well as civil rights.'[8] But over the last ten years feminists
have grown more careful about the meaning of 'emotion and
sexual freedom' for women in specific historical contexts. The
theme has been brought under critical scrutiny, for instance in
Martha Vicinus's *Independent Women: Work and Community for
Single Women 1850—1920* (1985)[9] and in the work of Sheila Jeffreys
and Margaret Jackson.[10]

Jane Lewis (ed.), *Labour and Love: Women's Experience of Home and Family,
1850—1940* (Blackwell, Oxford, 1986).
[5] J. A. and O. Banks, *Feminism and Family Planning in Victorian England*
(Liverpool University Press, Liverpool, 1964).
[6] Constance Rover, *Love, Morals and the Feminists* (Routledge & Kegan Paul,
London, 1970).
[7] Angus McLaren, *Birth Control in Nineteenth Century England* (Croom Helm,
London, 1978). See especially ch. 11, 'Feminism and fertility control'.
[8] Rover, *Love, Morals and the Feminists*, p. 145.
[9] Martha Vicinus, *Independent Women: Work and Community for Single Women
1850—1920* (Virago, London, 1985).
[10] Sheila Jeffreys, '"Free from all uninvited touch of man": women's cam-
paigns around sexuality, 1880—1914', *Women's Studies International Forum*, 6,

However, the interpretations put forward by Olive and J. A. Banks and Constance Rover have proved tenacious, and still echo in the literature. Patricia Stubbs, for example, confidently asserted in her study of *Women in Fiction* (1979) that nineteenth-century feminists 'were unaware of the part played by the family and its ideology in perpetuating women's oppressions'.[11] In accounting for the near-hysterical response which feminism aroused in some contemporaries, however, she has to concede that *potentially* feminism went far beyond limited demands for education, political rights, and jobs:

> In its furthest implications it was likely to question the very basis of social organisation — the family — and it contained the potential for direct confrontation with the dominant sexual ideology, which affected everyone, not just women. Not surprisingly then, it was seen by its opponents as a dangerous challenge to the stability of bourgeois society. The feminists themselves were the first to deny this. But if they were blind to the revolutionary possibilities of their movement, their opponents were not.[12]

Just why it should be likely that the *opponents* of a movement should enjoy a clearer idea of its potential than its *proponents* is by no means self-evident. In any case, and as the following chapters will illustrate, many nineteenth- and early-twentieth-century feminists were absolutely clear about feminism's challenge to contemporary forms of family life. Indeed, it was precisely their dissatisfaction with the family that fuelled their feminism.

It is not easy to define 'feminism'; there have been numerous attempts, but none is completely satisfactory. Most historians would agree that feminism has carried different meanings for

no. 6 (1982), and the same author's *The Spinster and Her Enemies: Feminism and Sexuality, 1880–1930* (Pandora, London, 1985); Margaret Jackson, 'Sexual liberation or social control? Some aspects of the relationship between feminism and the social construction of sexual knowledge in the early twentieth century', *Women's Studies International Forum*, 6, no. 1 (1983). See also Linda Gordon and Ellen Dubois, 'Seeking ecstasy on the battlefield: danger and pleasure in nineteenth century feminist thought', *Feminist Review*, no. 13 (1983).

[11] Patricia Stubbs, *Women in Fiction: Feminism and the Novel, 1880–1920* (Harvester, Brighton, 1979), p. 128.

[12] Ibid., p. 133.

4   *Introduction*

different groups of feminists at different points in history.[13]
Basically, feminists have seen themselves and can be regarded
as those who have identified a problem in the social relationships
existing between men and women, deriving from an imbalance
of power operating in favour of the former. However, there
have always been competing explanations and analyses of the
problem and these have given rise to different strategies for
change. The struggle for the vote in England between 1890 and
1914 represented a rallying point, allowing feminists of all shades
of outlook to find some common ground. But no simple consensus
characterized feminist attitudes to marriage, sexuality, or
family life.

In *Faces of Feminism* (1981) Olive Banks has claimed that
three different intellectual strands existed within the movement
between 1840 and 1961. These she identifies as Evangelicalism,
the Equal Rights and the Socialist traditions of feminism.[14]
Caroline Rowan has suggested that it is helpful to think in
terms of a 'spectrum of feminisms' coexisting in England around
the beginning of the present century, corresponding in part to
differences in social class and political outlook.[15] Both of these
writers have highlighted some of the ways in which differences
in class and political affiliation amongst feminists were reflected
in their attitudes to the family. We might consider it equally
possible that differing attitudes to the family may have influenced
feminist political allegiances during the period.

Olive Banks has contended that late-nineteenth- and early-
twentieth-century Socialism was characterized by deeply conservative views about the family, in marked contrast with the
Owenite Socialism of the early nineteenth century.[16] This conservatism surfaced particularly in the pursuit of policies to

[13] See, among others, O. Banks, *The Biographical Dictionary of British Feminists*,
Vol. I, 1880–1930 (Wheatsheaf, Brighton, 1985), pp. vii–viii; Banks, *Faces of
Feminism*, pp. 3–4; Carol Dyhouse, *Girls Growing Up in Late Victorian and
Edwardian England* (Routledge & Kegan Paul, London, 1981), pp. 139–44;
Philippa Levine, *Victorian Feminism, 1850–1900* (Hutchinson, London, 1987),
p. 14ff.
[14] Banks, *Faces of Feminism*, pp. 7–9 and *passim*.
[15] Caroline Rowan, 'Women in the Labour Party, 1906–1920', *Feminist
Review*, no. 12 (October 1982).
[16] Banks, *Becoming a Feminist*, p. 150.

'protect' wives and mothers in the working-class family and the labour market, most crucially through the defence of the ideal of the 'family wage'. She sees such policies as representing an important break with earlier traditions of 'equal rights' feminism, which had sought to strengthen women's position in the labour market, and, moving in the direction of economic individualism, had often implied a more radical critique of the family and the idea of a 'breadwinning' male. Caroline Rowan has described, similarly, how working-class women within the Labour Movement developed a feminist analysis which first and foremost asserted the value of a woman's role as domestic worker and child-rearer within the family,[17] an outlook which contrasted strongly with the individualism of many middle-class feminists.

However, it is important to recognize that although such divisions existed, they were by no means clearly drawn. Some working-class feminists, such as the ex-factory worker Ada Nield Chew, were as 'individualist' as middle-class feminists in their attitudes to women's economic independence.[18] And perhaps one of the most potentially radical of all critiques of the late-Victorian family came from a group of early-twentieth-century, largely middle-class Socialist feminists, the members of the Fabian Society Women's Group, who set themselves the task of thinking about how best to guarantee economic independence to women under Socialism in the years between 1908 and 1981. In practice, Labour politics and the emergence of particular concepts of social welfare in early-twentieth-century Britain certainly served to institutionalize a conservative vision of family life. But Socialist thinking about the family retained deep ambiguities throughout this period and beyond.

Much of the feminist criticism of, and invective against, the family in late-nineteenth-century England was not rejection of the family as a social institution in itself, still less of the family as an *ideal*. Rather it amounted to criticism of a particular

[17] Rowan, 'Women in the Labour Party'; see also the same author's '"Mothers, Vote Labour!" The State, the Labour Movement and working class mothers, 1900–1918', in *Feminism, Culture and Politics*, ed. Rosalind Brunt and Caroline Rowan (Lawrence & Wishart, London, 1982).

[18] Doris Nield Chew, *Ada Nield Chew: The Life and Writings of a Working Woman* (Virago, London, 1982).

manifestation of the family, that of the Victorian bourgeoisie. It was precisely their experiences of the Victorian patriarchal family — their experiences as dependent wives and daughters — which spurred many middle-class women towards developing a feminist viewpoint. The first chapter of this book therefore explores women's experiences of family life, and the discontents which fostered a critique.

The investigation of feminist attitudes to family life is not straightforward: the 'private' sphere of the family is less accessible to the historian than the 'public' arena of parliamentary and political debate. In recent years many feminists have adopted Kate Millett's term 'sexual politics' to indicate their understanding that power determines the structure of private, sexual and familial relationships and is not only contested in the public, more conventionally delegated 'political' arenas of social life.[19] Much of the resentment of and struggle against women's subordination has probably always taken place in the family, but these personal, political struggles have commonly been hidden from the public gaze. It is much easier to find out about women's organized campaign for the suffrage between 1860 and 1918 than it is to explore wider areas of feminist activity and thought during the period, and this is one of the reasons why historians have in the past so easily slipped into assuming an equation between suffragism and feminism. The sources which have been drawn upon in the process of carrying out research for this book have been extremely varied, and have included autobiographies, essays, polemical tracts, feminist journals and newspapers, histories, novels and other forms of imaginative literature. Even so, large areas of women's experience in the family remain shadowy. What follows should be regarded as an exploration rather than a definitive account.

[19] Kate Millett, *Sexual Politics* (Abacus, London, 1971).

1

Women's Experiences of Family Life: Towards a Feminist Critique

At the age of thirty-two, and in great agitation, tortured by despair at the seeming futility of her life, Florence Nightingale attempted to order her thoughts about the family and its constriction of women's lives.[1] She was well aware that in trying to give voice to the sense of injustice and oppression she felt, she was more likely to elicit anger than sympathy from the Victorian public. Men 'are irritated with women for not being happy',[2] she realized, all too clearly, and indeed it seems that it was in deference to the advice of the male intellectual establishment – represented here in the person of Benjamin Jowett, Regius Professor of Classics in Oxford – that Nightingale's three-volume book, *Suggestions for Thought to Searchers after Religious Truth*, was never published.[3] Jowett found her work too 'full of antagonisms', and strongly recommended some softening of its passionately feminist message. Nightingale set to and attempted to follow his advice, chopping and revising her manuscript. But although privately printed in 1860, the work was never to be formally published in her lifetime. A fragment of the whole

[1] Florence Nightingale, *Cassandra* (1852, revised 1859). This essay was published as an Appendix to Ray Strachey's *The Cause: A short History of the Women's Movement in Great Britain* (Bell, 1928), which has been reprinted by Cedric Chivers (Bath, 1974).

[2] Ibid., p. 396.

[3] Ibid. See also Elaine Showalter, *The Female Malady: Women, Madness and English Culture, 1830–1980* (Virago, London, 1987), p. 66.

finally appeared as an appendix (entitled *Cassandra*) to Ray Strachey's short history of the women's movement in Great Britain, *The Cause*, which was published in 1928.

Elaine Showalter has observed that 'in its history of thwarted publication, as well as in its accounts of women's confinement in the family and the psychic costs of that confinement', *Cassandra* affords 'one of the most striking examples of the silencing of female protest'.[4] There is a clear and disturbing parallel to be drawn between Nightingale's own attempts to trim her manuscript, to soften its antagonisms and to contain the force of its vehemence, and the very processes of social repression with which she was concerned. She herself saw the suffocation of women's ambitions, passions and intellects in the family as a warping of the spirit analogous to the process of physical stunting produced by the Chinese custom of binding young girls' feet.[5]

Private and public

I have chosen to begin with Florence Nightingale's testimony in *Cassandra*, because although it was written before the period with which this book is primarily concerned it is such a powerful statement of experience, and one which has resonated over the years: feminists could clearly identify with its 'antagonisms' in 1928 and indeed it can still be read with a shock of recognition by women today. Nightingale's bitterness about the female predicament ('Look at the poor lives we lead'[6]) was rooted in personal frustration. At the time of writing *Cassandra* she had found no outlet for her immense energies of spirit in the context of the family life which she shared with her parents and sister, and her frustrations kept her precariously close to the point of complete breakdown. Writing allowed her to reach beyond the confines and pain of her predicament towards some kind of social analysis. She saw that the family as she knew it — and her background, of course, was that of the wealthy Victorian

---

[4] Ibid.
[5] *Cassandra*, in Strachey *The Cause*, p. 396.
[6] Ibid., p. 399.

middle class — had entirely different meanings for men and women. For middle-class men, the 'private' sphere of the family offered a daily point of entry into the 'public' world of important issues; for women, it became a prison. Large purposes, be they social or intellectual, were denied to women, who would often 'Sink to living from breakfast till dinner, from dinner till tea, with a little worsted work, and to looking forward to nothing but bed'[7]. And yet the *idea* of the family was so sacred that women were willing to sacrifice *themselves* to it. Nightingale was too aware of her own struggles to assume that this was always an easy process: 'With what labour women have toiled to break down all individual and independent life, in order to fit themselves for this social and domestic existence, thinking it right!'[8] Her prose erupts with rage at both the costs of this sacrifice and also at what she sees as the 'hypocrisy' of women — particularly mothers — who teach their daughters to conform:

> her own sex unites against her ... they write books to persuade themselves that 'domestic life is their sphere' and to idealise 'the sacred hearth'. Sacred it is indeed. Sacred from the touch of their sons almost as soon as they are out of childhood — from its dullness and its tyrannous trifling *these* recoil. Sacred from the grasp of their daughter's affections upon which it has so light a hold that they seize the first opportunity of marriage, *their* only chance of emancipation. The 'sacred hearth'; sacred to their husband's sleep, their sons' absence in the body and their daughters in mind.[9]

This double-edged attitude to women, where they are both pitied (as victims) and yet resented (as oppressors of other women in the family) is a key theme in *Cassandra*, and there can be no doubt that even in the truncated version which eventually appeared in 1928 the dominant emotion is that of *rage*. Nightingale was infuriated with women for not puncturing through the idealized rhetoric of family life; in her mind it was *women* who needed to be aroused from ideological stupefaction into an awareness of their own deprivation:

[7] Ibid., p. 403.
[8] Ibid., p. 408.
[9] Ibid., p. 415.

Oh! Mothers, who talk about this hearth, how much do you know
of your sons' real life, how much of your daughters' imaginary one?
Awake, ye women, all ye that sleep, awake! If this domestic life
were so very good, would your young men wander away from it,
your maidens think of something else?[10]

Nightingale observed that some women rejected the idea of
marrying because they calculated that the costs of family life in
terms of its erosion of personal autonomy for women were too
great. The choice, for her, was a stark one: 'Some few sacrifice
marriage, because they sacrifice all other life if they accept
that.'[11] There can be no doubt that a sizeable minority of
middle-class women *did* see marriage as incompatible with any
life of social purpose and self-respect.[12] Nightingale herself chose
not to marry, as did Dorothea Beale and Frances Buss, the
two well-known pioneering headmistresses of the nineteenth
century,[13] and many other women engaged in educational,
social and political work made the same choice. Even when
they did eventually choose to marry, many feminists arrived at
the decision with trepidation, anxious about the loss of personal
freedom which this might entail. However, Olive Banks, who
has examined in detail the personal histories of a sample of
ninety-eight British feminists in the nineteenth and early twentieth centuries, has emphasized that although single women
played an important role in the development of feminism, the
women's movement could never at any time be described as a
movement of spinsters. Although a minority of the first generation
of women in her sample (that is, those born before 1828) ever
married, this minority was sizeable (46 per cent), and taking

[10] Ibid.

[11] Ibid., p. 407.

[12] See, for instance, Martha Vicinus, *Independent Women: Work and Community
for Single Women 1850–1920* (Virago, London, 1985) and Sheila Jeffreys, *The
Spinster and Her Enemies: Feminism and Sexuality, 1880–1930* (Pandora, London,
1985).

[13] Josephine Kamm, *How Different from Us: A Biography of Miss Buss and
Miss Beale* (Bodley Head, London, 1958). See also Carol Dyhouse, 'Miss Buss
and Miss Beale, gender and authority in the history of education', in *Lessons
for Life: The Schooling of Girls and Women 1850–1950*, ed. Felicity Hunt (Blackwell,
Oxford, 1987).

her sample as a whole the proportions were reversed, with over half the women she studied marrying at some point.[14]

In *Becoming a Feminist* Olive Banks set out to explore the life histories of feminists (including fourteen men classified as 'feminists', alongside the ninety-eight women), in order to learn about the ways in which their family backgrounds may have shaped their feminism. This involved her in exploring what sociologists have called 'families of origin' as well as 'families of destination'. In respect of the former her findings were less than conclusive and she has admitted that much of the evidence was rather slender.[15] She found a *slight* tendency for the women in her sample to have come from families where they had had rather cool or difficult relationships with their mothers, contrasting with comparatively affectionate ties with fathers, who were more encouraging of their daughter's ambitions or professional success. But not all those she studied fitted this pattern, and some of the women had been brought up by mothers who themselves espoused feminist convictions.[16] With 'families of destination' Olive Banks found a more clearly defined pattern, remarking on the extent to which the feminists in her sample 'sometime perhaps unconsciously, but often consciously' sought husbands who shared their views on marriage and family life, whilst others, 'fearing the effect of marriage on their freedom, avoided it altogether'.[17]

Banks's very interesting study raises a number of important questions. She herself is well aware of the difficulties of defining feminism, of selection, and of typicality. In the study being discussed (and also in her work more generally) she has tended to concentrate on the *public* face of feminism, and to use involvement in public political activism as a criterion for selection. In her own words, she singles out women who were 'activists' rather than 'sympathizers' for study.[18] This may be seen as a partial exploration, since there were undoubtedly huge numbers

[14] Olive Banks, *Becoming a Feminist: The Social Origins of 'First Wave' Feminism* (Wheatsheaf, Brighton, 1986), p. 35.
[15] Ibid., p. 26.
[16] Ibid., p. 28.
[17] Ibid., pp. 36–40.
[18] Ibid., p. 3.

of Victorian women who may have expressed feminist sympathies in their writing and in their lives whilst shunning political platforms, and even more whose immersion in what present-day feminists would call the 'sexual politics' of family life thwarted any possibility of getting near such platforms in the first place. But aside from these difficulties of definition, selection and representativeness there are complex questions which we need to ask about the nature of women's experiences and how the historian should set about exploring and making sense of these. The most obvious source of evidence available for the exploration of family backgrounds comes from autobiographical and biographical accounts, and Banks's study relies heavily on these. But there are problems in using and relying upon text of this kind. The writing of an autobiography involves an *interpretation* of experience; it is essentially an editing of one's life from a particular standpoint, and the stance will be affected by a number of considerations. One such consideration will be a consciousness of the effect of the account upon its audience. Most people writing autobiographies will be constrained by some awareness, for instance, of the feelings of any members of their family or friends still living who are likely to read about themselves in the text. Many (probably most) people have very strong feelings about their family lives, and many seek relief in trying to order these thoughts and feelings through writing. If the account is for publication, this equal imperative to mute straightforwardly personal testimony (or 'to soften antagonisms')[19] in deference to the feelings of others may intervene, and no doubt partly accounts for the fact that we can sometimes learn much more about a writer through his or her imaginative 'fiction' than through 'straight' autobiographical writing. For instance, it is probably the case that we can explore the attitudes of the twentieth-century feminist writer, Vera Brittain, to family life and relationships more fully through her novel, *Honourable Estate*, than through her much-celebrated autobiography of childhood and early life, *Testament of Youth*, published in 1933.[20]

[19] Cf. Jowett's advice to Florence Nightingale, n. 3 above.
[20] Vera Brittain, *Honourable Estate: A Novel of Transition* (Gollancz, London, 1936), and *Testament of Youth: An Autobiographical Study of the Years 1900–1925* (Gollancz, London, 1933).

Experience itself is rarely 'of one piece', and difficult to take
stock of. People's feelings about their families may be powerful,
but they are most often profoundly ambivalent; moreover they
show a marked tendency to change through time. In writing
about the past, one engages in a dialogue with what is remembered, but it is never possible wholly to resurrect an earlier self.
Again, if we look at Vera Brittain's writings about her family
background, the diaries which she kept as a young girl give a
very different picture of her relationships with her parents from
that which we might derive from *Testament of Youth*.[21] And yet
both accounts are in some sense 'true'.

The accounts which people render of their lives are necessarily
partial, their pattern rarely fixed. Autobiographies may supply
insights, but never the whole story. Biographies are even more
complex documents, involving as they must do an additional
dialogue; the interpretation, construction (and often justification)
of someone else's life. Insights into a writer's attitudes and
relationships can be derived from imaginative literature as well
as from autobiographical writing; indeed, the distinction between
'fact' and 'fiction' can often be seen as an oversimplified distinction and a misleading one. Historians need to recognize
these complexities. Whilst we may read everything which may
help to throw light on the lives of those in the past who interest
us, we must always read between the lines, and we must always
read with care. Exploring women's experiences of family life
forces one to be aware of these issues. If pressed to summarize
the attitude of most feminists towards the family in late-Victorian
and early-twentieth-century Britain I would find myself resorting
to (or taking refuge in) the concept of *ambivalence*. This is
undoubtedly partly because most people have always found
their greatest source of emotional support, and equally a source
of their greatest personal frustrations, in relationships with 'significant others' in the family. It is plain that the very force of a

---

[21] Alan Bishop (ed.). *Chronicle of Youth: Vera Brittain's War Diary, 1913–1917*
(Gollancz, London, 1981). For a discussion of some of the contrasts between
Vera Brittain's accounts of experience in her diaries and in *Testament of Youth*,
see Carol Dyhouse, 'Mothers and daughters in the middle class home,
c. 1870–1914', in *Labour and Love: Women's Experience of Home and Family
1850–1940*, ed. Jane Lewis (Blackwell, Oxford, 1986), pp. 42–4.

denunciation such as Nightingale's rested on the power of her attachments to the family in which she had grown up, and her attempts to wrest loose from such attachments induced in her a degree of somatic illness from which she was never entirely to recover.[22] In the rest of this chapter I shall attempt to sketch patterns of experience shared by many women in the living of their lives in the family through the years 1880–1939, and I shall concentrate on their frustrations, not because this was ever the whole picture, but because it was the sharing of common frustrations which made possible a feminist critique.

Images of constraint and belittlement

One way of exploring women's frustrations with family life is through the use of imagery and metaphor in their writing. I have already remarked upon the way in which Florence Nightingale saw the social construction of femininity in the family as a process of stunting a young girl's autonomy analogous to footbinding. Nightingale's little-known contemporary, a nonconformist schoolmistress called Mary Smith, similarly argued that lower down the social scale the 'feet of Englishwomen's souls' were crippled by an excess of small domestic tasks (especially needlework) which fell to their lot in childhood.[23] Olive Schreiner has her fictional heroine Lyndall lament to Waldo on this process of stunting and belittling, in *The Story of an African Farm* (1883):

> They begin to shape us to our cursed end ... when we are tiny things in shoes and socks. We sit with our little feet drawn up under us in the window, and look out at the boys in their happy play. We want to go. Then a loving hand is laid on us: 'Little one, you cannot go,' they say; 'your little face will burn, and your nice white dress be spoiled.' We feel it must be for our own good, it is so lovingly said; but we cannot understand; and we still kneel with one little cheek wistfully pressed against the pane. Afterwards we

[22] Cecil Woodham-Smith, *Florence Nightingale, 1820–1910* (The Reprint Society, London, 1952).

[23] Mary Smith, *The Autobiography of Mary Smith, Schoolmistress and Nonconformist: A Fragment of a Life* (Bemrose, London, 1892), p. 32.

go and thread blue beads, and make a string for our neck; and we go and stand before the glass. We see the complexion we were not to spoil, and the white frock, and we look into our own great eyes. Then the curse begins to act on us. It finishes its work when we are grown women, who no more look out wistfully at a more healthy life; we are contented. We fit our sphere as a Chinese woman's foot fits her shoe, exactly, as though God had made both — and yet He knows nothing of either. In some of us the shaping to our end has been quite completed. The parts we have not to use have been quite atrophied, and have even dropped off; but in others, and we are not less to be pitied, they have been weakened and left. We wear the bandages, but our limbs have not grown to them; we know that we are compressed, and chafe against them.[24]

The imagery of restriction here, of dwarfing or stunting, is powerful, and clearly it was passages like this which accounted for the impact of the novel on feminists at the turn of the century and beyond.[25]

Images of confinement, claustrophobia and belittlement abound in feminist discourse on family life. Home was frequently depicted as a prison, or a cage (even if 'gilded' or 'upholstered'), where young female fledglings had their wings clipped, as it were, against flight. Constance Louisa Maynard, the first Mistress of Westfield College, London, recalled that her experience of childhood and adolescence in the family home along with her sister Gazy was one of being 'shut up like eagles in a henhouse', with her mother being responsible for a constant 'pat pat patting down of all ambition' which might strengthen the resolve to lead an independent life.[26]

[24] Olive Schreiner, *The Story of an African Farm: A Novel* (Hutchinson, London, 1883), pp. 203–4.

[25] A pupil of Cheltenham Ladies' College at the end of the nineteenth century recalled that when a friend in her boarding house 'smuggled in *The Story of an African Farm*, just out, the whole sky seemed aflame, and many of us became violent feminists'. See A. Huth Jackson, *A Victorian Childhood* (Methuen, London, 1932), pp. 160–1. See also Vera Brittain's comment: 'To Olive Schreiner's *Woman and Labour* — that "Bible of the Woman's Movement" which sounded to the world of 1911 as insistent and inspiring as a trumpet-call summoning the faithful to a vital crusade — was due my final acceptance of feminism.' (*Testament of Youth*, p. 41.)

[26] C. B. Firth, *Constance Louisa Maynard, Mistress of Westfield College: A Family Portrait* (Allen & Unwin, London, 1949), pp. 54, 58.

Even as the product of an intellectual and privileged family in Oxford, growing up in the 1900s, Naomi Mitchison recalled her girlhood experience of feeling constantly 'netted by invisible rules'.[27] The twinned experiences of confinement and belittlement were also powerfully conveyed in the image of the doll's house, which gained widespread currency in feminist discussion after the production of Ibsen's play *A Doll's House* in London in 1889. Nora's rejection of her role as a child-wife in the play, her breaking free from family ties in a bid for personal maturity, caused heated public controversy, one product of which was the publication of alternative sequels to the play, with feminists (George Bernard Shaw, Israel Zangwill and Eleanor Marx) and anti-feminists (Walter Besant) attempting to drive home conflicting ideological points of view.[28]

Sisters and brothers

Families where there were children of both sexes afforded daughters scope for comparison of their own treatment and upbringing with that of their brothers, and the autobiographies of middle-class women abound with such comparisons. Particularly as puberty approached, girls were hedged around with many more restrictions on their freedom than boys, and girls were expected to defer to, and to dance attendance upon, their brothers.[29] Some women recorded that they accepted this as the natural order of things. M. V. Hughes, growing up in a middle-class family with three brothers in London in the 1870s, found that her parents presented a united front on the question of gender: 'My father's slogan was that boys should go everywhere and know everything, and that a girl should stay at home and know nothing.'[30] Her mother endorsed this with clear rules of

[27] Naomi Mitchison, *All Change Here* (Bodley Head, London, 1975), p. 24.
[28] See Walter Besant, 'The Doll's House − and after', *The English Illustrated Magazine*, (January 1890); George Bernard Shaw, 'Still after The Doll's House', *Time* (February 1890); and Eleanor Marx and Israel Zangwill, 'A Doll's House repaired', *Time* (March 1891).
[29] Carol Dyhouse, *Girls Growing Up in Late Victorian and Edwardian England* (Routledge & Kegan Paul, London, 1981), pp. 9−17.
[30] M. V. Hughes, *A London Child of the 1870s* (Oxford University Press, London 1977), p. 33.

precedence; boys were to come first: 'I came last in all distribution of food at table, treats of sweets and so on. I was
expected to wait on the boys, run messages, fetch things left
upstairs, and never grumble, let alone refuse.'[31] On one level
Hughes tries to give the impression that she accepted these
rules without resentment, and even with gratitude, noting that
she had never ceased 'to thank her mother for this early bit of
training',[32] and clearly deference to the male intellect became a
deeply internalized part of her personality, as any reader of her
autobiographical trilogy, *A London Family*, first published in its
entirety in 1946, will quickly learn.[33] But this is an example of a
text which is not easy to read as 'evidence' in any straightforward
way. Its tone is highly nostalgic and idealized, and the reader
cannot but wonder whether the writer has laboured over much
to present a rosy picture. In any case, there are hints of other
emotions, even if these are (or were) quickly suppressed:

'How I wish I were a boy!' Mother caught me saying this aloud
one day, and promptly told me that this was a wicked thought. She
did not go on to give a reason, but merely insisted that it was
splendid to be a girl, and with such exuberant enthusiasm that I
was quite convinced.[34]

Sometimes it took more than verbal persuasion: Molly records
a number of occasions when she dared defy the nascent
chauvinism of her brother Tom: he appears to have exacted
fealty with fines, regular finger-rappings, and a variety of other
kinds of physical force.[35]

Many women give much less ambivalent accounts of their
jealousies and resentments. Helena Swanwick, in the preface to
her autobiography, *I Have Been Young* (1935), confessed that one
of her main reasons for writing an autobiography was the need
to air the frustrations she still felt about the wasted opportunities

[31] Ibid., p. 7.
[32] Ibid.
[33] M. V. Hughes, *A London Family, 1870-1900* (Oxford University Press,
London, 1946).
[34] Hughes, *A London Child*, p. 33.
[35] Ibid., p. 129.

of her girlhood, contending that 'until a girl is given the same respect for her personality as a boy', we would never know the best of which women were capable.[36] Swanwick remembered that as a child she had felt some community with her brothers, and had developed a strong friendship with one of them in particular: 'Bernard was my "favourite brother". We used often to be in trouble together and, like a pair of young monkeys on one branch, found comfort in pressing our cheeks together. We formed a sort of union against the unkindness of Authority.'[37] But as adolescence approached, the bond between them weakened. This was made clear to Helena when she returned from a period she had spent at a school abroad, in Neuville:

> One dreadful day after my return from Neuville, when I went to him confident of his sympathy with my disgust at some prohibition laid exclusively on me, he replied carelessly, 'I suppose that's what it is to be a girl.' It seemed once and for all to dissolve our partnership and to drive me back on my loneliness. I forget what the prohibition was, but, rightly or wrongly, I know I felt it to be unjust and superfluous, and to set me at a disadvantage in relation to my brothers. That my 'favourite brother' should regard this as right and natural was bitter to me.[38]

Like many of her contemporaries, Helena was expected to spend large amounts of her time on domestic chores. This was common even when the family was comfortably middle class. Elizabeth Raikes, in her biography of Dorothea Beale, points out that much of Dorothea's girlhood was spent on 'the inevitable sock-darning which falls to a girl's position in a family of so many boys'.[39] Helena recorded that she had no cause for regret that she had thus acquired useful skills, but she had never fully fathomed why boys were exempted from this burden of family responsibility:

[36] Helena M. Swanwick, *I Have Been Young* (Gollancz, London, 1935), p. 16.
[37] Ibid., p. 57.
[38] Ibid.
[39] Elizabeth Raikes, *Dorothea Beale of Cheltenham* (Constable, London, 1908), p. 16.

I had mended my own clothes ever since I was eight, but now I had to help my mother to mend the household linen and all the 'men's' underclothes. What visions I have of piles of sheets to be turned sides into the middle, of shirt collars and cuffs to be replaced, of socks and stockings to be darned. It was fine discipline, and I grew quick and deft, and have all my life been glad of the skill I acquired. That was work which had to be done, and for some — to me inscrutable — reason boys were not expected to help with it.[40]

Jealousy of their brother's schooling is a constantly recurring theme of middle-class women's autobiographies. Again, Molly Hughes is deeply ambivalent: 'The boys had the advantage of me in going about, but I had the advantage of them in not being sent to school. Until my eleventh year I was saved from the stupefying influence of such a place.'[41] However, Molly clearly lived vicariously through her brothers' schooling at Shrewsbury and Merchant Taylor's; long sections in her auto-biography celebrate her brothers' school experiences, and she clearly regarded her own education — at the North London Collegiate School under Frances Buss — as a very inferior product to theirs.[42] Helena Swanwick wrote that on returning from Neuville (the school she had attended there had collapsed in 1876),

I could not help contrasting my condition with that of my three elder brothers, all at school and able to walk about freely in the day-time, while I was not allowed out alone and had to be content with some very poor piano lessons and a few desultory German lessons with two other girls who were quite beginners.[43]

Luckily for Helena, when she was fourteen years old her parents determined on sending her to Notting Hill High School, where she remembers that she 'passed four years of great happiness, and found myself'.[44]

---

[40] Swanwick, *I Have Been Young*, p. 58.
[41] Hughes, *A London Child*, p. 41.
[42] Ibid., pp. 54—8. See also M. V. Hughes, *A London Girl of the 1880s* (Oxford University Press, Oxford, 1978), *passim*.
[43] Swanwick, *I Have Been Young*, pp. 57—8.
[44] Ibid., p. 63.

In many cases it was not so much the exclusion from their brothers' schools which rankled, it was the greater degree of importance which girls perceived their parents attaching to the education of their sons, which inevitably suggested a different estimation of social value. Girls learned that they counted for less in the family, and they resented it. In *My Own Story* (1914) Emmeline Pankhurst remembered this:

> My own childhood was protected by love and a comfortable home. Yet, while still a very young child, I began instinctively to feel that there was something lacking, even in my own home, some incomplete ideal.
>
> This vague feeling of mine began to shape itself into conviction about the time my brothers and I were sent to school. The education of the English boy, then as now, was considered a much more serious matter than the education of the English boy's sister. My parents, especially my father, discussed the question of my brothers' education as a matter of real importance. My education and that of my sister were scarcely discussed at all. Of course, we went to a carefully selected girls' school, but beyond the facts that the headmistress was a gentlewoman and that all the pupils were girls of my own class, nobody seemed concerned. A girl's education at that time seemed to have for its prime object the art of 'making home attractive' — presumably to migratory male relatives. It used to puzzle me to understand why I was under such a particular obligation to make home attractive to my brothers. We were on excellent terms of friendship, but it was never suggested to them as a duty that they make the home attractive to me. Why not? Nobody seemed to know.[45]

Emmeline Pankhurst's feminism enabled her to analyse and make sense of the somewhat amorphous discontents she remembered experiencing in girlhood. Molly Hughes never developed a feminist viewpoint, and thus in writing about her past she either denies that she felt any disadvantage, or when relaying episodes which might suggest otherwise she is quick to dismiss these experiences as trivial or unimportant. Helena

---

[45] Emmeline Pankhurst, *My Own Story* (1914), quoted in Janet Horowitz Murray, *Strong-Minded Women and Other Lost Voices from Nineteenth Century England* (Pantheon, New York, 1982), p. 107.

Swanwick is quite clear about this process whereby a growing commitment to feminism — first discovered in the school library — both legitimated her experiences in the family and allowed her to see her personal frustrations in a social context:

It was greatly encouraging to find my own personal inarticulate revolts linked up with what I now recognised as a world movement. I had felt and resented the assumption that whereas education was of importance for my brothers, it was of no account for me. I resented also that I was required to render them personal services which they need not reciprocate. When they had done their lessons, they went to play, but when I had done mine, I very often had to mend their clothes and sort their linen and wash their brushes and combs. As I grew in my 'teens I resented the idea that I could not be allowed out after dark, even in frequented thoroughfares. When it was explained to me that a young girl by herself was liable to be insulted by men, I became incoherent with rage at a society which, as a consequence, shut up the girls instead of the men.[46]

Many women's autobiographies record moments of wishing that they had not been born female. Mary Carbery prayed to become a boy, and remembers her terrible disappointment at realizing the impossibility of this; she felt branded for ever with the mark of femininity/inferiority:

I had looked forward to being a boy and then a man. I felt so strong, and able to lead and protect those weaker than myself. And now to be set back for always among the women of the world, grandmothers, aunts, governesses, nurses, maids, dressmakers, washerwomen, sisters of mercy: all skirted people, afraid of mice.[47]

One is reminded of the attraction, for generations of young girls, of Jo March, the tomboy heroine of Louisa M. Alcott's *Little Women*.[48] Helena Swanwick wrote of her 'loathing' of 'feminine ideals'.[49] 'This business of becoming a young lady

---

[46] Swanwick, *I Have Been Young*, pp. 81–2.
[47] Mary Carbery, *Happy World: The Story of a Victorian Childhood* (Longman, Green, London, 1941), p. 138.
[48] Louisa M. Alcott, *Little Women* (Roberts, Boston, 1868).
[49] Swanwick, *I Have Been Young*, p. 57.

was continually besetting me,' wrote Naomi Mitchison recalling her childhood.[50] Becoming a young lady was a serious and sober business, involving

> a difference in behaviour, which must no longer be silly or careless, a lengthening of skirts to ankle length and putting up one's long maiden hair. The last was, to me, fiendishly difficult; I didn't want to be bothered with hairpins, nor did I think I looked any nicer with my hair bundled up behind.[51]

More restrictions, an end to 'tomboyish' behaviour, the letting down of skirts and the putting up of hair, these were the *rites de passage* into Victorian womanhood. And clearly, in Mitchison's and many other accounts, the business of putting up one's hair — a tricky one if it was strong and had a will of its own, because the myriad hairpins necessary had a habit of falling out and allowing strands to break free — stood as a metaphor for the struggle involved in the social construction of femininity.

Daughters and mothers

As models for daughters with wills of their own, mothers came in for a good deal of resentment. In *Cassandra* Florence Nightingale explodes with rage at the hypocrisy of mothers who 'cradle themselves in visions about the domestic hearth' and who 'teach their daughters to conform', but almost in the same breath she asks herself more soberly 'what else can they say to their daughters, without giving the lie to themselves?'[52]

Troubled relationships with mothers are a common theme of women's autobiographies, and especially of the life histories of feminists. Mothers usually provided their daughters with their earliest models of 'femininity' and daughters often found their mothers' lives wanting. Enid Starkie and Helena Swanwick both resented their mothers' deference to male judgement in public and economic affairs, and were acutely irritated by the

---

[50] Mitchison, *All Change Here*, p. 24.
[51] Ibid., p. 55.
[52] Nightingale, *Cassandra*, in Strachey, *The Cause*, p. 396.

way in which this was construed as proper wifely behaviour. Enid Starkie records that she fell out of sympathy with her mother when the latter made her hand round cakes decorated with anti-suffrage colours at a garden party organized for the benefit of the Anti-Suffrage League:

> Even at that time, small child that I was, my feminist instincts were outraged and I protested to my mother. She answered that she saw no reason why a woman should need a vote, since she could always influence public affairs through her husband, that she had in this way more power than she could ever hope to achieve with suffrage. Even then I wanted to do things myself, my own way, and not be obliged to use feminine wiles to get others to do them for me.[53]

Similarly, Helena Swanwick found herself acutely irritated by her mother's attitude to money. Even though Mrs Sickert professed some kind of sympathy for women's suffrage, Helena found her attitudes 'uncertain and inconsistent'.[54] Although she had means of her own, Mrs Sickert went through an elaborate charade of pretending that this was *not* the case, so as to safeguard her own sense of wifely dependence:

> She disapproved of the Married Women's Property Bill, saying that wives should be proud to let their husbands have the use of their money; wives ought to love their husbands, and if a woman had given a man her life it was a little thing to give him her wealth. She always felt it a grievance that her money had been strictly tied up in trust, and whenever she drew a cheque she handed the cash over to my father, so that she might have the pleasure of asking him for it, bit by bit.
>
> It was her luxury to pretend he gave it to her, and his eyes would smile at her as he drew out his purse and asked, 'Now how much must I give you, extravagant woman?' And she would say humbly, 'Well, Owlie, I must get some serge for the little one's suits, and a new hat for Nell, and I want to bring back some fish. Will fifteen shillings be too much?' So she would get a pound and think how generous he was. He used to argue with her that women

---

[53] Enid Starkie, *A Lady's Child* (Faber & Faber, 1941), p. 94.
[54] Swanwick, *I Have Been Young*, p. 84.

should have a right to their own property, because some women had bad husbands. But she wouldn't hear of that. 'Serve them right', she said, 'for marrying bad men.'[55]

Middle-class women's lack of entitlement to time and space in the bourgeois household often rankled with their daughters, who could not but perceive that the home was most generally run with the needs of their fathers being given clear precedence. Enid Starkie noted that her mother 'considered it right that the life of a wife, that the life of all women in a household, should revolve around its male head. Nurse, the maids, and even Lizzie the cook, accepted this attitude without question, and everything went smoothly.'[56] Ursula Bloom had a clear memory of her mother fretting when a maid failed to respond promptly to a ring of the bell from her father's study, whereas 'nobody would have been chivvied had it been Mrs Bloom's bell.'[57] Emily Shore's journal, published in 1891, contains a short dramatic sketch which she penned when she was thirteen years old and entitled *The Interruptions*, in which she graphically conveys the frustrations of women in the home when they attempted to get down to serious reading or study and found themselves constantly beleaguered by the queries of cooks, housemaids and nursemaids on trivial domestic matters.[58] When the bell rings for the umpteenth time that morning Emily's mother finally acknowledges defeat:

Mamma Oh dear! ... Emily, love, you must leave off your 'Sir Joshua Reynolds' now and put it away till after dinner.
Emily Yes, Mamma; but I have not read a page.
Mamma Well, it can't be helped, you know.[59]

Florence Nightingale's dissatisfactions with the family focused on this same theme: 'Women never have an half hour in all

[55] Ibid., pp. 84−5.
[56] Starkie, *A Lady's Child*, p. 36.
[57] Ursula Bloom, *Sixty Years of Home* (Hurst & Blackett, London, 1960), p. 116.
[58] *The Journal of Emily Shore* (Kegan Paul, Trench, Trubner, London, 1891), pp. 352−6.
[59] Ibid., p. 356.

their lives (excepting before or after anybody is up in the house) that they can call their own, without fear of offending or of hurting someone.'[60] And for the married woman, she contended, the situation became quite intolerable: some wives, she suggested, were driven to feign or exaggerate illness in order to fend off the incessant small claims of family life: 'A married woman was heard to wish that she could break a limb that she might have a little time to herself. Many take advantage of the fear of infection to do the same.'[61] Nightingale herself, of course, used illness as a refuge from the demands of her family.[62] A large proportion of the women who have bequeathed accounts of their upbringing in the last century shared the experience of having nursed sofa-ridden mothers at some point in their girl-hood: Anne Jemima Clough and Eleanor Sidgwick, née Balfour (the first two principals of Newnham College, Cambridge), Constance Louisa Maynard, and Helena Swanwick are all examples.[63] Middle-class women undoubtedly suffered ill health through constant childbearing, and we may speculate that many also suffered from *maladies imaginaires* and other neuroses that need to be seen in a social-psychological context. Winifred Holtby once pointed out that girls often approached puberty at the time when their mothers were going through the physical and nervous disturbances of the menopause, and that the image of their mothers as middle-aged 'physical crocks' could have a profoundly discouraging effect on their daughters.[64]

It is easy to find examples of Victorian daughters who re-nounced any claim to lives of their own in nursing aged relatives — particularly mothers — through long years of last illnesses, but it is less easy to know the truth of how they felt about doing so. Biographers are often bent on conveying an image of the saint-liness of their subjects and suggest that such sacrifices were

[60] Nightingale, *Cassandra*, in Strachey, *The Cause*, p. 402.
[61] Ibid.
[62] Woodham-Smith, *Florence Nightingale*.
[63] B. A. Clough, *A Memoir of Anne Jemima Clough* (Edward Arnold, London, 1897); E. Sidgwick, *Mrs. Henry Sidgwick: A Memoir, By Her Niece* (Sidgwick & Jackson, London, 1938); Firth, *Constance Louisa Maynard*; Swanwick, *I Have Been Young*.
[64] Winifred Holtby, *Women, and a Changing Civilisation* (1935; Academy Press, Chicago, 1978), pp. 101–2.

made without regard for self. Autobiographies and novels can give a very different picture. Constance Louisa Maynard, for all that she had internalized a religious ethic of self-abnegation, was clearly driven to distraction by looking after her mother. So, too, was Helena Swanwick. Helena, already chafing at her position as 'daughter-at-home', was fully determined that she herself would not commit 'mental suttee for domestic reasons',[65] when her father died suddenly, leaving her mother inconsolable.

> My mother was nearly mad with grief, and it happened that I was the person she wished to have constantly with her and the one upon whom fell the burden of her unreason. She had never slept alone, so I felt obliged to share her bedroom and I had no privacy, night or day. She made many good resolutions, one of which was that I should have a study in the house and carry out my projects of earning my living. She went so far as to furnish my father's studio as my study. But I soon found that if I sat up there to work, she spent her time in weeping downstairs. So I brought my work down to her sitting-room and did the best I could amidst the incessant interruptions which constituted her life.[66]

Women's novels furnish many examples of mothers, who, like Mrs Transome in George Eliot's *Felix Holt*, discovered painfully in middle life that they had 'selves larger than their maternity' and whose energies and egos, thwarted of legitimate purpose, caused havoc for those around them.[67] Alongside the development of psychoanalytic thinking in the present century such portrayals take on new complexity. Mrs Hilary in Rose Macaulay's *Dangerous Ages* (1921) is one such example, an ageing mother figure jealous and resentful of the children on whom she feels she has 'spent' her life, bankrupting herself in the process.[68] Macaulay's careful dedication of her novel to her own mother 'driving gaily through the adventurous middle years' makes clear her desire to differentiate the latter from Mrs Hilary. But the novel resounds with sharp insights into the nature of

---

[65] Swanwick, *I Have Been Young*, p. 136.
[66] Ibid., pp. 135–6.
[67] George Eliot, *Felix Holt, The Radical* (1866; Panther, London, 1965), p. 113.
[68] Rose Macaulay, *Dangerous Ages* (1921; Methuen, London, 1985).

women's predicament and conflicting needs within contemporary family settings at every point. There is undoubtedly a good deal of social observation — in itself a form of indirect experience — in it. Even more penetrating, and certainly more directly 'autobiographical', is the feminist writer May Sinclair's novel, *Mary Olivier: A Life*, which takes the mother — daughter relationship, through time, and with all its deep ambivalences, as the central theme of the book.[69] Mary adores, hates, resents and pities her mother in differing proportions at different moments, throughout her life, and when she nurses Mrs Olivier through the last years of the latter's life this is shown to be a profoundly complex experience for both women, necessitating an extraordinary amount of self-sacrifice on Mary's part, but also engendering celebratory feelings in her, a sense of triumph of the spirit. May Sinclair herself claimed in a letter which she wrote to Marc Loge, her French translator, that 'All this description of the inner life is as autobiographically accurate as I can make it', and she was a writer with a sound grasp of psychoanalytic theory.[70] Like life itself, the novel is almost impossible to summarize, and can be read in many different ways. In this sense it conveys more 'truth' about personal experience than do many of the less ambiguous and complex accounts of mother-daughter relationships in contemporary autobiographies.

It is clear from personal accounts of every kind that women's experiences of living at home as unmarried daughters in the middle-class family was a fertile breeding ground for social tension. It was at this stage that daughters were likely to rebel most fiercely against their mothers as role models. The endless round of ritualized social visiting, the minutiae of social etiquette, flower arranging, giving directions to the cook and producing poker-work for church bazaars offered scant food for the soul of a budding feminist, and women like Helena Swanwick, Vera Brittain, Katharine Chorley and Jean Curtis Brown were loud in their protests.[71] 'Paying calls' on female neighbours, with

[69] May Sinclair, *Mary Olivier: A life* (1919; Virago, London, 1980).
[70] Ibid.; see Introduction by Jean Radford.
[71] Swanwick, *I Have Been Young*, pp. 57–69; Brittain, *Testament of Youth*, p. 59; Katharine Chorley, *Manchester Made Them* (Faber & Faber, London, 1950), p. 153; Jean Curtis Brown, *To Tell My Daughter* (Rodney Phillips & Green, 1948), p. 89.

one's reticule stuffed with a range of appropriate *cartes de visite*, may have appeared socially obligatory in the eyes of many mothers, but the ritual frequently represented the ultimate in futile feminine activity for an intelligent girl. 'The day was indeed a black one', wrote Katharine Chorley, 'on which we found that our mothers had had their cards reprinted and that our names figured below theirs on the disgusting little white slips. But we, too, were drilled and disciplined.'[72] But Chorley herself found a way of working free of the confines of the leisured feminine society of the suburbs (aided by the changes precipitated by the First World War), and so did many of her contemporaries.[73]

Education and autonomy

There can be no doubt that changing provision in girls' education exacerbated the generational gap in outlook and aspirations between mothers and daughters towards the end of the nineteenth century and in the years preceding the War. In spite of the ladylike ethos which prevailed in many of the new or reformed girls' schools of the period, many of these schools provided a 'liberating' experience. Away from the demands of the family, many girls revelled in the luxury of acquiring time and space for themselves, and the scope for serious study.[74] Helena Swanwick has written movingly of her love of the order and regularity of her life at Notting Hill High School. It was there that her Headmistress inspired her with an 'intense desire to go to Girton College' to study economics.[75] Neither of her parents were sympathetic to this ambition, and Mrs Sickert especially wanted Helena to live the life of a 'daughter-at-home'. Even when Helena's Headmistress offered pecuniary help in the form of a scholarship, her mother refused to supplement this in order to meet the full cost of study, and it was only when a relative (whom Helena ever after thought of as her 'fairy godmother') undertook to settle the balance that Helena was

---

[72] Chorley, *Manchester Made Them*, p. 153.
[73] Ibid., p. 262ff.
[74] Dyhouse, *Girls Growing Up*, pp. 172–5.
[75] Swanwick, *I Have Been Young*, p. 115.

able to go to Girton.[76] Her description of her euphoria in finding herself thus afforded 'a room of her own' in which to study is worth quoting in full, encapsulating as it does the different aspirations of Helena and her mother:

> the social life of the College was to me so intoxicating that ... I was too excited to eat or sleep properly. To begin with, I now had a study as well as a bedroom to myself. My mother had brought me to Girton on the first day and we were shown round by an old student. The building was still in its infancy, and the only public room was the dining-hall; but I was impressed by it and by the long corridors, the 'gyps' wings', the wide stone stairs with their shallow rises. When the door of my study was opened and I saw my own fire, my own desk, my own easy chair and reading-lamp — nay even my own kettle — I was speechless with delight. Imagine my dismay when my mother turned to me with open arms and tears in her eyes, saying, 'You can come home again with me, Nell, if you like!' It was horrible. That which had enraptured me had struck here as so unutterably dismal that she was prepared to rescue me at all costs. I hardly knew how decently to disguise my real feelings. I could not help thinking how differently I should have answered if she had said as much ten years before.
>
> To have a study of my own, and to be told that, if I chose to put 'Engaged' on my door, no one would so much as knock was in itself so great a privilege as to hinder me from sleep. I did not know till then how much I had suffered from the incessant interruptions of my home life. I could have worked quite easily in a mere noise. I never found it at all difficult to do prep. in a crowded schoolroom. What disturbed my mind were the claims my mother made on my attention, her appeals to my emotions and her resentment at my interest in matters outside the family circle.[77]

School or College life supplied girls with role models very different from their mothers; there they came into contact with women who had forged new lifestyles for themselves outside 'the family circle', and a code of values which generally legitimated intellectual purpose. Women teachers often found themselves mediating between conflicting sets of values, intervening in family politics in order to defend their pupils' desire to study

[76] Ibid., p. 116.
[77] Ibid., p. 118.

against a parent's accusation of selfishness, futility, or neglect of family duty. Edith Morley's unpublished 'Reminiscences' recall her excitement as a young girl when Lilian Faithfull (recently appointed Vice-Principal of the Ladies' Department at King's College London), suggested that she read for the Oxford Examinations in English Language and Literature.[78] Edith was fearful that her parents would never agree. The resourceful Miss Faithfull countered with the suggestion that Edith engineer a dinner invitation for her at her home, and, this having been arranged, set about wheedling and flattering Edith's father into submission.[79] M. A. Hamilton records in her history of Newnham College that Mrs Fawcett wrote to one student's (Margaret Merrifield's) mother, begging her not to call her daughter away from study to attend to family duties.[80] Such cases were not at all unusual. Daughters themselves were sometimes driven to elaborate ploys to protect their desire to continue with their studies. One of the 'Girton Pioneers', Louisa Lumsden, recorded how she elected to live in lodgings during University vacations in order to evade her mother's insistence that she participate in the social round at home.[81]

Conflict between mother and daughter over concepts of family responsibility is easy to understand where a daughter cherished clear ambition, but the frustrations and the sense of vulnerability attendant on being a 'daughter-at-home' were very widely felt and might in themselves engender a feminist critique. Victor Gollancz, in the preface which he wrote to *The Making of Women: Oxford Essays in Feminism* (1917), contended that the predicament of middle-class girls living at home was one of 'the most pitiful results' of the present system of sexual inequality.[82] Such girls lived a life of complete aimlessness:

[78] Edith Morley, 'Looking before and after: reminiscences of a working life' (unpublished typescript, University of Reading Library), p. 26ff.

[79] Ibid., p. 33.

[80] M. A. Hamilton, *Newnham: An Informal Biography* (Faber & Faber, London, 1936), p. 112.

[81] Louisa Innes Lumsden, *Yellow Leaves: Memories of A Long Life* (Blackwood, Edinburgh, 1933), p. 53.

[82] Victor Gollancz (ed.), *The Making of Women: Oxford Essays in Feminism* (Allen & Unwin, London, 1917), p. 20.

From the moment at which their education is finished — an education the incompleteness of which is in itself due to the same false aim — they simply have to sit and wait — for a marriage that often never comes. At the age of eighteen or nineteen everyone has an instinctive longing for activity. Work of almost every kind seems to hold the promise of glorious happiness, for it offers the possibility of strife and victory. And the girl, seeing her brothers plunging into strife, or preparing themselves more completely by further education, must live a life of perpetual drift: she is waiting for something to happen instead of working towards a goal. But energies cannot be entirely suppressed; if they are denied their natural expression they will seek for some other outlet. One need be neither a doctor nor a psychologist to realise what would be the effect on the life of a nation if complete idleness were imposed on men between the age of eighteen and the age of twenty-five. But we impose this idleness on women; at a time when sexual impulses are at their strongest and the future course of life is being largely determined, we allow a girl, unrestrained by counterbalancing forces, to feed on herself.[83]

Gollancz's conception of useful work as involving 'strife and victory' reminds us that he was writing during the First World War, when a life of enforced leisure might have seemed particularly irksome to the daughters of the middle class. But there can be no doubt that even before the War discontents were rife. Josephine Pitcairn Knowles wrote a book which was published in 1913, entitled *The Upholstered Cage*, in which she attempted to anatomize and give vent to the countless frustrations and sense of social impotence experienced by 'girls-at-home' in the suburban middle class, the 'Mollusc Maries' unable to work, marry, or even secure an entrée into any congenial society.[84] Knowles tells us that her book grew out of two public lectures which she had previously delivered on the subject, and which had generated an enormous response.[85] Like Gissing's novel *The Odd Women* (1893),[86] *The Upholstered Cage* emphasized the extreme vulnerability of the middle-class girl without marriage prospects, who

---

[83] Ibid., pp. 20−1.
[84] Josephine Pitcairn Knowles, *The Upholstered Cage* (Hodder & Stoughton, 1913).
[85] Ibid., Appendix.
[86] George Gissing, *The Odd Women* (Lawrence & Bullen, London, 1893).

had been schooled without reference to the possibility of ever needing to earn a living. It was by no means uncommon, Knowles asserted, for a gentleman's daughter to be kept in entire ignorance of her father's financial status, yet she could be living in 'a fool's paradise'. Should her father die suddenly, or be reduced to bankruptcy, her position would be hopeless.

> The gentleman's daughter, brought up in an atmosphere of sheltered idleness, is suddenly, through the death of her father, thrust into the arena to earn her living without any previous training, and in consequence is thrust *down* to a lower plane to compete with the workman's daughter coming up. They meet on a mid level. The more refined girl is at a disadvantage, because she has lost her own sphere, and does not take kindly to the lower; it is always more stimulating to mount than to descend, and it is just this slow descending which makes so often a tragedy in women's lives. Many women seem to think that money just comes out of a bag, or can be fetched from a bank at any moment, but they would not be so foolish had they been trained to business ways when young or if the whole nature of investments and banking accounts were explained to them ...[87]

Knowles herself moved on to a feminist analysis of family life and the potential for social change, drawing upon the writings of Edward Carpenter and August Bebel.[88] But this problem of the inadequacy of the family to act as a safety-net for unmarried daughters was to remain a constant theme of feminist literature for a long period in the future. The impact of the First World War, in terms of the loss of young men's lives, served to reduce marriage prospects for many still further, and exacerbated the problem. As Rosaline Masson, writing for the feminist periodical *Time and Tide* in 1921, pointed out:

> Much of the home life of our country is built up on a substratum of obscure martyrdoms. It all goes on smoothly and unconsciously until some upheaval occurs — until the family is broken up by death, and then the luxurious hospitable family home belches forth dismayed spinsters into an unsympathetic world, to wander about

[87] Knowles, *The Upholstered Cage*, p. 163.
[88] Ibid., p. xxv.

as aimlessly, and seek cover as nervously as do wood-lice when the flower pot is lifted.[89]

Independence or marriage?

For some women the realization that they would need to make their own way in life through the precariousness of family finances or the death of a father came as a positive experience; pushing them in the direction of a personal autonomy which they might at some point learn to value very highly. Frances Power Cobbe, Dorothy Richardson, Hertha Ayrton and even to some extent M. V. Hughes are all examples.[90] Helena Swanwick was of course hungry for the opportunity to earn her own living, and the death of her father legitimized this desire for her. Rosaline Masson wrote of the pleasures inherent in acquiring the rights of 'the latch key and cheque book',[91] and many women have recorded their delight in receiving their first pay cheque. Sara Burstall (who eventually became Headmistress of Manchester High School for Girls) recorded her own feelings of celebration when she began her career in the 1880s as assistant mistress at the North London Collegiate School 'at what was for those times an exceedingly good salary, £120 per annum,' reflecting that:

Economic independence is, after all, one of the requisites of a full and happy life: 'To learn and labour truly to get mine own living', as the Church Catechism says, is not only a duty but a basis for better things. The joy and satisfaction of the modern woman's economic independence is sometimes not stressed as it should be in the many discussions on feminism.[92]

---

[89] Rosaline Masson, 'Dark stars', *Time and Tide*, 11 March 1921, pp. 226–7.
[90] Frances Power Cobbe, *The Life of Frances Power Cobbe by Herself* (Richard Bentley, London, 1894); J. Rosenberg, *Dorothy Richardson: The Genius They Forgot* (Duckworth, London, 1973); Evelyn Sharp, *Hertha Ayrton, 1854–1923; A Memoir* (Edward Arnold, London, 1926); Hughes, *A London Family*.
[91] Masson, 'Dark stars' pp. 226–7.
[92] Sara A. Burstall, *Retrospect and Prospect: Sixty Years of Women's Education* (Longman, Green, London, 1933), p. 91.

Sara's pleasure in teaching intensified her delight in this autonomy, and prompted her to add that: 'Apart however from
income, we teachers have the additional work which is happy
in itself, whether we get any pay for it or not. Indeed the first
time I cashed by cheque, I thought the shining sovereigns
passed across the counter were magical, for I should have been
glad to do the work for nothing.'[93] This by no means blinded
her to the fact that the majority of women in teaching depended
upon their work not just for their own livelihood, but often for
the support of others.[94]

Young women who had learned to value their often hard-
earned economic independence might be understandably ambivalent about marriage. In *Conflicting Ideals of Women's Work*
(1914), B. L. Hutchins asserted that 'Women ... cannot act
honestly so long as they depend for subsistence on father,
mother, husband or lover, and not on their own labour.' (Here
she was quoting the words of Karl Pearson, who as a young
man professed certain feminist views, although he was to modify
and renounce many of these later.)[95] Hutchins herself believed
that it was 'in the economic dependence of women on men that
we should look for the cause of such sex-antagonism as we see
today'.[96] Pointing out that 'a small, but growing proportion of
women have ... set themselves against the idea that they must
be, or pretend to be, grown up children all their lives, have
everything given to them and be completely dependent on
another person',[97] she argued that the idea of being reduced
once again to economic dependence on a male provider might
feel like a loss of personal dignity akin to an enforced return to
childhood.[98]

[93] Ibid., pp. 92–3.
[94] Ibid., p. 92.
[95] B. L. Hutchins, *Conflicting Ideals of Women's Work* (no publisher given;
London, 1914), p. 44. See also Karl Pearson, 'Woman and labour', *Fortnightly
Review* (May 1894). For further discussion of Pearson's views on the Woman
Question see, among others, Lorna Duffin, 'Prisoners of progress: women and
evolution', in *The Nineteenth Century Woman: Her Cultural and Physical World*, ed.
Sara Delamont and Lorna Duffin (Croom Helm, London, 1978), and chapter
4 below.
[96] Hutchins, *Conflicting Ideals*, p. 30.
[97] Ibid., p. 31.
[98] Ibid., pp. 31, 34.

Similarly the feminist writer Mabel Atkinson asserted (in a tract which she wrote for the Fabian Society in 1914) that:

> Few men understand what importance the middle class woman attaches to her economic independence . . . The life of the professional woman is often toilsome and often lonely, but the power of self-direction and self-activity which economic independence brings with it counts for much, and few women who have realised what sex-parasitism means, and have succeeded in emerging from it, will ever willingly return it.[99]

Atkinson analysed the predicament of those of her contemporaries whom she saw torn between their desire for marriage and children on the one hand, and economic independence on the other, in some detail:

> This dependence of the woman in marriage is unspeakably distasteful to one who has known or beheld the freedom of the woman who earns her own income and directs her own life. Such a woman may and does long for a mate and a child; nothing is more curious to one who knows from personal contact the newest phases of the women's movement than the extraordinary contrast between the caricature of the demands of the emancipated women and their real wishes. It is a common-place among professional women who are frank enough to take on the subject that their greatest grief is that they are childless; to some of them the mere organic craving for a child to care for and caress becomes an instinct so overmastering that it has to be recognised and conquered as an unhealthy and weakening obsession. Some of the more successful adopt children; some find relief in philanthropic and social work for children's benefit. The outsider may wonder why they do not marry. But marriage is extremely difficult for a woman of this type. While it is true that the normal woman, like the normal man, desires love and children, it is as untrue in her case as in his to declare that she desires nothing else. Society and custom place before the middle class woman two alternatives: independence, power and variety of experience, coupled with a barren celibacy; or marriage and maternity together with the monotonous life of housekeeping, and nine cases out of ten, subservience, social, intellectual

---

[99] M. A. Atkinson, 'The economic foundations of the Women's Movement', Fabian Tract, no. 175 (London, 1914), p. 14.

and economic, to the views and opinions of her husband. It is not to marriage and maternity as such that the modern woman is hostile. On the contrary she often regrets most bitterly her lack of those fundamental experiences of life. But she cannot, even if she would, give up her intellectual and spiritual freedom and her cherished 'economic independence'.[100]

For those women who *did* jettison their economic independence on marriage, the experience of 'being kept' could frequently prove galling. A key word in feminist discussion of the problems of 'the kept wife' in the period is the term *parasitism*: Mabel Atkinson refers to 'sex-parasitism' in the first of her passages which was quoted above. This image of the dependent middle-class wife as a social 'parasite' gained wide currency in feminist (particularly Socialist feminist) literature before the War, and especially after the publication of Olive Schreiner's influential polemic, *Woman and Labour*, in 1911, the first three chapters of which were entitled 'Parasitism'.[101] 'The one thing for which we think women should never be paid', insisted Maud Pember Reeves, introducing a discussion amongst members of the Fabian Society's Women's group in 1910, 'is the relationship of wife-hood.'[102] Feminist writers repeatedly testified to the sense of impotence experienced by married women who felt that they must account for every penny they spent, and whose only source of personal income came from savings out of 'housekeeping'. Sylvia Anthony quoted the lament of a young married woman whom she had overheard at a meeting of her local Women Citizens Association in the 1930s, who had interjected: 'It's horrid for a girl who's been earning her own living to have to ask her husband for the money every time she wants to buy a pair of shoes!'[103] She added that this longing to have 'some

[100] M. A. Atkinson, 'The feminist movement and Eugenics', *Sociological Review*, 1 (1910), pp. 53−4.

[101] Olive Schreiner, *Woman and Labour* (1911; Virago, London, 1978).

[102] Maud Pember Reeves, introductory lecture (summarized by Mrs Bernard Shaw), Fabian Women's Group, 'Summary of eight papers and discussions upon the disabilities of mothers as workers' (printed for private circulation, 1910), p. 5.

[103] Sylvia Anthony, *Women's Place in Industry and Home* (Routledge, London, 1932), p. 168.

money of one's own' was not limited to those whose husbands earned small incomes: 'One may hear it expressed, more hopelessly, by women whose husbands' incomes run to four figures and are not ungenerously spent.'[104] Anthony described a number of families of her own acquaintance riven by conflict ensuing from the husband's incomprehension of the wife's need for some kind of control of the purse-strings, concluding that 'there are many marriages in which the consciousness of economic independence of one partner on the other is a cause of estrangement which makes married life a continual misery, though they provide no motive for the husband to bring the marriage to an end, and deprive the wife of any power to do so.'[105]

The economic insecurities of a wife whose marriage came to an end, either through the death of a husband or through desertion or mutual disharmony, were of course a recurrent theme of feminist literature. But even those feminists who were most convinced in the equation between economic independence and self-respect, and most determined in their rejection of the idea of marriage as a dignified 'career' for women, had to recognize the problem that sexual inequalities were structured into the labour market. In *Marriage, Past and Present*, for instance, published in 1939, Margaret Cole reminded her readers of women's continuing insecurities in marriage, pointing out that the current legal situation allowed a husband 'magnificent freedom of testamentary disposition', he might leave all he had 'to his mistress or to a cats' home' and nothing could be done about it.[106] Yet she was forced to concede, ruefully, that 'with a very few exceptions, the educated woman, like her working class sister, will be better off *economically*, especially when she is over thirty or thirty-five, if she can find a man in something like her own economic condition who is willing to marry and to support her, even if she has to resign all thoughts of earning money herself.'[107] Good, well-paid jobs for working women, however able and well-educated, were still extremely rare. Wilma Meikle had made precisely the same point twenty-three years

---

[104] Ibid.
[105] Ibid., p. 169.
[106] Margaret Cole, *Marriage, Past and Present* (Dent, London, 1938), p. 157.
[107] Ibid., p. 154.

earlier: 'Feminine economic ambition is naturally blunted by the knowledge that while it is practically impossible for a woman to provide for her old age by her own earnings, there is always rather more than a sporting chance that marriage will give her security.'[108]

Writing during the First World War, Wilma Meikle had expressed a hope that the War might conduce towards a climate of opinion in which it would be 'as despicable for an able bodied, serviceably-witted woman to be wholly dependent upon a man's earnings as it is for an able-bodied man to be dependent on a woman's'. Only then, she ventured, would 'the ugly mercenary element in sexual relationships' be likely to disappear.[109] Whilst her hopes were to prove far from being realized, it is worth noting the very strong language which she used throughout her book *Towards a Sane Feminism* (1916) in condemning the role of the conventional middle-class wife dependent upon her breadwinner husband.[110] Both the language and the sentiments expressed typify a strand of feminist thinking which gained momentum during the period of suffrage activity and struggle on the eve of the War. Certainly this was a period when many feminists wrote to denounce marriage and contemporary family structures in their entirety. Cicely Hamilton, for instance, in *Marriage as a Trade* (1909), emphasized the degradation of wives as unpaid domestic servants, the personal property of husbands; a wife was 'not a human being', but a mere 'breeding machine and the necessary adjunct to a frying-pan'.[111] For Hamilton, and others like her, celibacy afforded the only possibility of survival.[112]

These denunciations of the position of 'the kept wife' echoed on through the inter-war period (and of course, beyond). Lady Rhondda (who had herself been married, although the marriage had been dissolved after the War), declared that 'the kept wife has no *raison d'être* as a person. She is an appendage, a 'dependant,

---

[108] Wilma Meikle, *Towards a Sane Feminism* (Grant Richards, London, 1916), p. 166.
[109] Ibid., p. 104.
[110] Ibid., *passim*.
[111] Cicely Hamilton, *Marriage as a Trade* (1909; The Women's Press, London, 1981), p. 50.
[112] Ibid.; see Introduction by Jane Lewis, and p. 145ff.

not a full human being.'[113] In her autobiographical *Notes on the Way* (1937) she railed against the fact that as a woman in public life, she was always receiving invitations from the *wives* of politicians to meet 'the ladies accompanying Members' at various conferences and functions. 'Do I want to meet these accompanying ladies?' she asked herself, 'I certainly do not.'

> For I know all about those ladies. I have met, alas, only too many
> of them ... The average kept-wife — potentially as interesting a
> human being as any other — is turned into something so deadly
> that — taken in the mass — any ordinary fully alive person will go
> miles to avoid having to meet her. Of the class as a whole it would
> scarcely be too strong to say that whilst in their youth, dull as they
> are to other women, they have sexual attraction for men, by the
> time they are middle-aged they have no attraction for anyone. That
> is why the poor things are reduced *faute de mieux* to herding together
> so much.[114]

This is hardly sisterly, but the edge of bitterness is tempered by Lady Rhondda's insistence that the women themselves are not to be blamed, but rather the social system which makes possible their leisured existence. And such scathing critiques of conventional wifedom were often in themselves fuelled by a kind of defensiveness; like Cicely Hamilton, and her friend and colleague Winifred Holtby, Viscountess Rhondda deeply resented what she saw as the patronizing sympathy of married women who professed pity for the plight of the spinster or the woman who chose to stand alone.[115]

Seeking autonomy within marriage

In her study *Becoming a Feminist*, which was discussed at the beginning of this chapter, Olive Banks concluded from her analysis of feminist marital experiences that the women in her

[113] Margaret Haig Mackworth (Viscountess Rhondda), *Notes on the Way* (Macmillan, London, 1937), pp. 97—8.

[114] Ibid., pp. 94—5.

[115] Ibid. See also Hamilton, *Marriage as a Trade*, p. 131, and Holtby, *Women, and a Changing Civilisation*, p. 124ff.

sample, if they did not shun marriage altogether, tended to have sought husbands broadly sympathetic to their views.[116] This is scarcely surprising. Generations of feminists have probably entered into the married state determined to do better than their mothers. An awareness of what they identified as the oppressive features of contemporary family life for women sometimes supplied a strategy or blueprint for what they hoped would be a new form of contract. Most famous in this context was of course the contract of marriage entered into by John Stuart Mill with Harriet Taylor, in 1851, in which Mill formally repudiated what they jointly defined as the most oppressive legal implication of contemporary marriage, which invested the husband with legal power and control over the person, property and freedom of action of the wife.[117] Although Mill's radicalism in this respect has been much celebrated by historians, as Olive Banks has pointed out, Harriet Taylor's views on marriage and family life, influenced by Owenite feminism, were much in advance of Mill's. She was much more aware than he was of the dignity of economic independence for women, and looked forward to a time of economic equality between the sexes which would make possible an end to all marriage laws.[118]

Countless women who agonized over the decision of whether or not to marry searched for some kind of reassurance from their potential husbands that these latter would continue to respect their autonomy and personal independence after marriage. Sometimes there were symbolic gestures, such as the omission of the word 'obey' from the marriage service.[119] Weddings were often muted affairs, divested of the elaborate ceremonial which might suggest that entry into the marriage state was *the* significant moment in a woman's life, that becoming a wife did not represent any key transformation in her personality. Some women kept their own names; others hyphenated their

---

[116] Banks, *Becoming a Feminist*, p. 39.
[117] Strachey, *The Cause*, p. 67.
[118] O. Banks, *The Biographical Dictionary of British Feminists*, vol. I, 1880—1930 (Wheatsheaf, Brighton, 1985), pp. 126—30 and 208—10; for Mill's relationship with Harriet Taylor see also Phyllis Rose, *Parallel Lives: Five Victorian Marriages* (Chatto & Windus, London, 1984), p. 95ff.
[119] Banks, *Becoming a Feminist*, p. 39.

own names with that of their husbands.[120] Vera Brittain tells us in her biography of Frederick Pethick-Lawrence that on the first anniversary of his wedding with Emmeline Pethick (who had been initially very reluctant to marry, given her commitment to a life of personal independence and social service), he presented her with a small apartment of her own, where she could work or rest uninterrupted by the claims of domesticity or family duty.[121] Similarly, in marrying Vera Brittain herself in 1925 George Catlin had made it quite clear that he would expect no sacrifice that would entail her compromising her own sense of personality, or her own literary career.[122]

Many feminists, then, went into marriage determined upon new kinds of contract and lifestyle; they had no intention of reproducing those patterns of family life which they had experienced as oppressive in their childhood. Their attraction to a particular kind of man was often premised on their conviction that this was someone with very different values and expectations from those cherished by their father, or their mother. Helena Swanwick, for instance, explained to her readers with great satisfaction the differences between her suitor, Frederick, and her mother:

> My mother had a great respect for Fred and grew to have some affection, but their points of view were very different. He told me when we were first engaged that she had tried to explain to him her objection to my professional work. 'Don't you see that I *can't* have her living in my house and earning her living like a man?' He had sadly to confess that he could not.[123]

In her long, semi-autobiographical novel *Honourable Estate* (1936), Vera Brittain traced this process of enlightenment through generations in some detail. Ruth Alleyndene and Denis Rutherstone enter marriage as personalities sharply differentiated from their

---

[120] Ibid.

[121] Vera Brittain, *Pethick Lawrence: A Portrait* (Allen & Unwin, London, 1963), p. 34.

[122] Vera Brittain, *Testament of Youth*, pp. 652–3; see also John Catlin, *Family Quartet: Vera Brittain and Her Family* (Hamish Hamilton, London, 1987), p. 101ff.

[123] Swanwick, *I Have Been Young*, p. 144.

parents. Ruth (a thinly disguised version of Vera herself) is the product of an upper-middle-class family established in the Potteries, but has outgrown her origins through higher education, travel, and her experiences of nursing through the traumatic period of the War. Denis's childhood (like George Catlin's) had been scarred by the internecine struggles between his parents, his intelligent, feminist mother driven to personal exhaustion and breakdown by the petty conservatism and pompous conventionalities of his clergyman father. Both Ruth and Denis are determined to learn through the mistakes of their parents, and they attempt a very different kind of union which will guarantee the independence of their separate personalities. Both continue in their careers and both (with the full-time assistance of a young lady from 'the Wellgarth Nursery Training School') look after the children.[124]

Many feminists undoubtedly made happy marriages and the success of these marriages clearly had much to do with the sense of equal partnership that evolved out of mutual respect for each other's autonomy and separate space. This was so with Barbara Leigh Smith's marriage to Eugène Bodichon, for instance, and in Josephine Butler's partnership with her husband George.[125] Both Helena Swanwick's and Vera Brittain's marriages similarly lasted for life. However, it almost goes without saying that it is no easy matter to 'take stock' of a marriage in simple terms of happiness, or success or failure. What one can say, in the case of these unions in particular and a number of others like them, is that the individuals concerned negotiated styles of partnership which allowed them, particularly the wives, to live lives which were markedly more independent than those of their contemporaries. In none of these cases was the woman's sphere of interest limited to that of the family, and further, in marriages of this type the wife's continuing interest in politics, literature and social affairs necessitated the forging of new patterns of family life; patterns sharply differentiated in many important respects from conventional middle-class forms. These new styles of partnership and family life were rarely forged

[124] Brittain, *Honourable Estate*, p. 549 and *passim*.
[125] Banks, *Biographical Dictionary*, pp. 27–30 and 41–5. See also Josephine Butler's *Recollections of George Butler* (J. W. Arrowsmith, Bristol, 1892).

without conflict and difficulty. Even those women who (like Helena Sickert and Vera Brittain) embarked upon married life with fairly well-defined feminist views and a clear sense of the pitfalls to be avoided found themselves chafing against some of the same constraints — both in the form of contemporary expectations and practical problems — that had helped to shape the lives of their mothers.

The newly-married Helena Swanwick set off for the north of England (her husband had a lectureship in Manchester) full of optimism and revelling in her escape from her mother. 'After twenty-four years of being "ridden on the curb"', she remarks in her autobiography, 'it was little short of heaven to share life with a man who was the most libertarian and unegotistic imaginable.'[126] Helena and Frederick were to live in Manchester for twelve years, but Helena confessed that she was never completely at home there. This was in part because she found the city ugly, and her health was never good whilst she lived in the North. But there were also the unforeseen problems of social intercourse when one was defined as 'a faculty wife'.

> At first my circle was a ready-made one. All the seventy 'College Ladies' called on me. I had to have an 'At Home Day' and was supposed to repay their calls within the term. After a time I lapsed badly. I found many of them unexhilarating, and once when I confessed this to Fred, he was grieved, and remarked, 'That's odd. I find my colleagues very good company in the Common Room, and I suppose their wives are their feminine counterparts.' To which I answered that this was not the case. Their 'feminine counterparts' would be colleagues of my own in common work in which we were engaged together. Too many of these ladies were not engaged in any work, and tea-table talk soon palled.[127]

This was a very common experience. Intelligent women often found it very difficult to adjust to the expectations of male-dominated academic society. However enlightened their husbands might have been, they deeply resented the notion that serious conversation was really a matter of college fellowship, appropriate at High Table or in the University common room,

[126] Swanwick, *I Have Been Young*, p. 144.
[127] Ibid., p. 145.

but out of place in the family drawing room. In her autobiography Josephine Butler recalled her frustrations at this sense of an exaggerated division between 'private' and 'public' life in Oxford in the 1850s, and explicitly related this to gender:

> this pleasant life at Oxford had its shadow side . . . Oxford was not then what it is now under expanded conditions, with its married fellows and tutors, its resident families, its ladies' colleges, and its mixed general social life. With the exception of the families of a few heads of houses, who lived much secluded within their College walls, there was little or no home life, and not much freedom of intercourse between the academical portion of the community and others. A one-sidedness of judgement is apt to be fostered by such circumstances — an exaggeration of the purely masculine judgement on some topics, and a conventional mode of looking at things.[128]

Josephine Butler admits to having felt grieved and insulted by the implicitly patronizing, and even misogynist, attitudes of George's academic colleagues. Her feminism was already well developed ('Every instinct of womanhood within me was already in revolt against certain accepted theories in society'), and she confesses that she found it almost impossible to maintain the silence expected of the young wife presiding over the tea-table in male company.[129]

Several decades later Margaret Cole recalled similar experiences of having felt cut off, as a woman and a wife, from Oxford society and discourse:

> I was not naturally cut out to be a don's wife. In London, I had had a job as well as a family, and a place in the front row of whatever was going on; if there was an interesting discussion I was in the middle of it. But in Oxford, it seemed to me, all the really interesting discussions, the occasions when something important was done, took place in colleges where women could not enter; even if you entertained a distinguished visitor, say R. H. Tawney, in your own home, you were only expected to feed him; after dinner, if not before, he went off and talked in a male common room. I did not find the routine occupations of female Oxford —

[128] George W. and Lucy A. Johnson (eds), *Josephine E. Butler: An Autobiographical Memoir* (J. W. Arrowsmith, Bristol, 1928), pp. 22–3.
[129] Ibid., pp. 23–4.

taking lessons in Spanish, for example, going to listen to Magdalen Christmas Carols in a high cold loft reserved for Ladies, having children to tea-parties, and escorting one's own to Greek Dancing lessons, dressed in tomato-coloured silk frocks — at all satisfying.[130]

Even more vehement was the protest registered by Vera Brittain, stranded as a young wife on the small-town American campus of Cornell University, to which her husband had repaired as a professor of the newly-founded Department of Political Science in the mid 1920s. Hankering after fame as a writer and political purpose Vera found herself quite unable to tolerate the society of campus wives 'who discussed babies, illnesses and domestic difficulties by the hour' and had come 'to regard literature and politics as "highbrow" and tiresome',[131] So desperate was she to differentiate herself from this female company that she found herself behaving like a 'supercilious intellectual', avoiding invitations to tea-parties and deftly snubbing any sympathetic enquiries on the part of other wives who were curious about whether she had any intentions of having children.[132]

The continuing struggle with domesticity

Although Vera herself was prepared in retrospect to describe aspects of her behaviour in Ithaca as 'malicious' and 'petty', this was not *just* unsisterly malice or intellectual snobbery. Much was at stake for her at this juncture. Her account of her time in America in *Thrice a Stranger* (1938) leaves us with no doubt about the pitch of frustration which she had reached, albeit in less than a year of marriage, over the social expectations surrounding her in her position as the young wife of a promising academic. Vera much resented being seen as George's wife rather than as an individual in her own right and she clearly dreaded the prospect of being submerged by domestic activity. She provides us with detailed daily time-schedules to demon-

---

[130] Margaret Cole, *Growing Up into Revolution* (Longman, Green, London, 1949), p. 110.
[131] Vera Brittain, *Thrice a Stranger* (Macmillan, New York, 1938), p. 57.
[132] Ibid., p. 58.

strate her desperate attempts to reserve time away from the business of getting meals and cleaning their apartment in order to concentrate on her writing.[133] Like so many women, she despaired of an 'overcrowded existence, so full of insignificant events which led nowhere'.[134] In England she had been accustomed to relying on a good deal of domestic help — a couple of years previously she had shared a flat in London with Winifred Holtby and they had experienced no difficulty in affording the services of a maid — but in America, domestic assistance was much less easily available. 'I have always detested domesticity', she wrote,

> as the unnecessary and too meekly accepted obstacle to women's achievement, the final and fundamental explanation of sex-inequality. Only those who appreciate the different qualities of work produced by complete and by partial concentration, can ever estimate the extent to which women's performances suffer from constant small interruptions and petty, time-wasting tasks.[135]

It is hard to imagine anyone less inclined towards meekly accepting a situation defined as impossible than Vera, and after a summer vacation in England at the end of the academic year, George returned to Ithaca on his own. Vera moved back into the flat with Winifred Holtby. But the marriage did not come to an end, although its pattern from then on became characterized by what Vera herself called 'semi-detachment'.[136] George continued to teach in Ithaca, Vera continued to live in London with Winifred, her existence punctuated by periods of travel abroad. When two children, John and Shirley, were born, they lived mainly with Vera and/or Winifred. When George visited England, he moved in with Vera and Winifred. The family and household, for all its unconventional pattern of relationships, remained a stable one.

Like Vera Brittain, Helena Swanwick found domestic organization more of a trial than she had expected:

---

[133] Ibid., pp. 47–8.
[134] Ibid., p. 49.
[135] Ibid., p. 53.
[136] Catlin, *Family Quartet*, p. 103.

For a good many years, whatever work I did was scrappy and such as I could take up or put down fairly easily. For I had to consider, not only the needs of my own little house and my over-worked husband, but those of his own family on the other side of Manchester. It seemed, on the whole, wiser to try to save rather than to try to earn money, although I was not without cravings for a profession.[137]

Helena buckled to and threw her energies into the business of dressmaking and learning to cook. She and Frederick were not particularly well off, but they were still securely established in that middle-class portion of the community which relied upon some paid domestic help — when this could be obtained. Here we find Helena, like so many middle-class wives of the period, discoursing at some length on various aspects of 'the servant problem':

Servants in Manchester were very hard to get and for the most part incompetent. We did not wash or bake at home, as so many Lancashire women did, and we gave the highest wages current at the time, and much leisure and freedom, yet in the first sixteen years of my housekeeping, eighteen 'generals' floated in and out of my employment, and very few of these were fit to be left in charge when we were absent.[138]

Feminist attitudes to domestic organization in the family will be explored further in chapter 3. Some women had the means (and the luck) to be able to secure the kind of live-in assistance which pre-empted problems: Helena Swanwick, writing in 1935, tells us that she eventually 'sailed into smooth domestic waters with the arrival of Agnes Rushton, who has been my faithful cook, housekeeper, nurse and friend for over thirty years';[139] and when Margaret and Douglas Cole, upon getting married in 1918, moved into a large house in Chelsea they 'inherited' Mrs Farrant, the then caretaker, who moved into the basement with the family as resident cook-housekeeper. She stayed with the Coles for ten years, accompanying them through their moves to

[137] Swanwick, *I Have Been Young*, p. 149.
[138] Ibid., p. 150.
[139] Ibid., p. 152.

Hampstead and then to Oxford, as Margaret put it, 'a grand windfall for a young couple who wanted to continue with their own outside works'.[140] Many middle-class wives undoubtedly did struggle to cope with much if not all of the domestic work generated by family living. Some made a virtue out of this, as we have seen the young Helena Swanwick did in the early days of her marriage. Other feminists emphasized the guilt which drove many of their contemporaries, however able as individuals, to struggle to try to conform to what they saw as the outmoded and oppressive ideal of the perfect homebody. Like Vera Brittain, Winifred Holtby deplored both the waste of talent and the self-deception which she saw this as involving:

> if it is true that many women better equipped to be engineers, lawyers or agricultural workers, waste their time on domestic activities, which husbands, sons or professional employees might more effectively perform, it is even more true that other women, who are naturally inclined to enjoy domestic work, use it as an excuse to do nothing and know nothing else. The consciousness of virtue derived from well-polished furniture or rows of preserved-fruit bottles is too lightly acquired. In too many small homes women use the domestic tradition to evade responsibility for everything else. 'Oh, I'm only a housekeeper. I'm a private person. My job lies within four walls,' they say, complacently, finding it easier to be a good housewife than a good citizen.[141]

For Holtby and for many other socially and politically minded feminists of the inter-war period, pride in being 'just a housewife and mother' was equivalent to a selfish opting out of communal concerns:

> So long as their own children are healthy and happy, why worry because others are ill and frightened? It is agreeable to distemper one's own nursery, bake crusts, squeeze oranges and mix nourishing salads; it is not agreeable to sit on quarrelling committees, listen to tedious speeches, organise demonstrations and alter systems, in order that others − for whom such wholesome pleasures are at present impossible − may enjoy them.[142]

[140] Cole, *Growing Up Into Revolution*, p. 81.
[141] Holtby, *Women, and a Changing Civilisation*, p. 148.
[142] Ibid.

Holtby, Vera Brittain and Viscountess Rhondda were all comfortably-off middle-class women who were able to delegate domestic work in their own households to paid servants. But this did not mean that they were blind to the social predicament of married women lower down on the social scale. In 1922, for instance, the feminist political weekly *Time and Tide* (on the board of which Viscountess Rhondda sat as a director) published a series of articles by Margaret Leonora Eyles entitled 'The woman in the little house', which attempted to speak for the experiences of the wives of the 'respectable' working class, imprisoned in the home and isolated from any opportunities for personal self-development or wider social involvement.[143]

The arrival of children in the middle-class family inevitably added to the task of domestic organization and encroached further on a mother's space for activities of her own. Some married women with feminist views remained childless, although this was not always a matter of choice. Neither Barbara Bodichon nor Helena Swanwick gave birth to any children, and although this was a cause of great sadness to both of them, it clearly guaranteed them more space for political involvement than they would have enjoyed as mothers. Olive Banks found that the married feminists in her sample had smaller families than was the norm for their contemporaries; and this was sometimes deliberate.[144] Even with domestic help and only a couple of children, middle-class women recorded the frustrations — the personal exhaustion, sleepless nights, and continual disruptions — as well as the joys of motherhood. Vera Brittain struggled to complete her book on women's work in modern England whilst pregnant with her first child.[145] The birth was a difficult one, and as a premature baby, John required very careful nursing. Even so Vera continued to write, merely commenting that:

[143] M. Leonora Eyles, 'The woman in the little house', *Time and Tide* (January — March 1922). These articles also appeared in the form of a book with the same title published by Grant Richards, London, in 1922.

[144] Banks, *Becoming a Feminist*, pp. 41—2.

[145] Vera Brittain, *Testament of Experience: An Autobiographical Story of the Years 1925—50* (Gollancz, London, 1957), p. 52ff.

The after-effects of mismanaged childbirth proved less easy to disregard than the malaises of pregnancy. But disregarded they had to be, since only through journalism could I make my one-third contribution to our joint household. When I left the nursing-home a woolly fog enveloped my mind, but within a few days I was again writing for the usual journals.[146]

In spite of the difficulties involved in living apart much of the time (which Vera attempted to 'think through' in writing a short book on marriage called *Halcyon; or The Future of Monogamy*, published in 1929)[147], Vera and George had planned a second baby.[148] Having failed, however, to conceive this second child by November 1929 Vera resigned herself to the possibility of having been rendered infertile through the damage she had suffered with John's birth and she turned her attention, instead, to planning a major book. When she suddenly realized that she was, after all, pregnant, her reaction was initially one of despair:

I had barely drafted half the first chapter when I realised that the elusive fourth member of our family would eventually appear. Theoretically, I ought to have been delighted; actually, I felt as though I had fallen downstairs. A book involving a large-scale reconstruction of the history, both national and personal, which had shaped my early life could not be tackled effectively with such a major diversion as a new baby just ahead.[149]

This conflict between the desire for children and the need for other forms of personal creativity is one which was felt by countless women in the past and indeed it still is, and will no doubt remain, a common experience. However the conflict is one which may be eased or exacerbated by circumstance; by class position, for instance, and by a range of additional factors such as social expectations, structures of family living, the avail-ability of domestic help and so forth; factors which do not remain static through history. In spite of her misgivings and

[146] Ibid., p. 54.
[147] Vera Brittain, *Halcyon; or The Future of Monogamy* (Kegan Paul, Trench, Trubner, London, 1929).
[148] Brittain, *Testament of Experience*, p. 59.
[149] Ibid., pp. 59–60.

frustrations, Vera Brittain was able to evolve a lifestyle which enabled her to combine motherhood, writing and political activity in an unbroken career. Other women tried to 'phase' their involvements in rearing children and other work in life. One is reminded of a letter which Mrs Gaskell penned, in the 1860s, by way of comforting and advising a harassed young wife and mother about reconciling herself to the postponement of her literary ambitions: 'When you are forty', she consoled, 'and if you have a gift for being an authoress you will write ten times as good a novel as you could do now, just because you will have gone through so much more of the interests of a wife and mother.'[150] One cannot but wonder whether the woman in question ever did write her book. Some women in their forties, their children grown, felt too old and bereft of the confidence that would allow them to rekindle the ambitions of their youth. Neville, the central character of Rose Macaulay's novel *Dangerous Ages*, at the age of forty-three, with two grown-up children and a disrupted medical career behind her, frets over her central purposelessness. As the wife of a successful politician, Neville feels herself a 'spectator' rather than a 'participator' in life; she has no personal achievements, only the love for her family, and she mourns over the waste of her intelligence, the sense of her brain 'squandered, atrophied, gone soft with disuse'.[151] 'How to be useful though married': Rose Macaulay reminds us, through Neville, that this problem, which barely existed for a husband, often became central for his wife when her children no longer demanded daily attention and nurturing.[152]

May Sinclair's novel, *The Creators*, which was first published in 1910, represents an extraordinarily astute exploration of some of the problems posed for women by contemporary structures of family life.[153] Jane Holland, the central character in the book, finds herself constantly torn between her artistic ambitions and her family. Unlike her friend Nina, who comes to look upon celibacy as an 'indispensable condition' for her art, Jane marries

---

[150] Quoted in Horowitz Murray, *Strong-Minded Women*, p. 90.
[151] Macaulay, *Dangerous Ages*, pp. 51–3.
[152] Ibid., pp. 204–6.
[153] May Sinclair, *The Creators: A Comedy* (Hutchinson, London, 1910).

and becomes pregnant. At first she manages to cope with the multifarious demands on her time, aided by the services of a highly efficient housekeeper. Even so the situation is highly tense. Jane's ambitions are construed as selfish by her husband's family: Gertrude, the housekeeper, comes to be seen as a more emulable model of devoted womanhood than she is, and there are undertones of rivalry between the two women over the affection of the children. Strain mounts, and Jane likens the quality of her life to the performance of a highly-trained juggler:

> she had so many balls to keep going. There was her novel; and there was Brodrick, and the baby, and Brodrick's family, and her own friends. She couldn't drop one of them.
>   And at first there came on her an incredible, effortless dexterity. She was a fine juggler on her tight-ropes keeping in play her golden balls that multiplied till you could have sworn that she must miss one.[154]

Brodrick's family watch on, unsympathetically, wanting her to fail. Jane's brother-in-law, Henry, a dyed-in-the-wool patriarch and doctor of the old school, labels her intellectual ambitions as unnatural, accusing Jane not only of overstraining her own reserve but of damaging the health of her 'delicate' second child.[155] The men close ranks, and determine to invest Gertrude with more authority over Jane's children. Close to desperation, and burning with the desire to put her foot through what she comes to see as a suffocating system of man-made rules for living, Jane requests that she be allowed to leave the family altogether for three months every year, in order to be able to concentrate on her own work. The doctor brother-in-law is horrified, but Jane's husband, Hugh, listens sympathetically to the request. There is an interesting dialogue in which Jane tries to convey to Hugh the frustration of trying to write in a family context, where her concentration is constantly punctured by the demands of others. Jane explains that another brother-in-law, John, who has recently become a widower, is continually

---

[154] Ibid., p. 349.
[155] Ibid., p. 404ff.

'dropping in' for sympathy. When Hugh asks why she does not send him away sometimes, Jane counters:

> But how can you when he's so unhappy? It would hurt him so. And yet, supposing you were to die, what would John say if I were to call on him at the works every day, and play with his dynamos to distract my mind, or sit with him in his office rumpling his hair and dislocating his ideas till he didn't know the difference between a steam-roller or an internal combustion engine? That's more or less what John does to me. The only thing to do is to get away.[156]

May Sinclair articulates much of her own experience through the creation of her fictional characters, such as Mary Olivier and Jane Brodrick, and her novels were read by women who recognized many of these experiences as their own. The marriage between Jane and Hugh in *The Creators* survives, but not without a good deal of conflict, difficult negotiation, and personal sacrifice. There are no simple solutions of offer; no unambiguously 'happy endings'. Women are faced with difficult choices in life, choices between careers, personal involvements and family relationships, and the author makes it clear that all choices have their costs. The novel ends on a questioning note, with the reader being asked to consider whether Jane is happy or not; a question which it is nigh impossible, of course, to answer.

[156] Ibid., p. 457.

2

The Economic Independence of Women in the Family

Celibacy, marriage and dependence

The desire to see more opportunities for women to earn their living was central to Victorian feminism. Around mid-century, Jessie Boucherett's Society for Promoting the Employment of Women had initiated a number of projects to train and employ women. Boucherett and the feminists of the 'Langham Place Circle' invested much of their faith in contemporary efforts to improve educational provision for middle-class girls, trusting that education would make women more employable.[1] To some extent it did, and the expansion in girls' secondary and higher education during the period in itself created scope for women to forge careers of some dignity, if rather less financial security, for themselves in teaching.[2] However, as Alice Zimmern, an early historian of women's education, lamented in the 1890s, although there had been much talk of late about new careers for women the 'very abundance of the talk' served 'to betray the poverty of the land'.[3] Of *new* careers there were very few, and the choices

---

[1] See among others, Ray Strachey, *The Cause: A Short History of the Women's Movement in Great Britain* (1928; Cedric Chivers, Bath, 1974); Lee Holcombe, *Victorian Ladies at Work: Middle Class Working Women in England and Wales, 1850–1914* (David & Charles, Newton Abbot, 1973); and Philippa Levine, *Victorian Feminism, 1850–1900* (Hutchinson, London, 1987).

[2] See Penny Summerfield, 'Women and the professional labour market, 1900–1950: the case of the secondary schoolmistress', in *Women, Education and the Professions* (History of Education Society, Occasional Publication no. 8, 1987).

[3] Alice Zimmern, *The Renaissance of Girls' Education in England: A Record of Fifty Years' Progress* (A. D. Innes, London, 1898), p. 246.

confronting women remained narrow. Clara Collet pointed out in a series of essays which she published on *The Economic Position of Women Workers in the Middle Classes* in 1902 that the prospects for even well-educated women in the labour market remained pretty bleak.[4] Improvements in women's education, in fact, were already being blamed for exacerbating the situation, and we find Alice Zimmern arguing that teachers and parents should aim to discourage girls whose fathers could comfortably continue to support them from hot-footing it after a career. 'Much may be done', she suggested, 'by mistresses at school to revive the dignity of home life, to check the untrue notion in the girl's mind that no work is worthy of the name unless it is paid for in coin of the realm.'[5]

The accusation that in seeking paid work a girl from a 'comfortable' home was behaving selfishly, allegedly depriving others more needy than herself of the opportunity to earn a living, was frequently voiced. However, there can be little doubt that the newer and reformed girls' secondary schools of the late nineteenth century did aim to encourage girls to look upon the prospect of earning their own living as preferable to marriage-for-marriage's-sake, or marriage simply as a meal-ticket.[6] And a considerable number of women came to look upon work not merely as a tolerable alternative to marriage but far more positively, as something central to their lives and self-respect. As we have seen, education and the struggle for professional status involved many women in painful conflicts with parents and families who were unsympathetic towards ambition in the female sex. It is scarcely surprising that such women tended to become jealous of the economic and personal independence which had cost them so much, nor that they frequently declined offers of marriage in their maturity. For many of these women, fearful lest marriage should shackle them with the constraints of family life from which they had previously found so much difficulty in escaping, celibacy represented a positive commit-

---

[4] Clara Collet, *Educated Working Women: Essays on the Economic Position of Women Workers in the Middle Classes* (P. S. King, London, 1902).

[5] Zimmern, *Renaissance of Girls' Education*, pp. 247–8.

[6] Carol Dyhouse, *Girls Growing Up in Late Victorian and Edwardian England* (Routledge & Kegan Paul, London, 1981), pp. 40–78, 170–5.

ment. Martha Vicinus's recent and fascinating study, *Independent Women*, sets out to explore the lives and loves of some of these single women for whom celibacy constituted the foundation for new patterns of lifestyle in late Victorian Britain.[7]

Historians have often portrayed nineteenth-century feminism as concerned mainly if not exclusively with the economic and social predicament of *unmarried* women. Victorian feminists are alleged to have devoted their energies to widening opportunities for single women in education and employment and to have stopped short of any thoroughgoing analysis of the problems of wives and mothers. However, this view has been overstated and it is possible to trace a strong current of concern for the economic position and problems of married women throughout the period 1860–1939. This concern surfaced initially in the campaign to secure women's rights to hold property within marriage. Indeed, the Committee formed by the young Barbara Leigh Smith (later Bodichon) in 1856, which set out to work for the reform of laws affecting women and identified the reform of the law relating to married women's property as its first goal, has sometimes been seen by historians as representing the beginning of an organized feminist movement in Victorian England. Herself possessed of an independent income, Barbara Bodichon was always acutely aware of the problems for women of economic dependency within marriage. Indeed, she did not believe that any real equality between men and women would be possible until this problem could somehow be resolved.[8]

The Married Women's Property Acts of 1870 and 1882 were identified by feminists as major landmarks along the route to women's emancipation, although some historians have doubted whether we can be justified in regarding their impact as revolutionary.[9] What they *did* secure was wives' entitlement to earn-

---

[7] Martha Vicinus, *Independent Women: Work and Community for Single Women, 1850–1920* (Virago, London, 1985).

[8] Barbara Leigh Smith Bodichon, *Women and Work* (C. S. Francis, New York, 1859), pp. 30–1, quoted in Mary Lyndon Stanley, "'One Must Ride Behind": married women's rights and the Divorce Act of 1857', *Victorian Studies* (Spring 1982), p. 372.

[9] For a full consideration of these Acts see Lee Holcombe, *Wives and Property: Reform of the Married Women's Property Law in Nineteenth-Century England* (Martin Robertson, Oxford, 1983).

ings and to property acquired through inheritance or gift. But the right to hold separate property, though it might be regarded as a *precondition* of economic independence, could, of course, do little to effect the latter in a society in which most women were locked into disadvantageous positions in the labour market and effectively prevented from acquiring property in the first place.

By the turn of the century the question of how to secure economic independence for women was increasingly identified as a key issue for feminists, many of whom became caught up in discussions about the extent to which material autonomy was possible within existing structures of marriage and the family. Attempts to think through the problem generated an impressive body of research and literature. Feminists with a leaning towards historical investigation eagerly set out to explore the economic position of women within the family in pre-industrial times; others embarked upon fact-finding missions and attempts to document the character and extent of women's work, both in and outside the home, in the 1900s. There was much speculative thinking and debate about the enormous range of issues — patterns of work, remuneration and dependency; the social arrangements for maternity and the support and upbringing of children, and so forth — which were perceived as relevant to this basic question of how best to secure some measure of economic autonomy for women.

Socialism and 'sex parasitism'

Probably the most sustained attempt to discuss and clarify these issues came from the Fabian Society Women's Group (FWG) which was set up in 1908 by a group of women who found themselves dissatisfied with the lukewarm commitment to feminism and women's issues they had experienced in Fabian Socialism.[10] The Fabian Women's Group had two objects. The first was actively to promote that equality between men and women in citizenship advocated by the parent society; the second

[10] Fabian Women's Group pamphlet, 'Three years' work of the Women's Group' (Library, London School of Economics, n.d. [*c.* 1911]).

was specifically to 'study the question of women's economic independence in relation to socialism'.[11]

Discussions among members of the FWG set out from the premise that economic independence for women was the major goal for feminists and that socialism had so far failed to recognize that women were the victims of patriarchy as well as capitalism. This position was stated quite explicitly in the papers published by the Group. A pamphlet published in 1911 entitled 'Three Years Work of the Women's Group', for instance, argued that:

> One of the driving forces of the woman movement today is the secret resentment of women against . . . economic dependence, and the subjection in which it keeps them. Socialists must recognise that women's economic revolt is not merely against the enslaving economic control of the capitalist, but against the enslaving economic control of the husband.[12]

And again, Mrs Bernard Shaw, introducing a summary of the Group's discussions in 1910, emphasized the crucial need for women to strive for self-support; warning her readers that:

> Socialism does not necessarily solve the problem, for we find that a great school of socialists holds that when security and a good wage shall have been brought within the reach of every head of a family the case of the dependent woman and children in each household can be left to that head to deal with. Such a state of things would amount to Socialism for men, but for most women would involve the subordination of the patriarchal family. We should think very long before we allow it to come about.[13]

Membership of the FWG in 1912 totalled around 230 women, most of them classifiable as educated and middle-class.[14] A questionnaire designed to elicit information about occupations and distributed to members in 1911 showed a solid core of

[11] Ibid., p. 1.

[12] Ibid., p. 9.

[13] Fabian Women's Group, 'Summary of eight papers and discussions upon the disabilities of mothers as workers' (printed for private circulation, 1910), p. 5.

[14] Sally Alexander, Introduction to Maud Pember Reeves, *Round About a Pound a Week* (Virago, London, 1979), pp. xiv, xvii.

professional women: teachers, lecturers, journalists and writers.[15]
It was recorded that many of the members were engaged in
unpaid domestic work, and it seems likely that the majority of
these were the wives and daughters of educated professional
men. Charlotte Wilson, as secretary, also recorded a list of
other societies to which members belonged, showing strong
links with suffrage societies and other women's organizations.[16]
Some women, such as B. L. Hutchins, were very active in both
the FWG and the Women's Industrial Council, which had been
inaugurated in 1894, growing out of the Women's Trade Union
Association and aiming to 'watch over the interests of women
engaged in trades, and over all industrial matters concerning
women'.[17] The minutes of the FWG show that members kept in
touch with suffrage organizations, the Women's Co-operative
Guild, the 'Right to Work' movement and a number of other
contemporary women's organizations, but the links with the
Women's Industrial Council (WIC) were particularly important
in the period leading up to the War.[18] This was partly because
of friendship networks and overlapping allegiances, but also
because the two societies functioned in a way which was often
complementary.

The WIC saw itself as involved in fact-finding, education,
and the politics of the workplace. The mainly middle-class
members of the Council sought to protect the interests of working-
class women by scrutinizing the working of the Factory Acts
and public health legislation, providing legal advice, and educating women workers in social questions, economics and legal
rights. They were also concerned to widen opportunities in
technical and vocational education for girls. As a context for
this kind of initiative, members committed themselves to investigating the facts and conditions of women's work during the
period, many of their findings appearing in the quarterly organ
of the WIC, the *Women's Industrial News*.[19]

[15] Fabian Women's Group, 'Three years' work', p. 20.

[16] Ibid., pp. 20−1.

[17] Ellen Mappen, *Helping Women at Work: The Women's Industrial Council
1889−1914* (Hutchinson, London, 1985), pp. 11−13.

[18] Fabian Society Women's Group, Minutes (Nuffield College Library,
Oxford) (available on microfilm, Harvester, Brighton).

[19] Mappen, *Helping Women at Work*.

Like the members of the WIC, members of the FWG were also concerned to learn more about contemporary patterns and conditions of women's work, but they were equally if not more committed to pursuing historical and theoretical lines of enquiry relating to their primary concern with the problem of securing economic independence for women under Socialism. In 1908 the group mapped out an impressive scheme of work, under three headings. In the first place they set out to determine whether women could legitimately be regarded as suffering 'natural disabilities' as productive workers by virtue of their sex, whether or not they were actively involved in childbearing. Next they planned to study women's economic status as productive workers and consumers in the past and in the present. Thirdly, they resolved to consider the ways in which social arrangements might be modified to free women both to work and to mother children in a way that would guarantee their sharing fully, as individuals, in the social wealth of the community.[20]

The Group adhered fairly closely to its proposed scheme of work. Summaries of papers and discussions on the disabilities of women as workers, and of mothers as workers, were issued for private circulation in 1909 and 1910.[21] By 1914 fifteen papers on the history of women's work had been given and lectures and discussion on the subject of women's economic conditions in the present had formed the basis of a volume edited by Edith Morley for the Group, entitled *Women Workers in Seven Professions*, published by Routledge in 1914.[22]

Between them the WIC and the FWG were responsible for or indirectly stimulated an impressive array of literature on women's work in the period preceding the First World War. Some members 'took stock' of existing literature: Lucy Wyatt Papworth

[20] Fabian Women's Group, 'Three years' work'.

[21] Fabian Women's Group, 'A summary of six papers and discussions upon the disabilities of women as Workers' (printed for private circulation, 1909), and 'A summary of eight papers and discussions upon the disabilities of mothers as workers'.

[22] Fabian Women's Group, 'Three years' work', p. 14; Edith Morley (edited for the Studies Committee of the Fabian Women's Group), *Women Workers in Seven Professions: A Survey of Their Economic Conditions and Prospects* (Routledge, London, 1914).

and Dorothy Zimmern, for instance, collected together and arranged an extremely comprehensive bibliography on *Women in Industry* for WIC, which was published in 1915.[23] There were also some important historical accounts. B. L. Hutchins, who was for some time editor of the *Women's Industrial News*, and who had co-authored *A History of Factory Legislation* with Amy Harrison in 1903,[24] published her important survey of *Women in Modern Industry* in 1915.[25] Alice Clark's *Working Life of Women in the Seventeenth Century* was influenced by the ideas of the FWG, and her research was indeed financed by a leading member of the FWG, Mrs George Bernard Shaw.[26] Mabel Atkinson's 'The economic foundations of the Women's Movement' appeared as a Fabian Tract in 1914.[27] By that time Lucy Wyatt Papworth, as secretary of the WIC, could report that the Council had concluded investigations into 117 different trades as well as having organized extensive inquiries into home work.[28] The Council also carried out a wide-ranging survey of married women's work, which was edited and published by Clementina Black in 1915.[29] Important publications on women's contemporary economic position by members of the FWG during these years included Ellen Smith's study of *Wage-Earning Women and Their Dependants* (1915),[30] a survey which helped to dispel the comfortable middle-class assumption that most women were supported by a male breadwinner, and contributed towards the

---

[23] *Women in Industry: A Bibliography*, selected and arranged by Lucy Wyatt Papworth and Dorothy M. Zimmern (The Women's Industrial Council, 1915).

[24] B. L. Hutchins and A. Harrison, *A History of Factory Legislation* (P. S. King, London, 1903).

[25] B. L. Hutchins, *Women in Modern Industry* (G. Bell, London, 1915).

[26] Alice Clark, *Working Life of Women in the Seventeenth Century* (1919; Routledge & Kegan Paul, 1982). For acknowledgement of the debt to Mrs G. Bernard Shaw see Alice Clark's preface, p. viii.

[27] M. A. Atkinson, 'The economic foundations of the Women's Movement', Fabian Tract, no. 175 (London, 1914).

[28] Mappen, *Helping Women at Work*, p. 18.

[29] Clementina Black (ed.), *Married Women's Work, Being the Report of an Enquiry Undertaken by the Women's Industrial Council* (1915; Virago, London, 1983).

[30] Ellen Smith, *Wage-Earning Women and Their Dependants* (Fabian Society, London, 1915).

feminist critique of the family wage expressed most notably in Eleanor Rathbone's writings, her essay on 'The remuneration of women's services' published in 1917,[31] and her subsequent book, *The Disinherited Family* (1924).[32] Mention should also be made of Maud Pember Reeves's *Round About a Pound a Week* (1913), based on the FWG's investigations into the daily expenditure of poor families in Lambeth, an account which made a strong immediate impact; impressing on the public the impossible predicament of working-class mothers trying to feed and clothe their families adequately in a context of desperate financial hardship and squalid, overcrowded conditions.[33]

All these texts have since become the 'classics' of women's social and economic history. Considered alongside other explorations and analyses of women's social and economic predicament which appeared around the same time, such as Olive Schreiner's widely read *Woman and Labour* (1911)[34] and the now less well-known works by Helena Swanwick (*The Future of the Women's Movement*, 1913),[35] and Wilma Meikle (*Towards a Sane Feminism*, 1916),[36] they demonstrate an impressive efflorescence of feminist thinking about women's working lives and economic position within the family in the period preceding and during the War.

The urgency of the need to find ways of guaranteeing some economic independence to women within marriage emerged as a dominant theme in this literature. As we have seen in chapter 1, many feminists had come to find the idea of being reduced to economic dependence degrading: they did not want to become 'kept women' at any price. 'The one thing for which we think women should never be paid', Mrs Pember Reeves had insisted, summarizing discussions of the FWG in 1910, 'is the relation-

[31] Eleanor Rathbone, 'The remuneration of women's services', *The Economic Journal* (March 1917).

[32] Eleanor Rathbone, *The Disinherited Family: A Plea for the Endowment of the Family* (Edward Arnold, London, 1924).

[33] Maud Pember Reeves, *Round About a Pound a Week* (G. Bell, London, 1913).

[34] Olive Schreiner, *Woman and Labour* (Fisher Unwin, London, 1911).

[35] Helena Swanwick, *The Future of the Women's Movement* (G. Bell, London, 1913).

[36] Wilma Meikle, *Towards a Sane Feminism* (Grant Richards, London, 1916).

ship of wifehood.'[37] Mabel Atkinson, Olive Schreiner, Alice Clark and many other feminist writers staunchly repudiated any notion of the economic dependence of a wife on a male breadwinner as 'natural' or as a universal feature of human society. For them, 'sex-parasitism' was a historically and class-specific phenomenon, and they all determined upon investigating its origins.

Schreiner's conviction was that those historical and particularly technological changes which had removed industry from the home had deprived middle-class women of social usefulness and reduced them to the 'parasitic' or doll-like status of fine-ladyism. Textile production had become concentrated in factories, and one by one, tasks which had traditionally been performed by the mistress of the household had become mechanized and the presence of large-scale industry often dependent on a male workforce. Her book was written in an intensely lyrical and polemic style:

> Our spinning wheels are all broken; in a thousand huge buildings steam-driven looms, guided by a few hundred thousands of hands (often those of men), produce the clothings of half the world . . .
>
> Our hoes and our grindstones passed from us long ago, when the ploughman and the miller took our place; but for a time we kept possession of the kneading trough and the brewing-vat. Today, steam often shapes our bread, and the loaves are set down at our very door — it may be by a man-driven motor-car! . . . The army of rosy milkmaids has passed away for ever, to give place to the cream-separator and the largely male-and-machinery manipulated butter pat. In every direction the ancient saw, that it was exclusively the woman's sphere to prepare the viands for her household, has become, in proportion as civilisation has perfected itself, an antiquated lie.[38]

Schreiner's proposals clearly had an inspirational effect on many, and *Woman and Labour* was sometimes referred to as 'the Bible of

---

[37] Maud Pember Reeves, introductory lecture (summarized by Mrs G. B. Shaw), Fabian Women's Group, 'Summary of eight papers and discussions upon the disabilities of mothers and workers', p. 5.

[38] Schreiner, *Woman and Labour* (1911; Virago, London, 1978), pp. 50–1.

the woman's movement'.[39] Her thesis embraced a number of important issues. She was well aware, for instance, of women's changing role in reproduction as well as production. Infant mortality rates had been falling, and women were bearing fewer children than they had in the past. Full-time mothering, she pointed out, had become reduced to an episode in most women's lives, particularly in 'higher' social groups:

> even those among us who are child-bearers are required in proportion as the class of race to which we belong stands high in the scale of civilisation, to produce in most cases a limited number of offspring; so that even for these of us, child-bearing and suckling, instead of filling the entire circle of female life from the first appearance of puberty to the end of middle age, becomes an episodal occupation, employing from three or four to ten or twenty of the threescore-and-ten-years which are allotted to human life. In such societies the statement ... that the main and continuous occupation of all women from puberty to age is the bearing and suckling of children, and that this occupation must fully satisfy all her needs for social labour and activity, becomes an antiquated and unmitigated misstatement.[40]

Schreiner's insistence that 'fully-developed natures need love and work', and her formulation of the demands of the Women's Movement, 'give us Labour and the training which fits us for labour', clearly articulated the goals of many of her contemporaries; she supplied a cogent analysis of the origins of middle-class feminism and at the same time she took cognizance of the position of working-class women. Industrialism, she claimed, had had the effect of confining women lower down the social scale to the lowest-paid and worst forms of drudgery. As standards of living rose, she predicted, 'female parasitism' would percolate down the class hierarchy.[41]

Mabel Atkinson's Fabian Tract, 'The economic foundation of the Women's Movement' (1914), offered an analysis which was in many ways similar to Olive Schreiner's, although her

[39] Vera Brittain, *Testament of Youth: An Autobiographical Study of the Years 1900–1925* (Gollancz, London, 1933), p. 41.
[40] Schreiner, *Woman and Labour*, p. 65.
[41] Ibid., p. 79ff.

approach was more that of the theoretical economist, her prose
style markedly less florid, and she was more centrally concerned
with social class. Like Schreiner she saw the impact of the
Industrial Revolution as having decisively altered women's role
in the family and in the economy. Prior to the Industrial
Revolution, the family had functioned as an economic unit in
which women had worked as the partners of men in production
primarily for use rather than exchange.[42] Here she quoted
examples of women's working lives in the sixteenth and seventeenth centuries. Fitzherbert's *Book of Husbandry*, for instance
(originally compiled in 1534 and reprinted by the English Dialect
Society in 1882), described the duties of the wife of a sixteenth-
century husbandman as encompassing a myriad of tasks: housekeeping, childcare, and the supervision of servants; but also the
supervision of milling, baking, brewing, dairy work, the care of
poultry and pigs, gardening, spinning, and the marketing of
any surplus produce.[43] Wives were often business partners in
their husbands' business enterprises and it was by no means
uncommon for them to continue running farms or shops after
their husbands' deaths. Industrialization changed all this.
Mechanization took work out of the home and the family was
broken up as a unit of production. Production for use rather
than for the market declined rapidly. Women's lives altered
beyond recognition but here class position was crucial. 'To
put it shortly, parasitism became the fate of the middle class
women, ruthless exploitation that of the working class women.'[44]
Working-class women and their children (who earlier had worked
equally as part of the family unit) were initially absorbed in
large numbers into the new factories. Atkinson pointed out that
the different experiences of working- and middle-class women
in this respect accounted for much of the controversy amongst
contemporary feminists. Middle-class women felt *excluded* from
work, mainly by middle-class men, whereas the main grievance
of their working-class counterparts was that *their* working hours
were too long and that they were carrying too heavy a burden:

[42] Atkinson, 'Economic foundations of the Women's Movement', p. 3.
[43] Ibid.
[44] Ibid., pp. 6–7.

What the woman of the proletariat feels as her grievance is that her work is too long and too monotonous, the burden laid upon her too heavy. Moreover, in her case that burden is due to the power of capitalistic exploitation resulting from the injustice of our social system. It is not due, or not at least, to any considerable extent, to the fact that the men of her class shut her out from gainful occupations. Therefore, among the working women there is less sex-consciousness. Evolving social enthusiasm tends to run rather into the channel of the labour revolt in general than into a specific revolution against the conditions alleged to be due to sex differences. The Working Woman feels her solidarity with the men of her class rather than their antagonism to her. The reforms that she demands are not independence and the right to work but rather the protection against the unending burden of toil which has been laid upon her.[45]

However Atkinson, like Schreiner, thought that one of the changes implicit in the present situation was that working-class women would seek 'protection' in the home and workplace at the expense of autonomy. In the long term, they might come to live through the same experiences of 'parasitism' as middle-class women.[46]

Rewriting history and anthropology

Members of the FWG put historical research high on their agenda of priorities, arguing that without a knowledge of the past it was impossible to comprehend the present, and bemoaning the fact that women and their concerns had been 'taken for granted and practically ignored by our historians.'[47] 'With all deference to Rogers, Ashley, Toynbee, Hasbach and Cunningham', wrote Charlotte Wilson in 1911, 'the economic history of this country from the point of view of the workers, to say nothing of the women workers, has yet to be written.'[48] A number of Fabian Women set out energetically to remedy this

[45] Ibid., p. 15.
[46] Ibid.
[47] Fabian Women's Group, 'Three years' work', p. 14.
[48] Ibid.

deficiency. Charlotte Wilson, Mabel Atkinson, B. L. Hutchins, Maria Sharpe Pearson, Elspeth Carr and several others contributed historical papers which were read before the group between 1908 and 1911. The fifteen historical papers which were recorded as having been completed by 1915 ranged widely, focussing on women in the Anglo-Saxon, medieval, Tudor and pre-industrial periods.[49] Themes of interest included the changing patterns and context of household organization, the extent of economic opportunities existing for women in different historical eras; women's contribution in various industries, such as wool, linen and mining; and the relationship between family structures and earlier modes of production and consumption.

Outstanding amongst feminist historiography in this context was Alice Clark's *Working Life of Women in the Seventeenth Century*, published in 1919. Clark's meticulously scholarly investigation was stimulated by a reading of Olive Schreiner: it was her reading of *Woman and Labour*, she claimed, which had impressed her with 'the sociological importance of past economic conditions for women', and 'the difference between reality and the commonly perceived generalisations as to women's productive capacity.'[50] Like Schreiner, Clark was convinced of the need for women to involve themselves in productive work as well as motherhood. She depicted seventeenth-century women as integrated within the family economy in a way which enabled them to combine work with motherhood more easily than their late-Victorian and early-twentieth-century equivalents. Capitalism had *reduced* women's role in production, and for Clark as well as Schreiner, the material rewards of industrial progress had to be weighed against this impoverishment of women's social and economic role. It is clear from the concluding pages of Clark's book that she saw women's exclusion from production as the root cause of their oppression in public life, underlying and making possible 'the organisation of a State which regards the purposes of life solely from the male standpoint.'[51]

Such feminist interpretations of economic history were directly at odds with orthodox accounts, which depended on a 'whiggish'

[49] Ibid., pp. 14—15.
[50] Clark, *Working Life of Women*, p. 308
[51] Ibid., p. 308.

belief in history-as-progress. Although the historical writings of
J. L. and Barbara Hammond, from a Socialist perspective,
were beginning to challenge complacency about the effects of
industrial capitalism on standards of living amongst the British
population, particularly by emphasizing the distress and disrup-
tion accompanying the early periods of technological change,[52]
the dominant interpretation of the Industrial Revolution was
still optimistic, emphasizing the long-term benefits of economic
growth. Accounts of the impact of industrial development on
the family tended to be coloured by this optimism, and owed
much to the tenets of social theorists such as Herbert Spencer,
who had seen the history of the family in 'civilized' society as a
key theme in social evolution and human progress. The nuclear
monogamous family of the Victorian bourgeoisie, headed by
the breadwinning husband, who relieved his wife from any
necessity of working for her own support, thus enabling her to
concentrate all her energies on the bearing and rearing of
children, represented for Spencer, as for many of his contemporaries, the high point of 'efficiency' in social organization.[53]
Indeed, this very exemption of women from economic activity
was used as an index of the progress made by societies moving
away from 'savagery' to 'civilization'.[54]

These contrasting explanations of economic change were lo-
cated in a wider context of controversy which raged not only
amongst economic historians, but amongst anthropologists
and others concerned with understanding the development of
the family in history. In her book *Patriarchal Precedents* (1983),
Rosalind Coward has drawn our attention to the explosion of
controversy amongst anthropologists and social theorists in late-

---

[52] J. L. and B. Hammond, *The Village Labourer 1760–1832: A Study in the
Government of England Before the Reform Bill* (Longmans, London, 1911); *The
Town Labourer, 1760–1832* (Longmans, London, 1917); *The Skilled Labourer,
1760–1832* (Longmans, London, 1919); and their later *The Rise of Modern
Industry* (Methuen, London, 1925).

[53] Herbert Spencer, *Principles of Sociology* (Williams & Norgate, London,
1876), vol. I; see esp. part III, 'Domestic relations'.

[54] Ibid. See also Lorna Duffin, 'Prisoners of progress: women and evolution',
in *The Nineteenth Century Woman: Her Cultural and Physical World*, ed. Sara
Delamont and Lorna Duffin (Croom Helm, London, 1978).

Victorian Britain.[55] This controversy centred upon interpretations of the function and history of the family and kinship and
on the changing relationships between men and women. Central
to this debate, Coward has shown, was the question of whether
the patriarchal family, generally assumed to be the basic unit of
human society, had indeed always existed, or whether patriarchy
had evolved out of earlier *matriarchal* social forms. 'It must
surely be no coincidence', she has written, 'that these debates
occurred at precisely the moment when nineteeth-century feminism made its impact.'[56]

Feminism did not merely enter into the discussion of what
was already an explosive area, it can be argued to have fuelled
the whole controversy. Even before the members of the Fabian
Women's Group attempted to systematize their historical inves-
tigations, groups of feminists had applied themselves to a scrutiny
of anthropological accounts of family history. In 1885 Eleanor
Marx and Edward Aveling had published an article entitled
'The Woman Question, from a Socialist point of view', in the
Westminster Review,[57] in which they discussed the ideas of the
German Socialist writer August Bebel, whose book *Die Frau in
der Vergangenheit, Gegenwart und Zukunft* had been translated into
English in 1885 as *Woman in the Past, Present and Future*.[58] Cheap
translations of Bebel's text were advertised in the columns of
the feminist newspaper *Shafts* in the 1890s.[59] The Marx–Aveling
article also recommended a reading of Engels's *Origin of the
Family, Private Property and the State* (first published in 1884) as
crucial reading for feminists.[60] These texts soon became familiar

[55] Rosalind Coward, *Patriarchal Precedents: Sexuality and Social Relations*
(Routledge & Kegan Paul, London, 1983).
[56] Ibid., p. 10.
[57] Eleanor Marx and Edward Aveling, 'The Woman Question, from a
Socialist point of view', *Westminster Review*, 6, no. 25 (1885).
[58] Ferdinand August Bebel, *Die Frau in der Vergangenheit, Gegenwart, und
Zukunft* (Zurich, 1883); translated by H. B. Adams Walther as *Woman in the
Past, Present and Future* (Modern Press, London, 1885).
[59] *Shafts, A Paper for Women and the Working Classes*, 28 January 1893, p. 199.
[60] Marx and Aveling, 'The Woman Question', p. 209; F. Engels, *Ursprung
der Familie, des Eigenthums und des Staats* (Zurich, 1884; the first translated
edition easily available was by E. Untermann, published by C. H. Kerr,
Chicago, 1902).

in 'advanced circles'. In London during the late 1880s, for instance, a small group of feminists and 'freethinkers' came together to form what they began by calling 'The Wollstonecraft Society', but soon renamed 'The Men and Women's Club', aiming for 'the free and unreserved discussion of all matters in any way connected with the mutual position and relation of men and women'.[61] Karl Pearson, Olive Schreiner and Maria Sharpe were three of the leading spirits. Reading lists compiled by Marie Sharpe, as secretary of the club, survive amongst the papers which are now in the archives of University College, London, and it is interesting to note that one of the earliest underlines 'work to be done on the Matriarchate', listing the anthropological writings of Bachofen, McLennan, Lubbock and Maine as critical sources.[62]

Two feminist writers in particular, Mona Caird and Emma Frances Brooke, both of them connected with Schreiner and the Men and Women's Club network, managed to familiarize themselves with the anthropological literature and made their own contributions to the debate. Mona Caird's *The Morality of Marriage, and Other Essays on the Status and Destiny of Woman* appeared in 1897, but was based on a series of articles which she had originally published in the *Westminster Review* between 1888 and 1894 (and which had generated an enormous amount of reader response and controversy).[63] Caird quoted the researches of Lippert, McLennan, Bachofen and Lubbock in support of her contention that patriarchy had evolved through marriage by capture and by purchase, superseding earlier social

[61] The archive relating to the Men and Women's Club is in the Pearson Collection, housed in University College, London. For recent accounts of the Club's doings and significance see Judith Walkowitz, 'Science, feminism and romance: the Men and Women's Club, 1885–1889', *History Workshop Journal*, no. 21 (Spring 1986), and Lucy Bland, 'Marriage laid bare: middle class women and marital sex, 1880–1914', in *Labour and Love: Women's Experience of Home and Family, 1850–1940*, ed. Jane Lewis (Blackwell, Oxford, 1986); see also ch. 4, below.

[62] Archive of Men and Women's Club, Pearson Collection, University College, London; see literature list by Maria Sharpe.

[63] Mona Caird, *The Morality of Marriage, and Other Essays on the Status and Destiny of Woman* (Redway, London, 1897). See also H. Quilter, *Is Marriage a Failure? . . . Letters to the Daily Telegraph in response to an article by Mona Caird* (Sonnenschein, London, 1888).

forms based on matriarchy and the descent of property through women. Like Engels, she concluded that the subordination of women was rooted in economics and the development of specific family forms and could no longer be seen as a reflection of human nature.[64] For Caird, it was inevitable that present-day feminism should challenge women's economic role in the family, since this was where the roots of oppression were to be found.[65] Emma Brooke's series of articles on 'The position of women: Its origin and history', published in the *Woman's Signal* in 1894, made very similar points.[66] Like Caird, she had found her imagination fired by anthropological speculation about matriarchal forms since these theories meant that 'The deeply-rooted idea of the natural subordination of women to men is thus negatived in the very earliest phase of what can be traced to human existence.'[67] Emma Brooke used her reading of Lubbock and other anthropologists to take issue directly with those ideas about women's economic dependence and social progress which Herbert Spencer had outlined in *Principles of Sociology*.[68]

Much was at stake in these controversies, and there can be no doubt that the feminist perspective appeared distinctly subversive. Spencer's conviction that the progress from 'savagery' to 'civilization' was accompanied by the marginalization of women in the economy had made it difficult for him to understand why women failed to enjoy this 'protection' in the patriarchal family; why late-nineteenth-century feminists sought new occupations for women and claimed 'rights' in the opportunity to work outside the home. He had suggested that this might be regarded as a temporary 'anomaly', traceable in part to demographic factors, that is to the current imbalance between the sexes in the population (what contemporaries dubbed the 'surplus women' problem); implying that were there enough men to go round, women would cease their clamour for economic

[64] Caird, *Morality and Marriage*, pp. 21–40.
[65] Ibid., p. 67.
[66] Emma Brooke, 'The position of woman: its origin and history', *The Woman's Signal, A Weekly Record of the Progress of the Woman's Movement*, 8 March, 29 March 1894.
[67] Brooke, 'The position of woman', p. 155.
[68] Ibid.

independence.[69] His sociological prose, however, had slid quickly into prescription when he had insisted that 'if women comprehended all that is contained in the domestic sphere, they would ask no other.'[70] Similarly Frederic Harrison, who also maintained that in a rightly ordered society woman would be 'relieved by man from the harder tasks of industry' so that she might concentrate on the home and the next generation, condemned the 'specious agitation' of the Women's Movement as threatening 'social anarchy'; and like Spencer, Harrison slid easily into a prescriptive tone. 'To keep the Family true, refined, affectionate and faithful', he urged, 'is a grander task than to govern the state; it is a task which needs the whole energies, the entire life of woman.'[71]

In spite of the hostile reaction which they often provoked, feminist theories about the social and economic history of the family blossomed in the period preceding the First World War. Thereafter some ground was lost. However, large-scale, ambitious histories of the family continued to contain a profound significance for feminism, and as the list of 'authorities' grew we find individual feminists grappling critically with the lengthy treatises of Westermarck, for instance, and Mueller-Lyer.[72] For Westermarck the history of human marriage was the history of a relation 'in which women have been gradually triumphing over the passions, the prejudices and the selfish interests of men'.[73] He held distinctly ambivalent views about the desirability of economic independence for wives and mothers. A mother's employment, he suggested, tended 'to weaken the ties between the members of the family, and the home may be badly managed'.[74] Contrasting with this value-stance, Mueller-Lyer's thesis, celebrating the Women's Movement as a key

[69] Spencer, *Principles of Sociology*, p. 792.
[70] Ibid.
[71] Frederic Harrison, 'The emancipation of women', *Fortnightly Review*, no. 298 (October 1891), p. 452.
[72] Edward Westermarck, *The History of Human Marriage* (Macmillan, London, 1894; F. Mueller-Lyer, *The Family*, trans. Stella Browne (Allen & Unwin, London, 1931).
[73] Westermarck, *History of Human Marriage*, pp. 549–50.
[74] Ibid., p. 90.

social advance heralding an era when women would be welcomed into all variety of activities and occupations (with changes in domestic organization to ease the combination of employment and motherhood), was more congenial to feminists of the 1930s. Indeed Mueller-Lyer's book *The Family*, originally published in Munich in 1912, was translated into English by the feminist Stella Browne in 1931.[75] Margaret Cole, writing in 1937, felt that there was little to be gained from speculative anthropology which attempted to settle the question of origins or to establish the historical precedence of one form of sexual relationships (polygamy/monogamy, matriarchy/patriarchy) over another.[76] The evidence was simply inadequate. There was much more to be learned from a study of the empirical anthropological investigations of authorities like Ruth Benedict and Margaret Mead, which emphasized the diversity of cultural patterns and family forms. Feminists could take heart, she argued, from work of this kind, since it implied fluidity and above all scope for social change.[77]

Feminist interpretations of nineteenth-century economic history also lost impetus after the First World War. It is significant that the one major study of women's work in the Industrial Revolution to be published in this period (by Ivy Pinchbeck in 1930) adopted a conservative ideological framework of analysis.[78] Pinchbeck's argument, contrasting strongly with that of Alice Clark, was that industrialization had solved more problems than it had created for women, at least in the long term. The shifting of industrial activity into factories had, she contended, improved conditions of home life and, most crucially, 'the industrial revolution marked a real advance, since it led to the assumption that men's wages should be paid on a family basis, and prepared the way for the more modern conception that in the rearing of children and in home-making, the married woman makes an adequate economic contribution.'[79] There were a

[75] Mueller-Lyer, *The Family*; see esp. pp. 352–6.

[76] Margaret Cole, *Marriage, Past and Present* (Dent, London, 1939), pp. 10–32.

[77] Ibid., pp. 29–32.

[78] Ivy Pinchbeck, *Women Workers and the Industrial Revolution, 1750–1850* (1930; Virago, London, 1981).

[79] Ibid., pp. 312–13.

number of contradictions in Pinchbeck's work, by no means successfully resolved. In her concluding paragraphs she admitted that 'It is only necessary to contrast the vigorous life of the eighteenth century business woman, travelling about the country in her own interests, with the sheltered existence of the Victorian woman, to realise how much the latter had lost in initiative and independence by being protected from all real contact with life.'[80] But she immediately qualified this by asserting that 'To contemporaries, however, the new independence of working women was an even more striking contrast.'[81] Pinchbeck referred here to *single* women. Whilst conceding that the Industrial Revolution had cost the majority of married women their economic independence, she was not prepared to look upon this as 'a retrogressive tendency', especially amongst the working class, where she contended that it made little sense for married women to seek to earn a wage, since 'her earnings rarely balanced the loss to the family from the non-performance of more important domestic duties.'[82]

Middle-class women and the marriage bar

All this would have been anathema to the members of the Fabian Women's Group, with their clearly stated and primary aim of working for economic independence for *all* women, whether or not they elected to become parents. For the majority of these women, 'the family wage' provided no solution, since in Charlotte Wilson's phrase it simply added 'the enslaving economic control of the husband' to that of capitalism.[83] The Group set out on something of a ground-clearing exercise between 1908 and 1910. Two early lectures by Edith Nesbit and Emma Brooke had raised controversial issues about the compatibility between motherhood and other vocations.[84] In response to this, the Studies Committee invited a series of speakers to discuss

[80] Ibid., p. 316.
[81] Ibid.
[82] Ibid., p. 312.
[83] Charlotte Wilson, in Fabian Women's Group, 'Three years' work', p. 9.
[84] Ibid., p. 10.

further the question of whether women could be regarded as suffering from any 'natural disabilities' as workers when they were not engaged in child-bearing, and secondly, to focus upon the disabilities of mothers as workers. Summaries of these papers and the ensuing discussions were printed and privately circulated within the Fabian Society in 1909 and 1910, and a conference, to which interested representatives from women's trade unions, teaching organizations and other groups were invited, followed in July 1910.[85]

These studies and discussions touched upon an enormous range of issues: physiological, anthropological, historical and economic. The first series of discussions resulted in a basic consensus that the so-called 'natural disabilities' of women had been greatly exaggerated. Summarizing, Emma Brooke gave short shrift to any notion that women were 'disabled' (through their menstrual cycles or any alleged incapacity for abstract reasoning) from carrying out responsible or productive tasks. 'The natural disabilities of women as workers', she concluded, 'have been, and still are, absurdly exaggerated.'[86] The second round of papers on mothers as workers raised thornier issues. The group were united in their distaste for 'parasitism' and agreed that all women, whether married or unmarried, who were not actively involved in the care of young children, should work for their own support. There was also a strong general feeling that 'the inevitable disabilities' of maternity, particularly when removed from a context of poverty and social disadvantage, had been much exaggerated. Dr Ethel Vaughan-Sawyer summed up her own paper on this theme by remarking that

> the inherent disabilities of maternity are few in number and not very serious. In many healthy women they are almost negligible. There is, however, a minimum of three months, two preceding and one following the confinement, during which, in the interests of both mother and child, no woman, however healthy, should be required to undertake any arduous duty.[87]

[85] Fabian Women's Group pamphlets, see n. 21 above.
[86] Fabian Women's Group, 'Summary of six papers', pp. 5–6.
[87] Fabian Women's Group, 'Summary of eight papers', p. 10.

Some members of the group concluded that many mothers of young children were quite capable of continuing self-support, especially if they had access to nursery facilities and flexible working arrangements. Maud Pember Reeves suggested that 'certain women, suited for the care of children, might choose to earn their living by taking daily charge of a carefully restricted number, their own and other people's; other women, whose abilities lay in a different direction, might spend the working hours of each day in another trade or profession.'[88] Both groups, she added, might profit from such an arrangement: 'The wife who earned her own money would be in a position of greater dignity and safety; and the mother who each evening received back a well nurtured and cared-for child would probably be a better mother than the harassed woman-of-all-work who now makes such an inefficient parent.[89]

There was a good deal of support for this viewpoint. Mrs Stanbury believed that it was crucially a question of earning power, suggesting that 'given an independent income of say, £100 a year, probably few mothers would desire to leave their young children for the entire day whilst they went out to work; but also practically no woman with £100 a year would choose to spend her whole time and energy in tending her children.'[90] She insisted that the real problem was that the working conditions of most women at the time, both inside and outside the family, were intolerable; however, the remedy lay not in driving women back into the home, but in fighting for conditions which were better suited to their needs. There was considerable interest in the views of the German feminist writer, Lily Braun (which were summarized by B. L. Hutchins), and which emphasized the advantages of crèches, communal kitchens and collective housekeeping.[91] Charlotte Perkins Gilman's ideas about collectivizing domestic work in order to free women for work outside the home were also summarized in a paper by Dr O'Brien Harris.[92]

---

[88] Ibid., p. 5.
[89] Ibid.
[90] Ibid., p. 29.
[91] Ibid., pp. 22–4.
[92] Ibid., pp. 25–7.

However, the feeling of the group was that even if such arrangements were feasible and became more widely implemented, motherhood would still leave most women economically vulnerable for a short period in their lives — probably around three months — each time they gave birth. Several contributors argued that the State should accept responsibility for its future citizens in this respect through the payment of a system of 'disability allowances' for mothers.[93] Maud Pember Reeves concluded her summary of the Group's discussions by suggesting that, should such a system of allowances be obtained from the state, and given some rationalization of 'the primitively chaotic economy' of the contemporary home, the women present were at one in believing that it was not only possible, but positively desirable, that mothers should take up the role of productive workers alongside men in any Socialist society of the future.[94]

Consonant with this viewpoint, the Fabian Women's Group was active in its opposition to contemporary attempts to impose restrictions on married women's work. In 1909 the Group raised the issue of the marriage bar, which some local authorities were invoking to dismiss women teachers, at the Fabian Society Conference, and the following year they co-operated with the Fabian Education Group to organize a discussion on the subject at Clifford's Inn.[95] Mrs A. K. Williams, the first woman Vice-President of the London Teachers Association, agreed to address the conference. Mabel Atkinson noted ruefully in 1914 that

In almost all occupations the public acknowledgement of marriage means for a woman dismissal from her post and diminished economic resources. This is the case in practically all the Government posts: women civil servants, including even factory inspectors and school inspectors, are compelled to resign on marriage. Even the women school medical officers of the L.C.C. [London County Council] are now forced to sign a contract stating that they will retire on marriage, and although the same rule is not so strict in private business, there, too, it is rare for married women to be employed.

[93] Ibid., p. 31.
[94] Ibid.
[95] Fabian Women's Group, *Minutes*.

Most women, that is to say, can only continue to preserve that
economic independence, so keenly appreciated and won by such
fierce struggles, on condition of compulsory celibacy and, what to
many women is far worse, compulsory childlessness.[96]

She took heart, however, from the growing refusal, amongst
middle class women, to accept this enforced choice: 'Against
this state of things a revolt is beginning which so far is barely
articulate, but which is bound to make itself heard in public
before long.'[97] In the same year, Edith Morley identified the
marriage bar as a key issue for feminists in the study of *Women
Workers in Seven Professions* which she edited for the FWG:

> Wherever the subject of the employment of married women is
> mentioned — and its crops up in most of the papers — there is adverse
> comment on the economically unsound, unjust, and racially danger-
> ous tendency in many salaried professions to enforce upon women
> resignation on marriage. It is clear that professional women are
> beginning to show resentment at the attempt to force celibacy upon
> them: they feel themselves insulted and wronged as human beings
> when, being physically and mentally fit, they are not permitted to
> judge for themselves in this matter.[98]

Morley expressed indignation at the cost involved in dismissing
women on marriage from jobs which were congenial to them, a
cost not only to the women themselves, in terms of their loss of
salary, but to the community, in terms of the waste of money
which had been expended on training. She also suggested that
women in happy marriages were probably better equipped to
endure the strain of demanding professional work than were
their unmarried equivalents.[99]

Atkinson and Morley both identified concerted opposition to
the marriage bar as a crucial strategy for feminists, only just
beginning to gather momentum; but it would have been difficult
for them, writing in 1914, to foresee the size of the task. During
the war, the need for women's work in both professional and

[96] Atkinson, 'Economic foundations of the Women's Movement', pp. 17–18.
[97] Ibid., p. 18.
[98] Morley (ed.), *Women Workers in Seven Professions*, p. xv.
[99] Ibid.

manual occupations served to conceal the strength of the latent ideological opposition to married women's employment. This became all too apparent in the 1920s. The Sex-Disqualification (Removal) Act of 1919 proved an illusory gain. Although it stated that neither sex nor marriage should disqualify anyone from appointments or professions, it seems to have been wholly ineffectual. At the beginning of the 1920s, public health authorities in Glasgow and St Pancras dismissed married women doctors, nurses and charwomen in their employ, in spite of loud opposition from feminists, and Dr Mabel Ramsay commented in a letter to *Time and Tide* in 1922 that marriage was coming to be regarded as the 'bar sinister' of women's work.[100] Against a background of growing competition for jobs, local authorities all over the country either sacked their married women teachers, or introduced new contracts requiring women to resign in the event of their marriage. Nottingham introduced the marriage bar in 1921. Lincoln sacked its 37 married women teachers in 1922. Leeds, Sheffield, Smethwick, Sunderland and Barnsley followed suit: only widows and those who could demonstrate that their husbands were economically dependent on them were allowed to keep their jobs.[101] By 1926 it has been estimated that about three-quarters of all local authorities operated some kind of marriage bar, providing for the resignation of women teachers on marriage and often involving the dismissal of serving teachers.[102]. London introduced a bar in 1923.[103]

The general rationale for dismissal was that 'women could not serve two masters', or as one member of the Herefordshire Education Committee claimed, 'There are few women in the world who could do two full-time jobs at one time.'[104] Not surprisingly, many women were incensed at rulings which not only deprived them of a livelihood and worthwhile occupation,

[100] *Time and Tide*, 13 January 1922; see also 17 March 1922, 26 May 1922.

[101] Geoffrey Partington, *Women Teachers in the Twentieth Century in England and Wales* (NFER Publishing, Windsor, Berks., 1976), pp. 28–31.

[102] Alison M. Oram, 'Serving two masters? The introduction of a marriage bar in teaching in the 1920s', in The London Feminist History Group, *The Sexual Dynamics of History, Men's Power, Women's Resistance* (Pluto Press, London, 1983), p. 147.

[103] Partington, *Women Teachers*, p. 33.

[104] Ibid., p. 31.

but which also implied that they were incapable of organizing their own concerns. The National Union of Teachers, although in theory opposed to the marriage bar, was in practice wedded to the interests of its male membership, and its male-controlled executive was highly ambivalent towards feminist issues such as equal pay or the marriage bar. Some action was taken in support of those dismissed, but support for their case was often lukewarm.[105] The feminist National Union of Women Teachers was much more energetic in its opposition to the marriage bar during the 1920s, although it lacked the resources of the parent union. When test cases against the unfair dismissal of women teachers in 1923 and 1925 were lost, and attempts to invoke the Sex-Disqualification (Removal) Act revealed as fruitless, the NUWT began to work with other feminist organizations like the Fabian Women's Group and the Open Door Council instead, in an attempt to influence public policy. This proved more successful, in a limited way. For instance, the NUWT sponsored the election of their representative, Agnes Dawson, to the London County Council in order to try to defend the interests of women teachers, and her activities helped bring about the abolition of London's marriage bar in 1935.[106]

However, writing in the 1930s, feminists like Winifred Holtby, Vera Brittain and Margaret Cole were ruefully aware of the continuing strength of public opinion reflected in the various restrictions still hedging around women's — and particularly married women's — right to employment on the same terms as men.[107] In *Women and a Changing Civilisation* (1935), Winifred Holtby argued that

there has been constant and recurrent opposition to the artificial restriction of women's labour. National and international societies have been founded to carry on the struggle. The Open Door International and the Equal Rights International are symptomatic of the tendency both of legislation and its critics to spread across

[105] Oram, 'Serving two masters?', pp. 143–4.
[106] Ibid., pp. 145–6.
[107] Winifred Holtby, *Women, and a Changing Civilisation* (1935; Academy Press, Chicago, 1978); Cole, *Marriage, Past and Present*; Vera Brittain, *Women's Work in Modern England* (Noel Douglas, London, 1928).

the frontiers of states and continents. The organisation of women
teachers and women doctors to uphold equalitarian principles
demonstrates the final solidarity of professional with industrial
women. But still in 1934, with the best intentions in the world,
public authorities dismiss married women employees upon marriage;
factories exclude them from special processes; unequal pay is given
for equal work. Still in the sacred names of motherhood and chivalry,
women are obstructed in their attempt to earn a living wage; and
still, because of their lower pay, they undercut men, lower wage
rates, and act as unwilling black-legs throughout industry.[108]

However, this 'final solidarity of professional with industrial
women' depicted by Holtby had never been wholly in evidence.
Feminists had been largely united in defending the rights of
'professional' women to continue with their careers after marriage, but the issue of 'protective' or 'restrictive' legislation in
relation to working-class women in industry had always proved
a rather more controversial issue.

Working-class women and the trade unions

Many feminists *were* united in defending the rights of *all* married
women to employment on the same terms as men, and they saw
no need for exceptions to this principle. In the later nineteenth
century, however, there had been heated controversy over
whether women needed 'special protection' against industrial
hazards in some branches of industry (such as those branches
of the pottery industry where white lead was used for glazing);
whether some industries were unsuited to women, and whether
their hours of work needed special regulation (whether, for
instance, nightwork should be permissible for women). Controversy also centred upon the clause in the Factories and Workshops Act of 1891, which stipulated that no employer should
'knowingly employ' any woman within a month of confinement.
Millicent Garrett Fawcett, Elizabeth Garrett Anderson, Cicely
Hamilton and others took an uncompromising line on such
issues, arguing that to classify women workers as in special

[108] Holtby, *Women, and a Changing Civilisation*, p. 82.

82   *The Economic Independence of Women*

need of protection in the labour market on account of their sex was an infringement of individual liberties and tantamount to treating them as minors, unable to look after their own interests.[109] This position was consonant with that adopted by the feminists of the 'Langham Place Circle' in the 1860s; Jessie Boucherett and Helen Blackburn, for instance, had consistently argued for 'a fair field and no favour' for women in the workplace.[110] Many of the early advocates of trade union organization for women, such as Emma Paterson and Ada Heather-Biggs, had fought for the same principles.[111] However, towards the end of the nineteenth century some of those working in the women's trade union movement had adopted a different stance and were more inclined to argue the need for protection. Clementina Black, for instance, who was elected secretary to the Women's Trade Union League after the death of Emma Paterson, was basically in sympathy with the aims of protective legislation, as was Beatrice Webb, both of them arguing that improved conditions for women would be likely, in time, to have a cumulative beneficial effect for all workers in industry.[112]

During the 1890s and in the first decade of the present century these issues were debated with increasing acrimony. In a tract which she wrote for the Fabian Society in 1896, Beatrice Webb insisted that the issue of protective legislation was a class issue, and she lashed out against middle-class feminists and those who she lambasted as 'capitalist's wives and daughters' who were seeking to alarm and confuse working-class women.[113] Beatrice Webb argued that 'The real enemy of the woman worker is not the skilled male operative, but the unskilled and

[109] See Report of Amendments to Factories and Workshops Bill, House of Lords, 23 July 1891 (*Hansard*): Earl Wemyss's motion for the omission of clause 16, discussion of communications from Millicent Garrett Fawcett, Elizabeth Garrett Anderson, Lady Goldsmid et al.

[110] Jessie Boucherett, Helen Blackburn et al., *The Condition of Working Women and the Factory Acts* (Elliot Stock, London, 1896).

[111] B. L. Hutchins, *Women in Modern Industry* (1915; EP Publishing, Wakefield, 1978), pp. 194ff.

[112] Ibid.; see also B. Webb, 'Women and the Factory Acts', Fabian Tract, no. 67 (London 1896); Barbara Drake, *Women in Trade Unions* (1920; Virago, London, 1984), pp. 27ff; and Teresa Olcott, 'Dead centre: the women's trade union movement in London, 1874–1914', *London Journal*, 2, no. 1 (May 1976).

[113] Webb, 'Women and the Factory Acts', p. 9.

half-hearted female "amateur" who simultaneously blacklegs both the workshop and the home.'[114] Most women in industry, she insisted, worked in separate branches or on different processes from men, in areas where sweated conditions, long hours, and low pay were the norm: in such areas factory legislation could only improve conditions and raise the status of the female worker. 'Unfortunately, working women have less power to obtain legislation than middle class women have to obstruct it',[115] she concluded, bitterly.

There can be no doubt that the divisions of social class — in terms of working conditions, and attitudes to work — did underlie much of the controversy over legislation and married women's right to work during these years. We may recall Mabel Atkinson's succinct discussion of the differences in her Fabian Tract, 'The economic foundations of the Women's Movement', in 1914, which emphasized the gulf in attitudes between middle-class feminists who consistently identified freedom to work as a *right*, whereas their working-class counterparts were bent rather on securing protection from an unending burden of toil both at home and in the workplace.[116] However, Beatrice Webb's analysis can be argued to have overstated the divisions. There were undoubtedly some working-class women who were as jealous of their autonomy in the labour market as their middle-class sisters; the ex-factory worker, socialist and trade unionist Ada Nield Chew is a good example.[117] And as B. L. Hutchins made clear in her study of *Women in Industry* (1915) there was always ample evidence of male trade unionists' attempts to exclude women from various trades on the grounds that their proper place was in the home.[118] Many women workers tired of repeatedly finding themselves acting as 'the shuttlecock between the opposing interests of the employer and the men's Union'.[119]

[114] Ibid., p. 15.

[115] Ibid., p. 9.

[116] Atkinson, 'Economic foundations of the Women's Movement', p. 15.

[117] Ada Nield Chew, 'The economic freedom of women', *The Freewoman*, 11 July 1912 (repr. in Doris Nield Chew, *Ada Nield Chew, The Life and Writings of a Working Woman*, Virago, London, 1982).

[118] Hutchins, *Women in Modern Industry*, pp. 191ff.

[119] Ibid., p. 193.

Arguments over the acceptability or otherwise of various forms of 'protective' legislation were then complex and contentious. They were rendered even more so in the context of the public debate over high infant mortality figures at the turn of the century, and particularly over the question of whether high rates of infant deaths could be linked with patterns of married women's work. The ideological climate guaranteed a public disposition to account for infant deaths in terms of inadequate mothering rather than poverty, and working-class mothers who were employed outside the home were seen as constituting a specific social problem.[120] Leading medical authorities such as Sir George Newman (Chief Medical Officer to the Board of Education) and Arthur Newsholme (Medical Officer to the Local Government Board) lent their backing to such interpretations.[121] Even when statistical investigations failed to demonstrate any clear connection between women's work and infant mortality, Newsholme's Reports on the subject to the Local Government Board revealed his ideological prejudices. Women's employment, he insisted,

> must, however, tend on balance to increase infant mortality and to lower the health of older children in the same family. Even when the mother's earnings are necessary for the breadwinning of the family such earnings are secured by some sacrifice of the interests of the next generation . . .

> In a wider sense, *all* industrial occupation of women whether married or unmarried, may be regarded as to some extent inimical to home-making and child care.[122]

---

[120] Carol Dyhouse, 'Working class mothers and infant mortality in England, 1895–1914', *Journal of Social History*, 13, (1979). See also Anna Davin, 'Imperialism and the cult of motherhood', *History Workshop Journal*, (Spring 1978).

[121] George Newman, *Infant Mortality: A Social Problem* (Methuen, London, 1906); Arthur Newsholme, *39th Annual Report of Local Government Board, 1909–1910, Supplement to Report of Board's Medical Officer, Containing a Report on Infant and Child Mortality* (PP 1910, vol. XXXIX); *42nd Annual Report of Local Government Board, Supplement Containing a Second Report on Infant and Child Mortality* (PP 1913, vol. XXXII); and *43rd Annual Report of Local Government Board, Containing a Third Report on Infant Mortality Dealing with Infant Mortality in Lancashire*, (PP 1914, vol. XXXIX).

[122] Newsholme, *Third Report on Infant Mortality* (PP 1914, vol. XXXIX), p. 19).

Statements of this kind were eagerly seized upon by male trade union leaders who resented women workers as a source of cheap competition in the labour market, and who were bent upon securing the principle of a family wage payable to the male breadwinner. Most notable in this context were the effusions of John Burns, who, as President of the Local Government Board, constantly inveighed against the evils of women's employment. In addressing two national conferences on Infant Mortality in 1906 and 1908, Burns portrayed women's work as responsible for infant deaths, rickety and anaemic children, broken homes, low wages, 'idle and loafing husbands' and unhappy and emasculated fathers. 'We have got to restrict married women's labour', he concluded urgently, 'as often and as soon as we can.'[123]

Resolutions passed at the 1906 Conference on Infant Mortality included a call upon the government to introduce further restrictions on married women's work, specifically through extending the provision of the 1891 Factories and Workshops Act by extending the prohibition on employment of women after childbirth from one to three months.[124] Partly in response to this, the Home Office embarked on a more systematic enquiry into the alleged effects of maternal employment on infant deaths, beginning in 1907. The evidence collected seems never to have been collated properly, at least in any published form.[125] Some of the reports of local investigations survive, however, and show interesting results. A careful inquiry which was carried out under the aegis of Dr John Robertson, Medical Officer of Health in Birmingham, in 1908, demonstrated unequivocally that in two of the poorest wards of the city the infant mortality amongst infants whose mothers were in employment was actually *lower* than amongst those whose mothers were not industrially

---

[123] *Report of Proceedings of National Conference on Infantile Mortality ... with Address by the Right Honourable John Burns, M.P.* (London, 1906); and *Report of Proceedings of Second National Conference on Infantile Mortality* (Westminster, 1908).

[124] Ibid.

[125] Home Office Correspondence (Public Record Office, PRO /HO 45 10 335/138532; HO 158/13, Circular dated 10 May 1907, no. 126388/9; 17 December 1907, no. 152746). See also reference in Ministry of Reconstruction, *Report of Women's Employment Committee* (1919), XIV, p. 52.

employed.[126] Commenting upon these findings, Robertson highlighted the key role of a mother's earnings in many working-class households. Working-class wives who shouldered the double burden of work in and outside of the home, he concluded, did so in order to secure extra nourishment for their children. Far from being stereotyped as 'inadequate mothers', they had to be respected as among the most capable and energetic members of the community.[127]

Hardly surprisingly, John Burns's near-hysterical denunciations of married women's work and his portrayal of working wives as bad mothers earned him the enduring enmity of many feminists. Ada Nield Chew wrote vigorously contesting his viewpoint in a number of articles, one of which was published in the suffrage journal, *The Common Cause*.[128] In the *Accrington Observer*, published in her native North-West, she staunchly defended the lifestyle of Lancashire working wives, angrily repudiating any contention that their economic independence as textile workers was secured at the price of domestic competence or the stability of family life.[129] Members of the Fabian Women's Group, notably B. L. Hutchins and Mrs Stanbury, deplored the 'ridiculously partial and unscientific manner and spirit' in which statistics on married women's work and infantile mortality were compiled.[130] The results of the Birmingham inquiry were greeted with great satisfaction as revealing a far more accurate indication of the real picture.[131] None of the women wanted to contest the fact that most working-class women lived lives rendered bleak through hardship and excessive toil. However, B. L. Hutchins, discussing Lily Braun's views on women and

[126] City of Birmingham Health Department, *Report on Industrial Employment of Married Women and Infantile Mortality* (Birmingham, 1910), Birmingham Reference Library, 22451.

[127] Ibid.

[128] Ada Nield Chew, 'The problem of the married working woman', *The Common Cause*, 6 March 1914, repr. in Doris Nield Chew, *Ada Nield Chew*, p. 232.

[129] Ada Nield Chew, letters to the *Accrington Observer*, 26 August 1913, 2 September 1913, 9 September 1913 and 14 October 1913. Repr. in Doris Nield Chew, *Ada Nield Chew*.

[130] Fabian Women's Group, 'Summary of eight papers', p. 19.

[131] Ibid., p. 22.

work, pointed out that factory work might be seen as 'the only form of labour which brings women into association with their fellows and carries with it a possibility of educating and enlightening them and evoking their capacity for organisation',[132] and she suggested that feminists might aim 'at better conditions and shorter hours, at maternity insurance and the establishment of well-ordered crèches, but not at the prohibition of married women's work'.[133] Mrs Stanbury ventured to challenge popular conceptions of the ideal, stay-at-home mother:

> The 'good mother' at home, leading a life quite incredibly bare and monotonous, day by day, year after year, with not a penny of her own, becomes extraordinarily like a fixture in her 'model' dwelling; and as a developing agent for her little child appears to have no value at all. To the superficial observer stagnation may easily be taken for serenity; inertia for nervous strength. In many cases her functioning degenerates into nagging the man for money, and fidgetting her child to keep quiet and 'clean'. In the case of a woman with more aspiration and more character such a life becomes prison-like and intolerable, and her children reflect her in their arrested development. She has no power of expansion. Better by far even the overworked woman, who sees and knows and is – who possesses her soul. The mother who goes out to work, however hardly she may be pressed by long hours, badly arranged work and underpay, is, to my comprehension, not only economically independent, but, other things being equal, more of an individual and therefore a better mother. Her life is not good, but it is relatively better.[134]

It was in this context of debate over the effects of married women's work on family life that the Women's Industrial Council set out in 1908 to conduct a detailed investigation into patterns of married women's work, the results of which were edited by Clementina Black and published in 1915.[135] The Investigation Committee, chaired by Clementina Black, included a number of women active in other women's organiz-

---

[132] Ibid., p. 23.
[133] Ibid.
[134] Ibid., p. 19.
[135] Black, *Married Women's Work*.

ations: B. L. Hutchins, for instance, as a member of the Fabian Women's Group, and others involved in the Women's Labour League. The survey was conducted on the basis of a detailed questionnaire and personal investigations in London, several large provincial towns in the North and Midlands, and it also extended to rural districts.[136]

It is significant that some dissension seems to have arisen during the progress of the inquiry, leading to the resignation of some of the members of the Council. Those resigning included Margaret MacDonald, who had initially been a member of the Investigation Committee, and others of her supporters in the Women's Labour League. It is difficult to retrieve evidence for all the details of disagreement, which seem to have focused upon organizational and procedural matters, but also to have involved a more fundamental divergence of opinion.[137] Most importantly, the Women's Labour League had, by about 1900, come to a position of defining the employment of the mother of young children as a social evil which called for legislation, and were coupling their demands for a family wage with the suggestion that mothers of children under five should ideally be excluded from the labour market. Hardly surprisingly, this did not go down at all well with feminists.[138]

The family wage and maternity endowments

Married Women's Work provides us with an immense amount of detail about both social conditions and attitudes. Clementina Black's introduction attempted a careful summary whilst maintaining a coherent feminist perspective. She began by squarely confronting the widespread popular prejudice against working wives and suggested that it was useful to divide married working-class women into four categories according to whether they did or did not earn, and if they were wage-earners whether they had become so in order to supplement an inadequate family

[136] Ibid., introduction by Ellen Mappen, pp. i—xv.
[137] Ibid., pp. viii—ix.
[138] Margaret Bondfield, *A Life's Work* (Hutchinson. London, 1949), pp. 38—42. See also Margaret MacDonald et al., *Wage Earning Mothers* (Women's Labour League, London, n.d.).

income or simply to acquire a better standard of life. Wives who worked in order to supplement an inadequate family income were, she emphasized, often amongst the hardest-pressed and most overworked members of the community, yet to accuse them of necessarily neglecting their children was unwarranted and unjust. Clearly, whether the children suffered or not depended upon the quality of any substitute arrangements made for their care. Women who chose to work even where there was no pressing economic need were often castigated as behaving reprehensibly, and yet they were often 'conspicuously competent' independent individuals who took pride and pleasure in being able to provide a more comfortable lifestyle for their children.[139] Black emphasized that she had not encountered *any* women willing to advocate legal restrictions on their right to earn. In her view, hardship was the direct result of inadequate wages: 'it must be repeated that what is wrong is not the work for wages of married women, but the under-payment, both of men and women, which compels some women to work who might gladly abstain, and compels those to spend many hours in work who might be glad to spend a few. Under-payment is the evil.'[140] There were a number of remedies which might be envisaged here, and the institution of a minimum wage, the endowment of mothers, or the establishment of a wife's entitlement to a fixed share of her husband's income might all potentially ameliorate conditions. In Black's estimate, the impact of poverty was merely compounded by inflexible social attitudes which insisted that all mothers should stay at home:

The assumption, however, that the existence of babies must and should in all cases and for ever prevent the mothers of them from going out to work would be rash. It is by no means always true that a mother is the person best qualified to take care of her infant. It may even conceivably be true that babies would be better off in the charge of an expert and that infant citizens may come to be tended, as boy and girl citizens are taught, in communities by trained persons.[141]

[139] Black, *Married Women's Work*, p. 7.
[140] Ibid., p. 13.
[141] Ibid., p. 6.

Black concluded her introduction to *Married Women's Work* by speculating on the changing pattern of family life, and her vision provides illuminating insights into feminist thinking on this subject on the eve of the War. 'It is possible', she suggested,

> that society is evolving in the direction of a family supported financially by the earnings of both parents, the children being cared for meanwhile and the work of the house being performed by trained experts. To me personally that solution seems more in harmony with the general lines of our social development than does any which would relegate all women to the care of children combined with the care of households.[142]

The fact that under conditions as they then obtained the majority of working-class wives worked because they had no choice in the matter was squarely faced by all the members of the Women's Industrial Council who contributed to the survey, and probably even by most middle-class feminists of the time. But they were highly suspicious of the kind of 'solution' envisaged by women closely allied with the Labour Movement who argued in favour of 'the family wage' and the exclusion of wives from the labour market. Such ideas were put forward by (among others) Margaret Macdonald and Katharine Glasier, the latter in an article originally appearing in the Independent Labour Party's journal, the *Socialist Review*, and reprinted in pamphlet form under the title *Socialism and the Home* in 1909.[143] Glasier's defence of the ideal of the family wage involved a somewhat frenzied attack on those advocating any form of state support for motherhood as 'unnatural', 'ludicrous' or 'monstrous'.[144] Those who valued their economic independence so highly were probably not fit to marry, she thundered, let alone to become parents.

> All over Britain to-day the Socialist propagandists of the Independent Labour Party are asking their vast audiences to plump for a father's right to work for a wage sufficient to keep his family, be it

---

[142] Ibid., p. 14.
[143] Katharine Glasier, 'Socialism and the home' (Independent Labour Party, London, 1909); see also Macdonald et al., *Wage Earning Mothers*.
[144] Glasier, 'Socialism and the home', p. 12.

large or small, just as our well paid civil servants have it today. There is not the least doubt about the response. Such demand as there may be in society for a "state maintenance of mothers" that leaves the fathers out of account is born either of the diseased conditions of present-day society, or of the sheerly individualist 'revolt' stage of our women's battle for freedom.[145]

But even some of the staunchest advocates of the family wage had to admit that such a system could not provide all the answers, and sometimes expressed grave doubts about the wisdom of attempts to extend legal restrictions on the employment of mothers. Anna Martin, who had a wealth of experience in working with families in the poorer districts of London, lent support to Clementina Black's contention that working-class women themselves were highly suspicious of attempts to 'protect' them from employment, albeit that the suspicion was based less on any feminist or political stance than on the simple fear for survival. In discussing the various proposals which had been mooted to ameliorate social conditions in the South Eastern district of London she noted that

> The proposal ... which strikes most terror to the hearts of the working women of the district is the threatened further limitation, shadowed forth by Mr John Burns, of the married women's permission to work. They do not realise the political danger of such a prohibition, which would inflict a serious disability on their class and come perilously near repealing, as far as they are concerned, the Married Women's Property Act, but they know from their own life experience the wholesale ruin that would result, under the present industrial system, from the passing of such a law ... the women are appalled at the idea of their liberty of action in this matter being forcibly taken from them. To do this, and to leave untouched the causes which drive them into the labour market seems to them about as wise a proceeding as trying to cure a broken leg by removing the splints.[146]

Few, if any, feminists would have argued that working-class women should be pushed into the labour market against their

[145] Ibid.
[146] Anna Martin, *The Married Working Woman: A Study* (National Union of Women's Suffrage Societies, London, 1911), pp. 40–41.

wishes, particularly if they were the mothers of very young children. And yet there was certainly a widespread suspicion of the Labour Movement's demands for a family wage payable to the male breadwinner. On the one hand, any such demand was guaranteed to undermine the feminist demand for equal pay. (In the teaching profession, for instance, men's opposition to women teachers' demands for equal salaries was precisely based on family wage arguments.)[147] On the other hand, it was difficult to see how a family wage system would cater for single women with dependants of their own, the section of the community whose needs were most frequently conveniently overlooked by wage theorists. Feminists had been made acutely aware of the numbers of these women, and their problems, by Ellen Smith's pioneering and detailed survey of *Wage Earning Women and Their Dependants*, which was published by the FWG in 1915.[148] Most fundamentally, however, objections to the family wage rested upon the fear that even in families where a husband was in regular employment and earning good money, a family wage system might well simply substitute one form of economic dependence for another, with women finding themselves at the mercy of their husbands rather than the capitalist employer.

Feminists showed more interest in a proposal formulated by Lady Aberconway, which envisaged legislation which would seek to guarantee a wife's entitlement to a proportion of her husband's earnings, thereby conferring upon her some degree of economic independence.[149] However, many – like B. L. Hutchins and Helena Swanwick – felt that even if legislation could be obtained in this respect it would prove extremely difficult to enforce.[150] Most feminists were more inclined to favour some scheme of maternity pensions, or the 'endowment of motherhood', financed directly through the State. Ideas in

[147] See, among others, Patricia Owen, '"Who would be free herself must strike the blow": The National Union of Women Teachers, equal pay, and women within the teaching profession', *History of Education*, 17, no. 1 (March 1988), p. 94.
[148] Smith, *Wage-Earning Women*.
[149] Discussed in Swanwick, *The Future of the Women's Movement* (G. Bell, London, 1913), p. 86.
[150] Ibid.; see also B. L. Hutchins, *Conflicting Ideals of Women's Work* (no publisher given; London, 1914), p. 65.

this area were much canvassed before 1914, and appeared to
have the double advantage of promoting economic autonomy
for women and also of legitimating the social value of child-
rearing. Mabel Atkinson contended that the endowment of
motherhood was 'coming to be realized more and more clearly
as the ultimate ideal of the feminist movement',[151] declaring
that

> No act of citizenship is more fundamental than the act of bringing
> into the world and protecting in his helpless infancy a new citizen,
> and therefore the most reasonable solution of the problem, though
> it may not be applicable in every case, is that women during the
> period when these activities must absorb their whole energies should
> be supported by a State endowment, but that this State endowment
> should not continue longer than the time during which they are so
> absorbed, and that at the end of that time they should be free to
> return to their former vocations.[152]

It was not possible to be dogmatic about the length of time
during which a woman would qualify for such support, Atkinson
insisted, since this would be likely to vary from industry to
industry, according to the nature of the work involved. But she
believed that it was crucially important to discuss maternity
pensions in conjunction with schemes providing for women's
return to the labour market, otherwise feminists might unwit-
tingly find their arguments taken up by those conservative
thinkers and eugenists who saw the state endowment of
motherhood as a way of encouraging women to accept that
'their real place' was in the home.[153] This problem had already
been appreciated by members of the FWG. In 1909, Emma
Brooke had warned that

> The state endowment of motherhood has a fascination for the mind
> as an expedient; but a hasty application of this idea, by men alone,
> will probably react disastrously on women themselves. Wrongly
> applied the State endowment of motherhood may bring the merely
> functional burden of maternity to press too heavily on individual

[151] Atkinson, 'Economic foundations of the Women's Movement', p. 23.
[152] Ibid., p. 21.
[153] Ibid., pp. 21–3.

mothers, and may result in reducing them to a slavelike powerlessness supported by law. This would be disastrous to true motherhood, and, with the mother, disastrous to the children and the race.[154]

There was indeed a danger that demands for 'the endowment of motherhood' would serve to unite a number of groups with radically different social and political viewpoints in England before the war. Henry Harben's tract for the Fabian Society, published in 1910, argued that the basic need for a system of maternity endowment, pensions or insurance was one on which the public was generally agreed: 'To raise the economic status of women by a method which would emphasise and appreciate at its full value their work as mothers of the race is an aim in which Suffragists and Anti-Suffragists, both male and female, find themselves in accord.'[155] One may recall that Remington, H. G. Wells's fictional politician in *The New Machiavelli* (1911), adopts the endowment of motherhood as his platform, with 'the good of the race' in mind, and finds himself applauded by benches of Imperialists in Parliament.[156] But Wells's own advocacy of schemes for maternity endowment, as promulgated in his *Socialism and the Family* (1906)[157] and elsewhere aroused the definite suspicions of many feminists as a controversy in the feminist journal *The Freewoman* made clear.

In the spring of 1912 *The Freewoman* published an editorial under the heading 'Woman: Endowed or Free?' arguing that a comprehensive system of maternity endowment might simply institutionalize women's 'parasitism'. At worst, this could degenerate into a system of wages-for-housework, simply turning wives into paid domestic servants. Feminists were exhorted to scrutinize all schemes for the endowment of motherhood with great care.[158] The front page of the following issue of the

[154] Emma Brooke, in Fabian Society Women's Group, 'Summary of six papers', p. 6.
[155] Henry Harben, 'The endowment of motherhood', Fabian Tract, no. 149 (London, 1910), p. 3.
[156] H. G. Wells, *The New Machiavelli* (1911; Penguin, Harmondsworth 1966), pp. 308–11.
[157] H. G. Wells, *Socialism and the Family* (Fifield, London, 1906).
[158] 'Woman: endowed or free?' in *The Freewoman*, 1, no. 15 (29 February 1912), p. 281.

journal carried a long letter from Wells in a mock-chivalrous tone arguing that the edition of *The Freewoman* had got it all wrong. Wells argued that there was a key distinction to be drawn between State endowment of *motherhood* and State endowment of *mothers*; the latter he considered misguided but the former to be defended as a wholly good thing. ('It's not human beings we want to buy and enslave, it's a social service, a collective need, we want to sustain.')[159] He proceeded to sketch in some of the provisions of what he believed would constitute a workable scheme. This failed to convince the editors, who referred in the next issue to the plan as 'hopelessly unsound'.[160] Whilst the controversy revealed the existence of some common ground between the protagonists — notably over the principle that endowment schemes should have as their basic aim the state support of children rather than their mothers — the feminists on *The Freewoman* retained their antipathy to any comprehensive scheme of endowment lest it should institutionalize women's dependence and under the guise of 'protecting' them, reinforce their disadvantages in the labour market.[161] They were particularly incensed by Wells's dismissal of what he designated their 'extraordinary assumption that women are, or can be made equivalent, economically to men',[162] since this *was* in effect what they defined as a major goal:

we do not regard it as a wise lead to women who are groping about amid social needs and responsibilities to find their destiny to suggest that they may, if they choose, establish a privileged caste and to foist it parasitically upon the labours of the community ...

What women want is their recognition of their right to work, their need for training for work and an *adequate monetary return* for work.[163]

---

[159] The text of Wells's letter was included in the editorial entitled 'Mr Wells to the attack: freewomen and endowment', *The Freewoman*, 1, no. 16, (7 March 1912).

[160] 'Woman endowed', *The Freewoman*, 1, no. 17 (14 March 1912).

[161] Ibid.

[162] H. G. Wells, 'Woman endowed', *The Freewoman*, 1, no. 18 (21 March 1912).

[163] *The Freewoman*, 1, no. 17 (14 March 1912), p. 323.

With these aims in mind, *The Freewoman* called an end to the debate, proclaiming its conclusion: 'We must resist the endowment, because it is not good for us. We can effect bolder things.'[164]

This stance was much less compromising than most, and indeed a careful reading of the articles themselves indicate that it was something of a rhetorical flourish. However, it demonstrates the uncertainty which existed amongst feminists on the issue of maternity endowment. Helena Swanwick's carefully written chapters on economics in *The Future of the Woman's Movement* (published in 1913) provide a further illustration of this ambivalence.[165] Swanwick entertained no doubts about the ways in which motherhood (or potential motherhood) currently affected the market value of women's work, but equally she saw that policies for endowment could be two-edged. Whilst less intransigent than the editors of *The Freewoman* over the subject of maintenance allowances for mothers (whether provided by individual husbands or through the State), she conceded that when reading Wells's 'enthusiastic description of how his endowed mothers will live' her soul became filled with 'an utterable sense of lamentation and mourning and woe'.[166] She concluded that she found it impossible to predict whether women of the future would 'choose to develop the family along individualist or socialist lines', but 'that they will not be content with things as they are' was a certainty.[167]

The most challenging thinking on the subject of the economics of the family wage and endowment systems in this period came in the aftermath of the First World War, and was represented on the one hand in ideas contained in the *Minority Report* which Beatrice Webb compiled for the Government's War Cabinet Committee on Women in Industry, published in 1919,[168] and on the other, in the work of Eleanor Rathbone.[169] Briefly sum-

---

[164] *The Freewoman*, 1, no. 18 (21 March 1912), p. 342.
[165] Swanwick, *The Future of the Women's Movement*, VII–XI.
[166] Ibid., p. 84.
[167] Ibid., p. 86.
[168] Beatrice Webb, *Minority Report* to the War Cabinet Committee's Report on *Women in Industry* (1919), (PP 1919, vol. XXXI).
[169] E. Rathbone, *The Disinherited Family* (Edward Arnold, London, 1924).

marized, Webb's *Minority Report* submitted that the present wage system represented chaos, and advocated its replacement by a system of clearly defined occupational or standard rates in all forms of employment, with no differentiation between male and female workers. She argued that there should be a legally enforced minimum wage based on the subsistence needs of an adult, below which no adult worker should be employed. This should be accompanied by legally enforced minimum conditions of employment and unemployment, which should again be identical for men and women. Most crucially, Webb insisted that a 'family wage system' raised more problems than it resolved:

> The assumption that men, as such, must receive higher pay because they have families to support; and that women, as such, should receive less because thay have no such family obligations, is demonstrably inaccurate to the extent of 25 or 50 per cent; and if wages were made really proportionate to family obligations, it would involve a complete revolution in the present methods of payment; it would be incompatible alike with Collective Bargaining and with any control by the workers over their conditions of employment, and it would lead to a disastrous discrimination against the married man or woman, and still more against parentage.[170]

In view of this, she contended that 'there seems no alternative — assuming that the nation wants children — to some form of state provision, entirely apart from wages, of which the present Maternity Benefit, Free Schooling and Income Tax Allowance constitute only the germ.'[171] She went on to urge the further investigation of the whole system of public provision for maternity and childhood through a separate Commission.[172]

These were radical proposals indeed, and if they had been acted upon, they would have carried far-reaching implications for feminists and indeed for the entire structure of women's work and patterns of family life. But the impact of the *Minority Report* was almost negligible, and its recommendations quite overshadowed by the much more conventional prescription of

---

[170] Webb, *Minority Report*: Summary of Conclusions, p. 255, para. 7.
[171] Ibid.
[172] Ibid., para. 8.

the main *Report*. These latter continued to sanction a system of wage rates which differentiated between the needs of men and women on account of the family responsibilities of the former.[173]

Eleanor Rathbone and family allowances

Eleanor Rathbone's campaign for family endowment spanned a long period, beginning in 1917 when she published her seminal article on 'The remuneration of women's services' in the *Economic Journal*[174] and founded the Family Endowment Society, and culminating in 1945, when family allowances became a reality, although the provisions which were then implemented bore little or no relation to the radical scheme which she had earlier envisaged.[175] As early as 1913, Rathbone's social investigation in her native city of Liverpool had imbued her with a profound sympathy for the economic plight of working-class mothers. During the war, she became interested in the way in which the separation allowances payable to the wives of enlisted men effected a marked improvement in the circumstances of these women, this improvement being primarily due to the fact that the allowances ('the largest experiment in the State endowment of maternity that the world has ever seen')[176] were proportioned according to the *size* of the families involved. Rathbone's article in the *Economic Journal* identified two major areas in which conflict and hardship were likely to crystallize after the War. In the first place, the withdrawal of separation allowances would mean a reversion to conditions whereby women were dependent upon 'the bounty of their husbands'. This would imply the reconstitution of the kind of anomaly whereby 'the quay-porter's wife who has been keeping eight children on a separation allow-

---

[173] War Cabinet Committee, Report on *Women in Industry*, see esp. part I, 'Introduction and recommendation', pp. 5–6.

[174] E. Rathbone, 'The remuneration of women's services', *Economic Journal* (March 1917); see also ch. IV in *The Making of Women: Oxford Essays In Feminism*, ed. Victor Gollancz (Allen & Unwin, London, 1917).

[175] See Hilary Land, 'The family wage', *Feminist Review*, no. 6 (1980), pp. 55–77; and Jane Lewis, 'Eleanor Rathbone and the family', Pioneers of the Welfare State 10, in *New Society*, 27 January 1983. Much of what follows has been derived from these sources.

[176] Rathbone, 'The remuneration of women's services', p. 55.

ance of 33s ... [was] ... reduced to her pre-war inferiority of income to her next-door neighbour, the ship-labourer's wife, who has maintained one child on an allowance of 17s 6d.'[177] Secondly, and as a result of government pledges and pressure from male trade unionists, vast numbers of the women who had entered industry in conditions of wartime labour shortages were likely to find themselves subject to new or to reimposed legislative restrictions upon their right to employment, or would simply lose their jobs. Women would not take kindly, Rathbone warned, to finding themselves treated once again as 'eternal blacklegs' or as 'industrial lepers', and any attempt 'to shut them up again in their compounds' after the war would inevitably be followed by the renewed expression of discontent in 'a much more vocal and embittered form'.[178]

The detailed consideration of these two related issues of women's place in industry and the problems associated with family support led Rathbone to her central concern, which was a sustained and comprehensive attack upon the whole idea of 'the family wage'. This, she maintained, was not only the main obstacle to equal pay, but a wholly 'indirect and clumsy method' of providing for the next generation. Indeed it represented the major obstacle in the way of women receiving any proper remuneration for their services both in industry, and in the home. A comprehensive system of state endowment providing for the cost of rearing children would go a long way towards solving many of these problems and constitute a much more equitable alternative.[179]

Eleanor Rathbone took over the Presidency of the National Union of Societies for Equal Citizenship (NUSEC) from Millicent Garrett Fawcett in 1919. With the suffrage issue settled, she made it her task to work for a new emphasis within feminism, one which would concentrate less on formal egalitarian goals and more on the specific needs and predicaments of mothers.[180]

---

[177] Ibid., p. 56.
[178] Ibid., p. 63.
[179] Ibid., pp. 63—8.
[180] Lewis, 'Eleanor Rathbone and The Family'; see also the same writer's 'Beyond suffrage: English feminism in the 1920's', *Maryland Historian*, 6 (1973); and *Women in England, 1870—1950* (Wheatsheaf, Brighton, 1984), pp. 102—6.

The fullest expression of her ideas on family endowment came with the publication of her major book, *The Disinherited Family*, in 1924. This represented an extraordinary achievement, challenging conventional economic theory and men's position within the family at every point. Rathbone contended that poverty could be best understood as the failure of the wage system to meet the needs of the population. Contemporary ideas of a family wage were based on the notion of the 'average' family being represented by a breadwinning husband, his wife, and three dependent children, whereas in fact only a tiny minority of families (less than 9 per cent) approximated to this norm.[181] If every man in the country were to be paid on the assumption that he supported a wife and three children this would mean that 'provision would be made for 3 million phantom wives, and for over 16 million phantom children in the families containing less than three children, while on the other hand, in families containing more than three children, those in excess of that number, over 1¼ million in all, would still remain unprovided for.'[182]

A detailed study of pre-war wage levels in Britain demonstrated anyway that the ideal of a minimum wage for men which would be sufficient for the support of 'a standard family' had never in fact been achieved. Basing her calculation on the estimates of Seebohm Rowntree's work on subsistence levels and using data on income supplied by Bowley and Sidney Webb, Rathbone showed that whether one took 25 shillings or 35 shillings as a subsistence family income real wages indicated that large numbers of men earned far less than this 'minimum': '32 per cent earned less than 25s when in full work and 74 per cent less than 35s; with a proportionately lower income when a normal amount of time off work is allowed for.'[183]

Even when a man was fully employed, and earning a 'family wage', there was no guarantee of him using it to provide for his wife and children; women were afforded little real protection by such a system, widows and orphans none at all. It was difficult to arrive at any realistic estimate of those women who in fact

---

[181] Rathbone, *The Disinherited Family*, pp. 16–17.
[182] Ibid., p. 20.
[183] Ibid., p. 26.

carried the major responsibility for dependent family members, Rathbone submitted, but contemporary estimates such as those arrived at by members of the Fabian Women's Group estimated that as many as 51 per cent of working women were wholly or partially responsible for dependents.[184]

In sum, *The Disinherited Family* supplied a powerful and comprehensive dismissal of the family wage as an economic ideal. Society had palpably failed to achieve such a wage; in all probability it was impossible to achieve out of contemporary resources, and indeed, supposing it were to be achieved, 'the waste at the one end and suffering at the other which it would entail' would be conspicuous.[185] In the second half of her book Rathbone set about examining more satisfactory alternative ways of providing for the population. She began with a detailed survey of experiments in family endowment as implemented abroad, in Australia and in various parts of Europe. She also focused her attention on the various kinds of objections mooted by opponents of endowment systems, before concluding with a discussion of the conditions of a scheme which she regarded as practical in the current context.

Rathbone's feminism supplied her with some sharply critical insights into the ideology of family life, and she understood the psychological difficulties inherent in patterns of dependency for women as well as their economic privation. The nineteenth century, she argued, had in some respects emancipated women from the most oppressive forms of marital and paternal power, and had supplied them new rights and opportunities of citizenship. Yet it had at the same time extended their economic dependence on the male. Was it fantastic to suggest 'that in accepting this new burden, the unconscious mind of man was aware that he was also securing a new hold over his dependants, more subtly effective than that which he was forgoing?'[186] She maintained a strong suspicion of what she called 'The Turk Complex', that male enjoyment of power which so often lurked under the mask of paternal protectiveness:

[184] Ibid., p. 159.
[185] Ibid., p. 268.
[186] Ibid., p. 270.

it is easy to see what satisfaction the institution of the dependent family gives to all sorts and conditions of men — to the tyrannous man what opportunities of tyranny, to the selfish of self-indulgence, to the generous of preening himself in the sunshine of his own generosity, to the chivalrous of feeling himself the protector of the weak.[187]

But, she insisted, 'A man has no right to want to keep half the world in purgatory, because he enjoys playing redeemer to his own wife and children.'[188]

Initially, Rathbone envisaged wage levels which would be based on the needs of a single adult. The endowment system would supplement these with cash allowances payable to the mother and each dependent child. The mother's allowance, she believed, would constitute community recognition of the value of maternity and also recognition of work done within the home. However, she recognized that there was a danger of such allowances being used to exclude women from the labour market, and later came to recommend a minimum wage sufficient for the maintenance of two people, with family allowances payable on account of each child, the amount payable dependent upon the age of the child.[189] Women with only one or two children of school age might then find it more acceptable, Rathbone suggested, to return to work. She was vehemently opposed to any idea that the payment of family allowances should depend upon a mother staying at home. If women wanted to use part of the allowances to engage domestic help for the care of their children whilst they themselves returned to work, she felt that this would be perfectly appropriate. Rathbone was also convinced that such a system of family allowances would improve the portion of single women, in that it would strengthen their case for equal pay.[190]

However, in spite of the feminism apparent in such proposals and inherent in her critique of existing patterns of dependency and family life, there were elements of conservatism in Rathbone's

---

[187] Ibid.
[188] Ibid., p. 273.
[189] Lewis, 'Eleanor Rathbone and the family', p. 138.
[190] Rathbone, *The Disinherited Family*, pp. 297–9.

outlook. As the feminist historian Jane Lewis has pointed out in her recent analysis of Rathbone's work, she retained a fundamental conviction that the mother was the best and proper guardian of the young child, and felt that for the majority of women, maternity would involve staying at home.[191] In politics Rathbone was a pragmatist, and prepared to work with allies of - radically differing political stances in pursuit of any concrete, short-term goals which she could identify as conducing towards a better deal for women and children. Hence during the 1930s, as Lewis has described, her campaign for family allowances tended to become submerged in her work to alleviate family poverty generally and her involvement with the Children's Minimum Council, an organization which she launched in 1934 to press for levels of unemployment assistance which would make possible a higher standard of nutrition amongst the populace.[192]

Many of the more egalitarian-minded feminists found themselves out of sympathy with this drift and with Rathbone's influence within NUSEC. Like the feminists in the Fabian Women's Group on the eve of the First World War, they were deeply suspicious of the conservative potential of any alliance between advocates of family endowment, or 'the protection of motherhood', and eugenists and trade union leaders keen to exclude married women from the labour market. Women teachers — particularly members of the feminist National Union of Women Teachers — feared that their case for equal pay would become weakened and sidetracked by demand for family allowances. Conflict over these issues, and particularly over the vexed question of protective legislation and maternity leave, came to a head within NUSEC in 1926 and 1927, with the more stringently egalitarian feminists transferring their allegiance to the newly-constituted Open Door Council, the Six Point Group, or the Women's Freedom League — all of these committed to opposing legislation which singled out women for special treatment in the occupational arena.[193] When family allowances eventually bacame a reality, under Beveridge's ad-

---

[191] Lewis, 'Eleanor Rathbone and the family', pp. 138—9.
[192] Ibid.
[193] Lewis, 'Beyond suffrage', p. 12ff.

ministration in 1945, they were implemented in a way which fulfilled nothing of the radicalism of Rathbone's early visions. They constituted a small supplement to wage levels, a slight adjustment in the distribution of national income. That they were made payable to mothers, rather than to fathers, could be attributed to feminist pressure, but not much else.

Some inter-war views on economic independence

It can be argued that divisions amongst feminists frustrated the achievement of any distinctively feminist economic theory of the family and women's work in the inter-war period. The conflicts were related to the divisions of social class, but not exclusively so, and they were focused very much on disputes around the family wage and over issues of 'protection' in the labour market. But it is important to bear in mind the context in which these debates were taking place: feminists were on the defensive, and the disagreements amongst them amplified by the economic and political instabilities of the 1920s and 1930s. The work of women as heroines of production during the First World War was quickly forgotten: as Margaret Cole put it, 'Public opinion, less than a year after the War, was calling these women limpets, and urging, in a slightly mixed metaphor, that they should be combed out.'[194] Engulfed by the strength of the 'back-to-the-home' movement in the 1920s, women found it hard to rally to the urgent injunctions of *Time and Tide* headlines exhorting them to 'Stick To Your Job'.[195] We have seen that the vigour with which employers erected or resurrected marriage bars in industry, teaching public administration made it impossible for many women to stay in work. During the 1930s, developments abroad began their deeply disturbing effect. Writers like Winifred Holtby, Vera Brittain and Margaret Cole cast nervous glances in the direction of Germany, Italy and the USSR, where fascist and communist regimes embarked on highly contrasting and portentous experiments in 'family policy' which clearly carried enormous but as yet unknowable implications

[194] Cole, *Marriage, Past and Present*, p. 106.
[195] *Time and Tide*, 22 April 1921, p. 378.

for the status and lives of women. Margaret Cole, writing in the late 1930s, was forced to conclude that in the light of these developments, the future social position of women could at best be described as 'uncertain'.[196]

However, a careful reading of Sylvia Anthony's book, *Women's Place in Industry and Home*, published in 1932, shows that something of a tradition of feminist thinking on economics, women and the family had been built up through the period from 1890 to 1930.[197] The book was dedicated to the memory of Maria Sharpe Pearson, the earnest young feminist who, prior to her marriage to Karl Pearson in 1890, had acted as secretary to the Men and Women's Club, carefully compiling reading lists and abstracting from papers on a highly diverse series of subjects which had ranged from sexuality, prostitution, and women's independence through the appeal of Ibsen's dramatic heroines to the economic and social foundations of primitive matriarchy.[198] Sylvia Anthony was able to draw upon the detailed work of Alice Clark and the feminist historiographers of the 1900s, and her overall analysis owed much to the arguments and insights of Beatrice Webb, the Fabian Women's Group, and Eleanor Rathbone.

The sexual division of labour, Anthony insisted, was a *social* construction. It was rooted in history, but alongside the development of capitalism in nineteenth-century England it had assumed a form which had proved increasingly disadvantageous to women. The time had now come when women's work within the home was 'considered and officially described as the antithesis of gainful occupation'.[199] The economic security of childbearing women was less than that of almost any other members of the community. Partly as a result of their 'peculiar economic impotence and dependence', women's health was neglected, and of seemingly little concern to the State. Directly linked with poverty, the physical costs of maternity were appallingly high —

---

[196] Cole, *Marriage, Past and Present*, p. 141.
[197] Sylvia Anthony, *Women's Place in Industry and Home* (Routledge, London, 1932).
[198] Papers relating to Men and Women's Club, in Pearson Collection, University College, London.
[199] Anthony, *Women's Place*, pp. 65–6.

it was now more dangerous to be pregnant, Anthony contended, than to follow any other business or employment.[200] Women's work both in and out of the home was desperately in need of a wholesale social re-evaluation. Equal pay, family allowances, and more flexible forms of organization both in the workplace and in terms of domestic arrangements were urgent priorities. Feminists should continue to fight for a society which would allow them to mother children without sacrificing the dignity and security of economic independence which could basically only be derived from work outside the home.[201]

[200] Ibid., pp. 66, 179.
[201] Ibid., pp. 186ff., 224.

3

Domestic Organization

The 'servant problem'

Discussions of domestic organization amongst feminists were inevitably shaped by the experience and sometimes by the assumptions of social class. Upper-middle-class women might take the ministrations of servants for granted. They might regularly discuss 'the servant problem' in terms of the difficulties they experienced in terms of obtaining the services of reliable and efficient employees, but they knew little about the drudgery of daily domestic chores. Naomi Mitchison recalled that during her girlhood any 'tidying and washing up was just left. In the morning it was done. One was unfamiliar with the process. Dusters, soap, soda? These belonged to another world.'[1] Servants with their separate entrances and staircases protected their employers from the dirt and drudgery that might contaminate the refined status of the latter. They acted as a buffer between the middle-class household and the outside world which both protected and confined the middle-class woman.[2] Symbolically, it was often unheard of for the wife or daughter of a middle-class household to answer her own doorbell. Edith Morley, growing up as the daughter of a surgeon-dentist in late-nineteenth-century Bayswater recorded: 'I still remember the shock of surprise I underwent when, for the first time in my experience, a friend opened her own front door when I went to

---

[1] Naomi Mitchison, *All Change Here* (Bodley Head, London, 1975), p. 90.
[2] For a fuller exploration of some of these ideas see Leonore Davidoff, 'Class and gender in Victorian England', in *Sex and Class in Women's History* ed. Judith Newton, Mary Ryan, and Judith Walkowitz (Routledge & Kegan Paul, London, 1983), esp. pp. 27–8.

call. I was not allowed to do so even if I happened to be in the hall when the bell rang and knew who was likely to be there.[3] However, engaging and supervising the activities of servants could constitute a burdensome and time-consuming activity for the mistress of a household, and within the home, the existence of servants guaranteed time and space to middle-class women less than it did to men. We may recall Ursula Bloom's memories, referred to in Chapter 1, of how her mother would fret when a maid dallied in answering the bell from her father's study, and how she pointed out that 'nobody would have been chivvied had it been Mrs Bloom's bell.'[4]

If all women, whatever their class position, can be seen to have felt responsible to some degree for domestic organization, the gulf between the servant-keeping classes and the majority was still often enormous and painfully apparent. In a letter which Virginia Woolf penned to her friend Margaret Llewelyn Davies in 1931 this distance of the middle-class feminist from the domestic lives and experiences of working-class women is directly confronted.[5] Virginia Woolf wrote of the 'contradictory and complex feelings' which had beset her as an observer at a meeting of the Women's Co-operative Guild in Newcastle in 1916 and of the difficulties she had experienced in empathizing with the predicament of working men's wives, and with their demands for hot water, labour-saving appliances and housing reform: 'after all the imagination is largely the child of the flesh. One could not be Mrs Giles of Durham because one's body had never stood at the wash-tub; one's hands had never wrung and scrubbed and chopped up whatever the meat may be that makes a miner's supper.'[6]

The number of domestic servants in the population remained high throughout the period with which this book is concerned. In 1891 there were 1,386,167 domestic servants in England and

[3] Edith Morley, *Looking before and after: reminiscences of a working life* (unpublished typescript, University of Reading Library), p. 21.

[4] Ursula Bloom, *Sixty Years of Home* (Hurst & Blackett, London, 1960), p. 116.

[5] Virginia Woolf, letter to Margaret Llewelyn Davies, in M. L. Davies (ed.), *Life as We Have Known It: by co-operative Working Women* (1931; Virago, London, 1977), pp. xvii–xxxxi.

[6] Ibid., p. xxiii.

Wales, a figure which represented 34 per cent of all women registered as 'employed'.[7] The numbers actually increased by 16 per cent between 1920 and 1931, from 1,148,698 to 1,332,224, although according to the 1931 Census the latter figure had come to represent only 23 per cent of women occupied.[8] However, only a minority of upper-middle-class homes at the turn of the century (those with an income of around £300 per year, or more), could call upon the attentions of two or three living-in servants. Around three-quarters of the late-Victorian middle class had incomes well below this level, and these households could not usually afford to employ more than one servant, the general skivvy, or maid-of-all-work.[9] Women discussing the problem of domestic service at a Conference arranged by the National Union of Women Workers (NUWW) in Brighton in 1900 noted that 60 per cent of the 'servant keeping classes' kept only one domestic servant, and another 20 per cent only two.[10] It was argued that the remaining 20 per cent of privileged households where more than two servants might be employed suffered comparatively few problems in obtaining them, because they could often offer relatively high wages and better conditions; it was 'easier for them to arrange regular free times for their servants than it [was] for the busy mother of a household who can afford to pay only one servant to help her in her never-ending and multifarious duties'[11] The unpopularity of domestic service was inescapable, and demonstrated repeatedly by the fact that wherever alternative forms of employment became available, such as factory work, young girls showed little hesi-

[7] Leonore Davidoff, 'Mastered for life: servant and wife in Victorian and Edwardian England', *Journal of Social History* (Summer 1974), p. 410.

[8] Pam Taylor, 'Daughters and mothers — maids and mistresses: domestic service between the Wars', in *Working Class Culture: Studies in History and Theory*, ed. John Clarke, Chas Crichter and Richard Johnson (Hutchinson, London, 1979), p. 121.

[9] Patricia Branca, *Silent Sisterhood: Middle Class Women in the Victorian Home* (Croom Helm, London, 1975), pp. 38–48; and Theresa McBride, 'As the twig is bent: the Victorian nanny', in *The Victorian Family*, ed. A. S. Wohl (Croom Helm, London, 1978), pp. 44–5.

[10] Mrs P. Bunting, 'Domestic service', paper read at the National Union of Women Workers' Conference held at Brighton, 23–26 October 1900 (papers published by P. S. King, Westminster, 1900), p. 164.

[11] Ibid., p. 165.

tation in opting for them. Single servants were often overworked and socially isolated, 'captive employees' with little time of their own and subject to endless infringements of personal liberty.[12] Autobiographical material and the evidence of oral history make it clear that large numbers of women resented and felt humiliated by the conditions of service. Middle-class women who contemplated 'the servant problem' endlessly discussed these issues and emphasized the need to guarantee 'free evenings' to their maids and to treat them with more consideration, but they could not eliminate the resentments which the basic relationship of social subordination implied. After the First World War, women who had gained experience of factory work were extremely reluctant to contemplate going back into service; it was only the absence of alternatives, in many cases, which drove them into it.[13]

In this context it was scarcely surprising that middle-class women became increasingly preoccupied with questions of domestic organization and the issue of how to minimize household chores. For feminists, and other women who sought personal fulfilment in some form of activity outside the home, these problems quickly became acute. Some were lucky and managed to secure the services of loyal and efficient housekeepers who stayed with them for many years and in some cases developed into lifelong companions and friends. This was the experience of Helena Swanwick with Agnes Rushton, who cooked and kept house, nursed and cared for her for over thirty years.[14] The scientist Hertha Ayrton, shortly after her marriage in the 1880s, found herself the recipient of money from her feminist friend Barbara Bodichon. She immediately engaged a housekeeper whose services freed her to pursue her researches in electricity. Her biographer recalls that when Madame Curie visited Mrs Ayrton she expressed

> admiration for the way in which the latter managed to organise her household and to delegate work to others, so as to free herself for

[12] Taylor, 'Daughters and mothers', p. 125.
[13] Ibid.; see also Gail Braybon and Penny Summerfield, *Out of the Cage: Women's Experiences in Two World Wars* (Pandora, London, 1987), p. 143.
[14] Helena M. Swanwick, *I Have Been Young* (Gollancz, London, 1935), p. 152.

her scientific labours; and the opinion was worth having, for Madame Curie's problem in Paris, where she was both Professor of Physics and the mother of two young children, was not unlike her friend's problem in London.[15]

Other women were not so lucky. Again, we may recall Vera Brittain's frustrations with domestic chores, when she found herself responsible for cleaning the four-roomed campus flat which she shared with her husband George at Cornell in the 1920s.[16] But even those feminists who did manage, like Helena Swanwick, 'to sail into smooth domestic waters' with the help of loyal housekeepers might reflect on the fact that they had merely succeeded in solving on a personal, individual level what remained for many women as an intractable social problem. Swanwick digressed at some length on the problems of resident domestic service in her autobiography, arguing the need for 'a corps of well-trained and reliable outside workers'. She claimed that she would have gladly employed such outside workers had they existed, and records that 'at one time I had serious thoughts of throwing myself into a large scheme for their training and registration; but other claims and other work intervened.'[17]

Co-operative households

During the period with which this book is concerned, one of the most sustained attempts to reassess the nature of contemporary domestic arrangements from a feminist and socialist perspective came from Jane Hume Clapperton, whose books, *Scientific Meliorism* (1886) and *Margaret Dunmore; Or A Socialist Home* (1888), have now largely been forgotten.[18] Clapperton also outlined her ideas in a series of articles which were published in the feminist newspaper *Shafts* in 1893, under the title 'Reform

[15] Evelyn Sharp, *Hertha Ayrton, 1854–1923: A Memoir* (Edward Arnold, London, 1926), pp. 128–9.
[16] Vera Brittain, *Thrice a Stranger* (Macmillan, New York, 1938), pp. 47–53.
[17] Swanwick, *I Have Been Young*, p. 150.
[18] Jane Hume Clapperton, *Scientific Meliorism and the Evolution of Happiness* (Kegan Paul, London, 1885); *Margaret Dunmore; or A Socialist Home* (Swan Sonnenschein, Lowry, London, 1888).

in domestic life, as required by scientific sociology'.[19] Contending that existing domestic arrangements were wholly unsatisfactory from the viewpoint of both mistresses and maids, Clapperton advocated co-operative styles of living in the form of 'Unitary' or 'Associated' homes, where several families of like-minded individuals might come together in order to share the burden of household tasks and break down the psychic isolation of the isolated family unit. Middle-class women would thus be freed from the 'greasy domesticity' of the little villa, a home system which she believed calculated to foster nothing but 'smallness and meanness of mind'.[20] Domestic service might disappear as a system of personal slavery ill befitting a free society. Middle-class people would increasingly have to do their own work, but in a shared community this would lost its stigma of inferiority and come to be seen as dignified service to one's fellows. The performance of household tasks would be rendered much more efficient and less onerous with the advent of large communal kitchens, laundries and washhouses and the adoption of 'scientific methods'. Both men and women would benefit from this, since more of their time would be freed for other kinds of activity, such as the better education of children. Clapperton owned herself greatly inspired by 'the communistic experiment made by Robert Owen and his followers, at Tytherly, Hampshire', noting that although the experiment had in effect failed, it had in certain important respects proved highly successful:

The working members declared they would rather live on an Irish diet of potatoes than go again into the old world — as, alas! they were ultimately compelled to do — and residents and boarders, of whom there were many in the community, 'all regretted the end of their tenancy' ... the cause of the wreck of the enterprise was purely commercial ... The whole history of this experiment proclaims the abudant existence of raw material ripe for the construction of the social fabric of a new order, provided the baser elements — the pounds, shillings, and pence — that must enter into the enterprise are justly, ably and fitly handled in relation to the future, as

[19] Jane Hume Clapperton, 'Reform in domestic life, as required by scientific sociology', *Shafts* (April, May and June 1893).
[20] Ibid. (April 1893), p. 32.

well as the present, and with scrupulous regard to interests that are general and not special to a few favoured individuals.[21]

In the light of her understanding of Owen's experiment in Hampshire, Clapperton submitted that private property ought not to be relinquished in her scheme of practicable 'Unitary Homes', but repeatedly emphasized the necessity to establish such centres on a careful financial basis.[22]

In her novel *Margaret Dunmore* she set out to explore the details and potential advantages of such arrangements. An experiment in communal living ('La Maison'), is made possible on the basis of money supplied by the heroine, Margaret Dunmore, inspired by the Socialist ideas of her French friends and influenced by the experiment of Owen, the Phalastères and the Bible Perfectionists of Oneida Creek. The ideological conviction underlying the whole experiment is that socialism calls for radical changes in lifestyle which will foster those changes in individual personality which alone can facilitate genuine social progress. The novel focuses upon the aspirations, conflicts and development of those individuals who participate in the venture, charting the ways in which their values and relationships are transformed. Personal possessiveness diminishes, as does patriarchal authority. Ideals of masculinity and femininity become less polarized, in that women are shown as becoming more authoritative and serious-minded, and men more involved with their children. There is a good deal of discussion about sex roles, and the sexual division of labour, although the novel depicts no revolutionary changes in this respect. Much space is devoted to the institution of new forms of educational practice designed to foster the higher social purpose.[23]

Jane Hume Clapperton corresponded with the members of the Men and Women's Club, and sent them a copy of her book on *Scientific Meliorism*.[24] Her publications appear to have been reasonably widely reviewed, and her articles in *Shafts* must

---

[21] Ibid. (May 1893), p. 42.

[22] Ibid.

[23] Clapperton, *Margaret Dunmore*.

[24] Papers relating to Men and Women's Club, in Pearson Collection, University College, London; see correspondence from Jane Clapperton (10/29).

114 *Domestic Organization*

have succeeded in introducing her ideas to many feminists. However, her ideas about the reorganization of domestic life do not appear to have generated as much discussion among English feminists as those of the American writer, Charlotte Perkins Gilman, whose influential *Women and Economics*, and *The Home, Its Work and Influence*, were published in 1898 and 1903 respectively.[25] In the latter text, particularly, Gilman supplied a radical critique of the existing arrangement of home life. Surveying history, she argued that the home had conspicuously failed to develop alongside other social institutions and had become a repository of primitive industry and conservatism, a 'prison' and a 'workhouse' for most women, a 'private harem' for men. Like modern feminists, she was concerned with what she identified as the exaggerated division between public and private social worlds, a division which had damaging implications for both sexes, but particularly for women: 'With the steadily widening gulf between the sexes which followed upon this arbitrary imprisonment of the woman in the home, we have come to regard "the world" as exclusively man's province, and "the home" as exclusively woman's.'[26] Technology had potentially rendered obsolete many of the material foundations of domestic ideology, but society had as yet failed to recognize this:

> The domestic hearth, with its undying flame, has given way to the gilded pipes of the steam heater and the flickering evanescence of the gas range. But the sentiment about the domestic hearth is still in play. The original necessity for the ceaseless presence of the woman to maintain that altar fire — and it was an altar fire in very truth at one period — has passed with the means of prompt ignition; the matchbox has freed the housewife from that incessant service, but the *feeling* that women should stay at home is with us yet.[27]

This confining of women in the home, Gilman emphasized, entailed an enormous cost in terms of the loss, to society, of a

---

[25] Charlotte Perkins Gilman, *Women and Economics: A Study of the Economic Relation Between Men and Women as a Factor in Social Evolution* (1898; Harper & Row, New York, 1966); *The Home, Its Work and Influence* (Charlton, New York, 1903).

[26] Gilman, *The Home*. (Charlton, New York, 1910), p. 22.

[27] Ibid., p. 37.

vast reserve of productive labour. The home was often praised, or sentimentalized, as a haven of privacy for the individual. However, as every wife who 'kept house' soon learned, it afforded little time or space for her to concentrate on any worthwhile task:

> The mother – poor invaded soul – finds even the bathroom door no bar to hammering little hands. From parlour to kitchen, from cellar to garret, she is at the mercy of children, servants, tradesmen and callers. So chased and trodden is she that the very idea of privacy is lost to her mind; she never had any, she doesn't know what it is, and she cannot understand why her husband should wish to have any 'reserves', any place or time, any thought or feeling, with which she may not make free.[28]

Both sexes, then suffered from these 'hopelessly restrictive' conditions.[29] But Gilman was at pains to point out that she was not in any way attacking marriage, or the family as an ideal – it was the conditions and structure of contemporary family life which cried out for reassessment. Society was apt to confuse domestic arrangements with family life. 'This business' (of 'keeping house', or 'home-making'), she insisted, 'is not marriage, it is not parentage, it is not child-culture. It is the running of the commissary and dormitory departments of life, with elaborate lavatory processes.'[30] In economic terms, Gilman drew attention to the waste of endless repetition of 'plant' – ('twenty kitchens, where one kitchen would do') – inherent in current conditions.[31] Her conclusion was that if all this waste, in both human and material terms, was to be avoided, new forms of socialized and professionalized domestic organization had urgently to be evolved.

The kind of practicable alternatives which Gilman came to envisage included 'kitchenless houses', communal social and dining facilities and professionalized domestic support services organized on a commercial basis. These ideas were explored

---

[28] Ibid., p. 40.
[29] Ibid., p. 113.
[30] Ibid., p. 69.
[31] Ibid., p. 118.

more fully in her novel, *What Diantha Did*, which she published
in serial form in the American journal *The Forerunner*, in 1909–
10.[32] Diantha Bell, the heroine of the novel, establishes a res-
taurant, kitchenless dwellings and hotel apartments, backed by
cooked food delivery and cleaning services, in 'Orchardina', a
town in California. The capital for this fictional venture is
supplied by a young wealthy widow, Viva Weatherstone, whose
investment proves extremely profitable. As Dolores Hayden,
who has extensively studied Gilman's ideas, points out, Diantha
is celebrated as the successful feminist entrepreneur.[33] The
scheme, though radical, is so only within well-defined limits.
Domestic organization remains a female responsibility, and social
hierarchy, in terms of the gulf between female 'management'
and the workforce of albeit well-paid and contended domestic
employees, remains intact. Hayden emphasizes that although
Gilman always described herself as a socialist, she was keen to
dissociate herself from any 'narrow and rigid' analysis of the
class struggle propounded by the 'Marxians'. She was far more
at ease with Fabian Socialism.[34]

What Diantha Did was given a rather mixed review by the
English feminist journal *The Freewoman* in 1912. The book itself
was considered 'well worth reading', though Diantha herself
was lampooned for her sentimentality and religiosity: 'Diantha,
in fact, besides her excellent head for business, has a real,
womanly, pulsing, American heart, and though she does not
seem to think the Deity can do much in the way of pushing a
cooked-food delivery concern, she throws herself heavily on His
mercy in moments of emotional crisis.'[35] More soberly, the
reviewer expressed some doubt over the feasibility of Gilman's
vision, submitting that private agencies aiming to supply domestic services at acceptable rates would probably turn out to be

[32] C. P. Gilman, *What Diantha Did*, serial novel in 14 parts, in *The Forerunner*,
(November 1909 to December 1910); subsequently published by T. Fisher
Unwin, London, 1912.
[33] Dolores Hayden, 'Charlotte Perkins Gilman and the kitchenless house',
Radical History Review, no. 21 (Winter 1979–80), pp. 230–2. See also the same
author's *The Grand Domestic Revolution: A History of Feminist Designs for American
Homes, Neighbourhoods and Cities* (MIT Press, Cambridge, Mass., 1981).
[34] Hayden, 'Charlotte Perkins Gilman', p. 232.
[35] *The Freewoman*, 29 February 1912, p. 296.

as exploitative of labour as existing arrangements, if they were to prove commercially viable in English cities.[36]

Gilman's ideas were nevertheless much discussed in England, particularly by the Fabian Women's Group in the 1900s. She had established connections in this country in the course of a visit in 1896, when (as Mrs Stetson) she had travelled around the North and Midlands alongside Ada Nield Chew and Amy Morant, disseminating Socialist ideals with the Clarion Women's Van.[37] The minutes of the Fabian Women's Group also record a reception which the Group planned to welcome her on a visit in 1913.[38]

There was already some interest in schemes for co-operative housekeeping amongst the members of the Fabian Society. In 1898, the architect Ebenezer Howard, inspired by his reading of Edward Bellamy's *Looking Backward* (1888), and by the ideas of another American reformer, Marie Howland, had published his celebrated *To-Morrow: A Peaceful Path to Social Reform*.[39] Together with his colleagues Raymond Unwin and Barry Parker, Howard developed the idea of Co-operative Quadrangles, designed to recreate the social coherence of rural villages; residential units planned with the aim of facilitating the sharing of basic domestic services. H. G. Wells was greatly enthusiastic about the idea of building 'kitchenless houses', the potential of which he celebrated in *A Modern Utopia* (1905).[40] Dolores Hayden has described how Wells put pressure on Howard to introduce co-operative housekeeping in his Garden City at Letchworth, in 1909, Wells claiming that 'in a few short years all ordinary houses would be out of date and not saleable at any price'.[41] Howard saw 'Homesgarth', a development of thirty-two kitchenless apartments at Letchworth into which he and his wife

[36] Ibid.
[37] Julia Dawson, 'The Clarion Women's Van', *Labour Annual* 1897, pp. 184–5.
[38] Fabian Society Women's Group, Minutes of Executive Committee, 1908–1919 (Nuffield College Library, Oxford) (Available on microfilm, Harvester, Brighton).
[39] Ebenezer Howard, *To-Morrow: A Peaceful Path to Social Reform* (Swan Sonnenschein, London, 1898).
[40] H. G. Wells, *A Modern Utopia* (Chapman & Hall, London, 1905).
[41] Hayden, *The Grand Domestic Revolution*, p. 231.

moved in 1913, as a venture which would liberate women's energies and go some way towards solving both 'the servant question' and 'the woman question', both amongst the most vexed social issues of the day.[42] A handful of similar projects followed: 'Meadow Way Green', also in Letchworth, which included a central dining room (1915–24); 'Guessen's Court' in Welwyn (1922); and Waterlow Court (built by Baillie Scott and housing professional women) in Hampstead Garden Suburb in 1909.[43]

Support for such adventures in communal living was canvassed by the Society for the Promotion of Co-operative Housekeeping and Household Service, under the enthusiastic leadership of Alice Melvin, a feminist active in *Freewoman* Discussion Circles, in the years before the First World War. Alice Melvin's articles in *The Freewoman* in 1912 were prefaced by inspirational quotations from Gilman's writing, and her arguments owed much to this source.[44] The Society professed a dual aim: it wanted both to extend the principle of co-operation in housekeeping, and to widen the scope of housecraft as a profession for educated women.[45] The extent of the Society's membership is not known, but Melvin claimed that she was currently 'in touch with hundreds of would-be tenant-members and scores of educated women, waiting and training to take up house-craft as a profession in connection with co-operative housekeeping, which could be organised by the society anywhere round London'.[46] She identified a number of potential strategies. Associations might be formed which could rent suitable, adjoining houses, furnishing and fitting those communal rooms such as dining rooms, library and kitchens, and providing unfurnished rooms for members who wished to subscribe. Or more ambitiously, estates could be developed along 'garden city' lines, with public facilities and meals services, and tenancy agreements similar to

[42] Ibid.
[43] Ibid., pp. 231–7.
[44] Alice Melvin, 'Co-operative housekeeping and the domestic worker', *The Freewoman*, 4 April 1912; 'Abolition of domestic drudgery by co-operative housekeeping and the mother', *The Freewoman*, 23 May 1912.
[45] Ibid., 11 April 1912, p. 410.
[46] Ibid.

those of Hampstead and other Co-Partnership Tenant Societies. A key feature of the schemes envisaged by Alice Melvin was the provision of facilities for child-care:

> A day-nursery, in charge of competent and qualified nurses, would also be established on the estate in order that busy mothers could at any time leave their children in safe custody, and clean and comfortable surroundings, while they went about their business elsewhere.[47]

She saw mothers as amongst the main beneficiaries of such centres, alongside 'that large, rapidly-growing, and hitherto unprovided for class, the educated women workers'. 'Teachers and professional women generally', Melvin contended,

> are at present confronted with a choice of evils.
> They must either live in a boarding-house, without privacy or congenial company, or else take rooms and do their own domestic work after the business of the day, which has probably been long and tiring, is over. The love of privacy, and a place of their own, usually leads them to adopt the latter alternative, and they are obliged to muddle on as best they can. Nothing is more distressing than to come home after a tiring day's work, and then to have to set to and prepare one's own meals, to say nothing of the cleaning and mending which will also demand attention; yet this is what many thousands of women do to-day, not because they like it, but because it is the best they can do under the circumstances.[48]

In the main it seems to have been this group of single, professional women for whom experiments in co-operative living exerted an appeal, for instance, in Hampstead Garden Suburb.[49] Feminist newspapers of the time constantly featured articles on the difficulties experienced by single, working women in finding suitable living accommodation in the city, and their loneliness and isolation outside work hours. Martha Vicinus has drawn our attention to a competition organized by the journal *Work and Leisure* (a paper for 'working ladies') in 1887, inviting sugges-

[47] Ibid., p. 411.
[48] Ibid.
[49] Hayden, *The Grand Domestic Revolution*, p. 237.

tions for the 'Erection, Arrangement and Management of a block of Associated Dwellings adapted to the needs of single women at 10–50 shillings per week',[50] and to 'The Ladies' Dwelling Company' which built a large residential home in Lower Sloane Street towards the end of the century.[51] 'Residential chambers' for professional women afforded small flats and companionship to those on modest incomes. However, the key problem was always that of finance. Not only were the majority of women's earnings very low, driving many to take cheaper lodgings in 'Homes for Working Girls' or small private houses, but capital for more adventurous residential experiments, let alone for the construction of purpose-built estates, was simply not forthcoming. Hayden has pointed out that the financiers who supported Ebenezer Howard's early initiatives at Letchworth were lukewarm about co-operative domestic arrangements, as a result of which the earliest buildings there were conventionally designed houses incorporating private kitchens.[52] Alice Melvin's articles in *The Freewoman* emphasized problems of capital availability and called upon wealthy women to come forward and support such projects:

This is a woman's question, and by women it must be worked. Rich women! here is a work for you to help forward. To help house the brain workers who need an individual home. Give us builders and capital and within twelve months we could house hundreds of families, hundreds of bachelor workers under the co-operative scheme.[53]

Significantly, in the feminist fictional Utopias of the period which celebrated the benefits of co-operative or communal living arrangements, it is usually a wealthy widow or heiress who acts as fairy-godmother in supplying capital for such schemes. In Clapperton's novel it is Margaret Dunmore, in Gilman's, Viva Weatherstone. In 'George Egerton's' short story, *The Regeneration*

---

[50] Martha Vicinus, *Independent Women: Work and Community for Single Women, 1850–1920* (Virago, London, 1985), pp. 296ff.
[51] Ibid.
[52] Hayden, *The Grand Domestic Revolution*, p. 231.
[53] Melvin, 'Co-operative housekeeping', p. 412.

of Two (1894),[54] a rich widow establishes a co-operative in her country home, providing work and shelter for fallen women in the neighbourhood. History furnishes fewer examples of such benefactresses than does utopian literature.

There were a number of feminists who worked energetically to promote changing forms of domestic organization, both in London and the Provinces, although documentary evidence for such ventures is often sparse and difficult to locate. Louisa Martindale, for instance, a feminist living in Sussex in the 1890s, was an enthusiastic promoter of communal kitchens.[55] Mrs Martindale was active in many areas of the women's movement; she was a lifelong suffragist, and keenly committed to working for better conditions for governesses and shop assistants in Brighton.[56] She was also a strong advocate of higher education for women. Both of her daughters, Hilda and Louisa, went on to forge impressive careers in fields which were only beginning to open up for women, Hilda in factory inspection and the Civil Service, Louisa in medicine. Hilda recorded that her mother lectured on co-operative kitchens to the Women's Liberal Association, and to Brighton Women's Co-operative League in the 1890s.[57] At the 1900 Conference of the National Union of Women Workers, which was held in Brighton, a Mrs Aldrich, from Burgess Hill, delivered a paper on 'The management of a modern household', which she based partly on notes which were supplied by her friend Mrs Martindale.[58] Both women emphasized the need for a more 'professional' and 'scientific' approach to household work if women from lower-middle-class and artisan homes were to be liberated from the constant round of domestic drudgery which currently inhibited their involvement in any activity outside the home. They drew

---

[54] George Egerton, 'The Regeneration of Two', in *Discords* (Elkin Mathews & John Lane, London, 1894). 'George Egerton' was the pseudonym of Mary Chavelita Dunne. See G. Egerton, *Keynotes and Discords*, with a new introduction by Martha Vicinus (Virago, London, 1983).

[55] Hilda Martindale, *From One Generation to Another, 1839–1944* (Allen & Unwin, London, 1944).

[56] Ibid., pp. 13–32.

[57] Ibid., p. 41.

[58] Papers from 1900 Conference of the National Union of Women Workers held in Brighton (P. S. King, Westminster, 1900), pp. 173–80.

attention to the success of some employers' initiatives in supplying canteens for their workforces, which they felt feminists might learn from:

> The heads of our large factories have doubtless found that in order for people to be able to *work* well, they must be fed well. In connection with Colman's factories the Carron Works' kitchen (Norwich), which has as for its object the sale of good food at cheap rates, was started in 1868. In 1874 fresh premises had to be provided. In the first year 9,677 pints of tea and coffee were sold and 13,990 dinners (dinners varying from a penny to fourpence each). In 1895, 99,962 pints of tea and coffee, and 32,729 dinners were sold.[59]

Municipal or people's kitchens might be started under the supervision of local authorities, Mrs Aldrich submitted, pointing out that in Austria and Germany a number of such centres were flourishing:

> There are kitchens in Vienna, Prague, Christiania, and Berlin. Those in Berlin (probably opened earlier than the others) were started by the Emperor and Empress with some money which had been presented to them. In Vienna there are twelve kitchens started about twenty-six years ago. These supply food to about five thousand people daily. They are largely patronised by poor students; the food, which is very nourishing, is cooked by steam, therefore nothing is spoilt by smoke or by being burnt. The people carry away the food in every sort of pot and pan, but, apparently, the hot-water 'carriers' in use elsewhere are less appreciated here.[60]

Mrs Aldrich, described how Mrs Martindale had made several attempts to induce London firms to supply a cooked-meals service. Her early attempts had met with little success because the food provided had not been good enough. However, she had recently discovered a large catering firm in the West End who were prepared to work to her suggestions. 'The dinners sent were quite satisfactory', wrote Mrs Martindale:

[59] Ibid., p. 178.
[60] Ibid., p. 179.

Later on, the caterer, his chef, and staff all went to the Kensington Co-operative Stores. He has done as I suggested: designed a dinner carrier, had dishes made for meat, tins for soup, jars for sauces, all warmed by hot water. He is also having made a tin stand on the gas stove or fire to be filled with boiling water, into which the dishes are placed directly they arrive. This he proposes to send to families paying by the month or quarter.[61]

Since then, Mrs Aldrich noted, the Reformed Food Company in Victoria Street, Westminster, had also taken up these ideas, and were supplying vegetarian food in a 'take-away' service. She ended her lecture on a note of exhortation to her audience. Whilst conceding that at present only a tiny number of people were reaping the benefit of such initiatives, the potential scope of such improvements was immense, and women should battle away at the social conservatism which alone impeded them.[62]

The retreat from household reorganization

While some women struggled to effect changes of this kind, the feminists in the Fabian Women's Group and the Women's Industrial Council continued to invest a good deal of faith in fact-gathering and systematic research into problems of domestic organization. In 1914, the FWG instituted a 'Committee to Reorganize Domestic Work', which defined its purpose as being: 'To devise some scheme for organising the necessary domestic work of cleaning and feeding the community in order that women should be free to choose their occupation, whether domestic or otherwise, and to collect information to this end.'[63] Mrs McKillop was elected chairman of the Committee, whose members included Ernestine Mills, Elspeth Carr, and Mrs Herbage Edwards. Characteristically, at the first meeting on 12 March in 1914 the members decided that the collection of information should be its first priority. It was agreed that they

---

[61] Ibid., pp. 179–80.
[62] Ibid., p. 180.
[63] Minutes of Domestic Relief Committee, Fabian Society Women's Group Papers (Nuffield College Library, Oxford), 12 March 1914.

should seek the co-operation of members of both the Women's Industrial Council and the Women's Co-operative Guild. They set themselves the task of collecting data from the census on the numbers of women currently engaged in domestic service, and sought to explore girls' attitudes to domestic employment. Members also decided that they would attempt to analyse their own problems of household organization and in particular the difficulties arising from attempts to combine housework with employment outside the home. Typed circulars were distributed to this end, together with questionnaires which would give information on the size of household, its location and so forth.[64]

The inquiry does not appear to have yielded any useful results. It was probably very small-scale. The Minutes of the FWG do not state how many questionnaires were actually distributed, but only twenty-seven were returned. The attempt to collect information on time spent on household work failed, since many of the completed questionnaires omitted details on this, and in the rest the answers were so divergent that no conclusion could be drawn. The suggestions which were put forward as likely to reduce the burden of domestic drudgery were none of them very revolutionary, and some of them rather trivial. It was mooted, for instance, that *rounded* corners in cornices and mouldings were less likely to trap dirt than right angles, and that hearthstoning doorsteps or polishing brass door-knobs was a waste of time. Some correspondents raised the possibility of co-operation in purchasing food or labour-saving devices, but in a rather lukewarm way.[65]

The Committee seems to have lost impetus at this point. There was a somewhat desultory attempt to collect newspaper clippings relating to experiments in new forms of domestic organization. A cutting from *The Sydenham, Forest Hill and Penge Gazette*, dated 9 October 1914, for instance, has survived in the archives, describing the Lewisham Women's Franchise Club's establishment of premises from which orders would be taken from local residents for domestic services. The Club advertised its intention of employing its own contingent of trained and uniformed servants who would be despatched to the homes of

[64] Ibid.
[65] Ibid., April–October 1914.

members for the performance of specific tasks. The scheme
seems to have been envisaged as an emergency scheme planned
to alleviate 'war distress' and we know little about its outcome.
Ernestine Mills wrote to the *Daily Chronicle* calling for the institution of communal kitchens and more local agencies supplying
domestic services, again emphasizing their expediency in wartime.[66] A conference was arranged in March 1915, where Mrs
Bernard Mole spoke on the advantages of co-operative households, but this again met with a disappointing reception. A few
more meetings were planned — in May 1915, Mabel Atkinson
and May McKillop spoke on 'The household problem and its
solution', and 'The sociology of the servant' — but after this the
Committee seems to have fallen apart.[67]

A much more systematic attempt to gather information on
domestic work was made by the Women's Industrial Council
on the eve of the war. The WIC survey, however, focused
specifically on the problems of domestic service and much less
on the possibilities of household reorganization. The results
were published in the form of a short book, *Domestic Service*, by
C. V. Butler in 1916.[68] The Investigation Committee which the
WIC set up to carry out its survey was chaired by Clementina
Black, and its secretaries included May Barlow, Lucy Wyatt
Papworth, M. S. Barton and Mrs Bernard Drake.[69] Two sched-
ules were drawn up at the outset: one, consisting of a series of
'leading statements' on various aspects of service, was circulated
'to be discussed on paper' by employers all over the country.
The second schedule consisted of a series of brief questions,
with spaces for replies and suggestions, and was distributed
(largely through the Domestic Servants' Insurance Society) to
women currently in service. A total of 708 replies were received
from employers, 566 from servants. In addition, Butler claimed
that the Committee had received 'hundreds' of letters from
interested parties seeking to report on their experiences.[70]

[66] Ibid., correspondence dated 17 August 1914.
[67] Ibid., May—June, 1915.
[68] C. V. Butler, *Domestic Service: An Enquiry by the Women's Industrial Council*
(G. Bell, London, 1916).
[69] Ibid., p. 6.
[70] Ibid., pp. 5—6.

Butler claimed that the investigation was mounted in an attempt to 'weigh impartially' all the varied and often conflicting attitudes to service from both employers' and employees' perspectives. She began her report by pointing out that the 1911 Census showed a total of 1,359,359 women and girls (and 54,260 men and boys) as currently employed in in-door domestic service, a sector which constituted the largest form of employment in the country. At the same time there was a 'constant undersupply' of such labour, and it had to be readily conceded that indoor service was a highly unpopular form of employment.[71]

If more evidence were needed, the WIC questionnaires certainly yielded some unforgettable testimony to this unpopularity. One respondent summed up her experience of service as 'prison without committing crime', others complained of being treated as 'a despised race', 'machines', 'dogs', 'reptiles' or 'cattle'.[72] The catalogue of grievances was depressingly familiar: the stigma of caps and aprons, no time off, squalid and poky basement bedrooms, loneliness and lack of liberty. Yet the Council also received evidence from servants who described themselves as working for kind and considerate employers, and as content in their work. Butler emphasized that the main area in which the replies received from mistresses and maids conspicuously differed was over the general question of there being a social stigma attached to service.

Almost all the large number of mistresses who wrote about this either denied that maids were despised by any one, or else replied virtually, *'honi soit qui mal y pense'*; — maids were well quit of the company of any people, young men or others; who could despise so honourable a calling.[73]

Yet she had to concede that 'The maids ought to be the more reliable when they describe the caste difficulties that they actually experience, however unreasonable these may be.[74] Some mistresses put the blame on elementary education for having

[71] Ibid., pp. 9–12.
[72] Ibid., pp. 29,34,36.
[73] Ibid., p. 36.
[74] Ibid.

raised the aspirations of working-class girls beyond their lot. For instance, one employer wrote:

> I have invariably found that the more education the worse the servant ... I consider the Council education has ruined girls for service, and caused them to be ambitious beyond their capabilities, looking down upon domestic work when they have no qualification for any other work or profession. I would suggest that quite half the girl's school life should be solely occupied with domestic training, and that some system of apprenticing girls to good housekeepers might be practicable.[75]

But whilst admitting that this lady would 'probably find many to agree with her', Butler rejected the idea that the goals of education were misplaced, and contended that broader horizons and opportunities for self-development could only effect improvement in the situation. Indeed, the main argument of her whole report was that 'raised conditions of service' would be best secured through education and training, as well as more definite hours and contracts, and a good deal of space was given over to describing Board of Education and local authority initiatives in this area.

Even without the benefit of hindsight there is something rather lame about Butler's belief that 'public opinion' could be 'worked on' to help raise the status of domestic service, and to 'inculcate wholesome views about the dignity of labour in the girls' own class'. Reading the report, one cannot help sensing her arguments as going against the tide of her own observations and evidence, hence perhaps the tone of exhortation which seeps in here and there. In her own conclusion Butler submitted that the present period could best be understood as one of transition, which afforded definite scope for improvement in conditions, whilst admitting that the whole system was really something of an anachronism: 'It seems probable that the whole organisation of domestic service will in due course be transformed as it is brought more into line with other forms of women's employment.[76]

[75] Ibid., p. 26.
[76] Ibid., p. 99.

Clementina Black and federated households

Butler's report stopped short of exploring what an alternative system might look like. However, the minds of some of those working with her on the project were certainly active in this direction. One of the most coherently thought-through schemes of alternatives came from the Investigation Committee's chairman, Clementina Black, who published a short book entitled *A New Way of Housekeeping* in 1918.[77]

Clementina Black's book was based on a series of articles which she had originally written for the suffrage paper, *The Common Cause*, in the late summer of 1916. In a footnote to the book she tells us that she had not read Charlotte Perkins Gilman's novel, *What Diantha Did*, until after having delivered her first lecture on the subject of 'federated households'.[78] Although her ideas are not unlike Gilman's, a main point of difference is that where the latter held that household reorganization afforded scope for business enterprise, Black maintained that any commercially inspired venture would be doomed to failure since individual and collective convenience would be subordinated to the profit motive.[79]

Like Gilman, Black repeatedly emphasized the *wastefulness* of current forms of housekeeping, which monopolized the labour of two-thirds of the women in the community. She pointed to the loss of life amongst young men involved in the War and argued that the country would need to call upon all its reserves of labour in the post-war period:

> The only labour reserve upon which it can reckon consists of women who have not hitherto been employed in economically profitable work. Of these the greatest number have been engaged in some branch of housekeeping. Any reorganisation of housekeeping, therefore, which, without relaxing family ties or diminishing domestic comfort, releases women for other occupations will be of national benefit.[80]

[77] Clementina Black, *A New Way of Housekeeping* (Collins, London, 1918).
[78] Ibid., p. 129.
[79] Ibid., pp. 129–30.
[80] Ibid., p. ix.

Reform of domestic life should be seen as a national duty. Again, like Gilman, Black emphasized the 'cultural lag' exemplified in current practice; housekeeping had failed to respond to technological advance, and represented 'a chaos of makeshifts',[81] The system of living-in service was a 'semi-feudal relic'.[82] At the same time, the claims advanced by some would-be reformers who believed that all families could cope with their own domestic work were unrealistic, and here Black highlighted the predicament of working wives and the mothers of young children, whom she saw as particularly in need of domestic assistance.

The only solution, Black maintained, was more co-operative practice. But she remained sceptical about most contemporary experiments in communal housekeeping for three reasons. They had tended to founder, in the first place because they had sought commercial viability, secondly because they had relied on management by amateurs rather than highly-trained professionals, and thirdly because they had probably envisaged 'too much community of life'. 'People do not want to pool their lives', Black insisted, 'they only want to get their food and their service properly organised.'[83] She proceeded to outline in some detail the kind of project which she thought viable. A group of about thirty or fifty householders, living close to each other in a street, square or block of flats, might come together to form a committee. This committee would of course include women, but Black felt it important to emphasize that it should also include men: 'Many business questions will come before the committee, upon which the opinion of people possessing legal, financial and commercial training will be of great value, and at present such training is seldom a possession of women.[84]

Once constituted, the committee would set about establishing a house which would act as a 'domestic centre', fitted up with store places, kitchens, dining-rooms, offices and 'lodings for a nucleus of resident servants'. It would next seek to appoint a highly-trained manageress. It was crucial that her salary should be a substantial one, because the range of her duties would be

[81] Ibid., p. 52.
[82] Ibid., p. 20.
[83] Ibid., p. 55.
[84] Ibid., p. 56.

wide and she would carry a good deal of responsibility for ordering and equipping the domestic centre, catering arrangements, and interviewing and employing subordinate workers.[85] Here Black gave full play to her imagination over the decor and decorum of such a project:

> If she [i.e. the manageress] is a wise woman she will make it her first aim to foster a spirit of cheerfulness throughout every department of the Centre; will insist upon light walls and gay colours, and choose for the servants a uniform that will be not only useful but pretty. Pink, for instance, is one of the best wearing as well as the most festive of tints.[86]

The manageress would appoint a secretary who would deal with accounts, paper work, and answer the telephone. Food — unadulterated and wholesome — would be purchased in bulk, at favourable prices, directly from contractors. The kitchen would employ up-to-the minute technology, and store-rooms lined with a rodent and insect-proof 'glazed cement'. Meals could be enjoyed either in the communal dining-room, or residents' own homes, since menus would be circulated nightly and householders would simply relay their orders for the following day over the internal telephone. Women would no longer be faced with the tiresome task of waiting in all day to receive parcels or arrange for the carrying-out of household repairs. The Centre would see to all that, and more:

> At the Centre also parcels will be received for any resident whose house is temporarily empty; letters will be sent on during holidays; pet animals, whose existence so grievously complicates weekend absences for their owners, will be received as temporary boarders, and enthusiastic gardeners will be able to leave instructions for the punctual watering of cherished flower-beds or vegetable patches.[87]

Children (as well as pets) might be catered for in the domestic centre, for if householders saw fit, there could be no objection

[85] Ibid., p. 58ff.
[86] Ibid., p. 60.
[87] Ibid., p. 66.

to the organization of a crèche or a Montessori School.[88] Indeed, the Centre might develop into an educational institution in another direction, too, since it could also provide classes and lectures for young servants:

A deliberate organisation of classes and of brief lectures may very naturally arise. One can imagine such headings as: *The right way to scrub and the wrong*; *How to deal with painted surfaces, oilcloth and cork carpet*; *The usefulness and the dangers of turpentine*. Attendance at such instruction for a certain time might perhaps be made a condition of engagement for young new-comers. Examinations and certificates might be established, and the holding of the latter might be made a necessary step towards the attainment of a higher grade in the rank of the federation's servants.[89]

There is little evidence of Black envisaging any challenge to the hierarchy of social class, or to the sexual division of labour. Servants would be better trained, and better paid; they would be freed from the 'semi-feudal' conditions of residence in private households and their conditions of employment would more nearly approximate to those of other waged workers, but they would remain servants. And most servants would be women, although

The heavy work of the federation will probably provide whole-time employment for one man, or perhaps two men, who will clean all doorsteps and outside brasses (until the spread of general intelligence eliminates such labour), carry coals (until the committee supersedes coal by some system of central heating), clean windows (with a proper safety seat), clean boots and shoes (with a proper labour-and-leather saving machine) and work the electrically-driven vacuum-cleaner, an instrument much more powerful than any single householder could afford.[90]

Women would undoubtedly turn out to be the major beneficiaries of federated households, Black argued:

[88] Ibid., p. 78.
[89] Ibid., p. 74.
[90] Ibid., pp. 67–8.

No doubt many a woman living in a federation will still perform various domestic operations, just as many a man in his spare hours likes to do a job of home carpentering or to paint his summerhouse; but she will no longer feel obliged to do so daily with unbroken regularity nor to do so as a duty.[91]

The passage makes it clear that she is thinking of the middle classes, and indeed it is the assumption of the book that middle-class families must take the lead in such reforms. However, Black insisted that the need for domestic reconstruction was if anything *more* pressing lower down the social scale: 'Unless, however, such schemes spread to the clerk, the artisan, and, finally to the poorest class of industrial workers, the reform will not be complete.'[92] Referring her readers to the recent publication of *Maternity: Letters from Working Women* (1915), which provided ample evidence of the hardships and suffering experienced by working-class mothers at the turn of the century, she contended that co-operation could be seen as a crucial strategy for improving the quality of these women's lives.[93] Indeed, the very existence of the Women's Co-operative Guild testified to working-class women's recognition of this fact, and the Guild had fostered the spirit of co-operation and the organizational abilities which would facilitate reform. In the past, Black considered, working-class women had shown themselves somewhat conservative in their attitudes to housekeeping, but the wartime experience of public kitchens, works canteens and hostel-living had probably softened this conservatism. In some parts of the country – in Lancashire, for instance – she felt confident that domestic federations could succeed.[94] However, the reader cannot but note that the cost-benefit analysis of federated households which she attempts in her book is anchored pretty securely upon the assumption of middle-class incomes.

[91] Ibid., p. 95.
[92] Ibid., p. 110.
[93] Ibid., p. 111. See also Margaret Llewelyn Davies (ed.), *Maternity; Letters from Working Women* (G. Bell, London, 1915).
[94] Black, *New Way of Housekeeping*, p. 112.

Middle-class feminists and working-class households

Middle-class feminists such as Clementina Black were by no
means ignorant of the circumstances of working-class women's
lives, and indeed, one of the major and enduring achievements
of organizations such as the WIC and the FWG lay precisely in
documenting these lives. It is as a result of what Ellen Mappen,
a historian of the WIC, has called the 'social feminism' of the
middle-class women who established these organizations that
the early-twentieth-century public were made aware of the
experiences of women both in service and in industry, and as
wives and mothers in the home.[95] Against a dominant tendency
inherent in middle-class ideology to blame working-class women
for domestic disorganization, and to argue that ignorance of
domestic skills and inefficiency in household management lay
at the root of 'the social problem', feminists such as Black and
Maud Pember Reeves regularly and persistently emphasized
poverty and low wages as the real issue.[96] They staunchly
defended the competence of working-class mothers who managed, often with considerable ingenuity, to feed and clothe their
families whilst living on the edge of destitution. Maud Pember
Reeves's publication of *Round About a Pound a Week* in 1913
made a major impact in this context.[97] Based upon the FWG's
investigation of the budgets and daily circumstances of working-
class mothers in Lambeth between 1909 and 1913, the book
clearly hammered home the message that where families were
wholly deprived of decent housing, domestic equipment and
adequate food and clothing, any attempt to seek improvement
through training in housewifery or more efficient forms of domestic organization was doomed to failure.

[95] Ellen Mappen, *Helping Women at Work: The Women's Industrial Council
1889–1914* (Hutchinson, London, 1985), pp. 1–27.
[96] See, among others, Carol Dyhouse, 'Good wives and little mothers:
Social anxieties and the schoolgirl's curriculum, 1890–1920, *Oxford Review of
Education*, 3, no. 1 (1977); Anna Davin, 'Imperialism and the cult of motherhood', *History Workshop Journal* (Spring 1978); Sally Alexander, Introduction to
Maud Pember Reeves, *Round About a Pound a Week* (Virago, London, 1979).
[97] Maud Pember Reeves, *Round About a Pound a Week* (1913; Virago, London,
1979).

Social investigations of working-class home life carried out by middle-class women during the late nineteenth century and after were, of course, part of a well-established tradition of home-visiting and 'feminine philanthropy'. But they were sometimes distinguished by an implicit, if not an explicit, feminism, in that they identified themselves firmly with the perspectives and predicament of women in the community. This was so, for instance, with Florence Bell's study of working-class life in Middlesbrough, in Yorkshire, *At the Works*, which was first published in 1907.[98] Like Maud Pember Reeves, Lady Bell set about exploring every detail of domestic organization in the families she studied, concluding similarly that current social conditions imposed a near-impossible task upon the wives and mothers of the poor. The same detailed exploration and careful documentation of the domestic circumstances of working-class women was apparent in the Women's Health Enquiry Committee's investigation, which began in 1933 and published its report, written by Margery Spring Rice, as *Working Class Wives, Their Health and Conditions*, in 1939.[99] Again, this survey identified extreme poverty and a near-total lack of time and facilities for leisure as responsible for crippling the lives of working-class housewives. Here again, the feminism is implicit rather than explicit in the perspective of those who carried out the inquiry, which was careful to emphasize its 'entirely non-political basis'.[100]

Neither was there a lack of interest amongst feminists in the domestic lives of working-class women slightly higher up the social scale. In his study of social conditions in York, which was published in 1901, Seebohm Rowntree had felt constrained to comment on the domestic drudgery and social isolation which impoverished the lives of the wives of the better-paid artisans and workmen with whom he came into contact:

No-one can fail to be struck by the monotony which characterises the life of most married women of the working-class. Probably this

[98] Lady Florence Bell, *At the Works: A Study of a Manufacturing Town* (1907; Virago, London, 1985).
[99] Margery Spring Rice, *Working Class Wives: Their Health and Conditions* (Penguin, Harmondsworth, 1939).
[100] Ibid., p. 21.

monotony is least marked in the slum districts where life is lived more in common, and where the women are constantly in and out of each other's houses, or meet and gossip in the courts and streets. But with advance in the social scale, family life becomes more private, and the women, left in the house all day while their husbands are at work, are largely thrown upon their own resources. These, as a rule, are sadly limited, and in the deadening monotony of their lives these women too often become mere hopeless drudges.[101]

In 1922 *Time and Tide* took up this theme by serializing articles by Leonora Eyles, later extended into a book, entitled *The Woman in the Little House*.[102] These articles set out to anatomize the predicament of 'Annie Britain' a prototype suburban housewife typically married to a 'respectable' working man and living in a tiny, rented, badly-constructed and labour-intensive house in somewhere like Peckham, Ilford or Woolwich. Although their incomes were by contemporary standards not high (before the War they had probably lived on a wage of around thirty shillings, afterwards, £3–4 per week), such families did not lack housing or food. But Eyles argued that the modest little homes had become 'cages' or 'coffins' to their cramped inmates, the women toiling daily through endless rituals of child-care, cleaning, ironing and mending; engaged in a perpetual struggle with leaky boilers, smoky chimneys and wet washing. Above all, these women were lonely, bored and exhausted. 'Going to the pictures' often represented their only leisure activity, and this more for the opportunity to drowse than for entertainment:

The 'Tower' in Peckham is one of the most frequented rest cures I ever heard of. I have watched tired, dull women thronging in the afternoon, always with one baby and several small children ... A baby, nursed in its mother's arms in a warm, music-laden atmosphere will go to sleep; the bigger children will sit quietly, interested by the pictures part of the time, part of the time overawed by the

[101] Seebohm Rowntree, *Poverty: A Study in Town Life* (Macmillan, London, 1901), pp. 77–8.
[102] M. Leonora Eyles, 'The Woman in the Little House', *Time and Tide*, 20 January 1922–10 March 1922; see also the same author's book, *The Woman in the Little House* (Grant Richards, London, 1922).

policeman-like commissionaire at the door who, they are told, will 'fetch them' if they fidget. And so the mother rests.

... later I worked for a time in a picture palace in a poor district and used to see row after row of weary women drowsing with babies in their arms; some of them stayed two hours, some of them four, quite oblivious to the fact that they had 'seen' the programme round already.[103]

Like many of her contemporaries, Eyles put her faith in co-operation as a crucial strategy for improving the quality of these women's lives. Co-operative stores, she argued, would improve the standard of commodities which could be bought on a modest income; co-operative kitchens could supply better meals than could be contrived in inadequate private kitchens, and co-operatively organized crèches would afford the leisure and space for self-improvement and civilized social intercourse which the women needed above almost anything else. It was a deep-rooted conservatism, she believed, which stood most in the way of such improvements.[104]

Eyles claimed particular knowledge of the circumstances of working-class women because she herself had known poverty and hardship. Middle-class feminists were often acutely aware of their own economically privileged position and sometimes attacked each other for their ignorance of working-class women's lives, often in seeking to establish their own credentials as *bona fide* reformers or socialists. In seeking to gain access to the Trades Union Congress which was held in Liverpool in 1890, for instance, we find Eleanor Marx insisting that she worked a typewriter, and could thus be regarded as a genuine 'working woman', unlike Clementina Black, who had 'never done a day's manual labour' in her life.[105] Or we find Beatrice Webb, as described in the previous chapter, herself from a highly privileged middle-class background, lashing out vehemently against 'the capitalists' wives and daughters' whom she accused of knowing nothing about the interests of working-class women.[106] This

---

[103] Ibid., *Time and Tide*, 24 February 1922, p. 176.
[104] Ibid.
[105] Yvonne Kapp, *Eleanor Marx: The Crowded Years, 1884–1898* (Virago, London, 1976), p. 394.
[106] Beatrice Webb, *Women and the Factory Acts*, Fabian Tract, no. 67 (London, 1896), p. 9.

was an overstatement. Albeit that experiences of domestic and occupational life could vary so immensely between social classes, there were many middle-class feminists involved in social work who were far from being completely ignorant of the predicament of working-class women.[107]

Even so, class divisions certainly inhibited feminist attempts to find creative and enduring solutions to problems of domestic organization. Most crucially, the gulf which separated women in little houses like 'Annie Britain' from middle-class feminists like Vera Brittain was the economic difference which enabled the latter to continue to 'buy in' domestic help. Few middle-class feminists could envisage lives without service and the schemes for communal housekeeping or federated dwellings envisaged by Charlotte Gilman or Clementina Black still tended, as we have seen, to leave both social hierarchy and the sexual division of labour relatively intact. Equally importantly, social divisions between working- and middle-class women in this period, as described in the last chapter, tended to polarize over attitudes to employment outside the home. For middle-class women, work outside the home was conceived of as a right, or a privilege; whereas lower down the social scale women might identify their very source of oppression in what was effectively experienced as the dual burden of housekeeping and paid labour. It was the desire to shed half of this burden, as we have seen, which could lead wives to identify themselves with working men's demands for 'a family wage'. Ideologically, this demand often functioned in association with an expressed desire to emphasize the dignity of domestic work and raise the status of the housewife in the community.[108] Such goals, often articulated by Labour women in conjunction with demands for better housing, undoubtedly had a conservative effect. As we have

[107] See, for instance, Ellen Mappen's discussion of the 'social feminism' of middle-class women like Clementina Black in *Helping Women At Work*, pp. 11–27. On Clementina Black see also Liselotte Glage, *Clementina Black: A Study in Social History and Literature* (Carl Winter, Heidelberg, 1981). I am indebted to Olive Banks for this reference.

[108] Caroline Rowan, 'Women in the Labour Party, 1906–1920', *Feminist Review*. no. 12 (October 1982). See also the same author's '"Mothers, Vote Labour!" The State, the Labour Movement and working class mothers, 1900–1918', in *Feminism, Culture and Politics*, ed. Rosalind Brunt and Caroline Rowan (Lawrence & Wishart, London, 1982).

seen, many of the feminists who interested themselves in schemes
of domestic organization commented upon the conservatism of
working-class women. Caroline Rowan has pointed out that
communal facilities such as municipal kitchens and day nurseries,
insofar as they were introduced in order to free women for
factory work during the 1914—18 war, generally met with a
contradictory response from Labour women. They might be
welcomed as easing the burden of housework, but equally they
were sometimes seen as undermining the family by encouraging
mothers to go out to work. The result was that those advocating
communal facilities tended to emphasize that their aim was not
primarily one of freeing women for employment, but rather that
of ensuring that women secured more leisure and space for the
kind of personal development which would help them to become
better wives and mothers.[109]

Education for housework

There was also something of a convergence between Labour
women's emphasis on the importance of the home, and the
need to raise the status of domestic work, and the arguments of
those middle-class women who sought to solve 'the servant
problem' through similar means. The conservative potential of
these demands was exemplified in popular demands for increasing the emphasis on domestic skills in the education of girls and
women. Feminists themselves were often very divided upon this
issue. We have seen how C. V. Butler's investigation of domestic
science for the WIC devoted considerable space to detailing
Board of Education and local authority initiatives in devising
schemes for the education of girls in housewifery, although
Butler admitted that this was a somewhat controversial area:

> On the one side, employers may say cheerily that half or the whole
> of the school time of all 'working-class' girls over ten should be
> spent in domestic work, and some practical-minded parents would
> welcome this; on the other, enthusiasts for literary education cry

[109] Ibid.

out against calling down too soon the 'shades of the prison house', and entreat that the curriculum should not be made too utilitarian.[110]

She herself thought that a compromise was possible, but noted that there had undoubtedly been a 'decided recrudescence of interest' in household management during the last decade, pointing to the lead taken by King's College for Women, which had introduced its three-year course in 'Home Science' in 1908 as evidence of this.[111] Even so, she judged that there was some consensus of opinion amongst those circularized by the WIC that not nearly enough secondary schools contrived to include 'domestic subjects' in their curricula.[112]

It is notable that where the WIC interested itself in the promotion of technical education for women its initiatives stopped short of challenging the sexual divisions which structured the contemporary labour market. As Ellen Mappen has pointed out, there was no suggestion that girls should acquire skills to compete with men, rather they should be trained for dressmaking, laundry work and domestic industries.[113] Members of the Council consistently advocated the need for domestic economy schools which would include training for motherhood, and submitted a plan to the London County Council for the training of children's nurses in 1898. In 1911 the Council opened its own nursery training school in Hackney, envisaging that this would not only prepare working-class girls for their futures as wives and mothers, but also increase the supply of trained children's nurses available to the middle class.[114]

The question of whether housewifery should be elevated to the status of a 'science', which could be studied at every level from the Board School to the University, provoked a good deal of dissension amongst feminists.[115] The institution of the King's College Course in Home Science aroused the acrimony and derision of some contributors to *The Freewoman*, who jeered at

[110] Butler, *Domestic Service*, p. 77.
[111] Ibid., p. 83.
[112] Ibid.
[113] Mappen, *Helping Women at Work*, p. 24.
[114] Ibid.
[115] C. Dyhouse, *Girls Growing Up in Late Victorian and Edwardian England* (Routledge & Kegan Paul, London, 1981), pp. 165–9.

the 'mole-eyed . . . imbecility' of those who they claimed could not see that 'a Housewives' Degree' was 'a retrograde scheme perpetuating woman's inferiority'. 'There are no reasonable grounds for raising the estimation in which housework is held socially', inveighed one contributor to the debate: 'This estimation is far too high already, and housework absorbs the energies of many intelligent women, who, but for the social status which it is unfairly accorded, would be honestly ashamed of not attempting something better'.[116] In an editorial entitled 'The Drudge' which was featured on the front page on 8 February 1912, *The Freewoman* declared that the housewife was an anachronism:

> The housewife holds an office the business of which has become effete . . . With the advent of machinery and the factory, women got their marching orders, 'Out of the home', exactly as did men. Men obeyed them much more readily because they had so often before received such. To leave the home was no novelty to them. In war and in the hunt, they had become accustomed to moving afield. Women made no voluntary movement, though circumstances were strong enough to push millions of the less strongly entrenched out into the open world. Yet, after a century and a half of 'Industrialism', women are still fondly imagining that their highest destiny is in 'The Home', and that they can earn their salt by the pottering little duties to be found there.[117]

The business of child-care, *The Freewoman* contended, needed thoroughly rethinking. Not all women were drawn to it as a full-time occupation. Some undoubtedly were, and the best solution was surely to effect economies of scale whereby such women would assume responsibility for the day-time care of perhaps eight to ten babies whilst their mothers involved themselves in other kinds of work. These women should receive the kind of specialist training in child psychology that teachers currently benefited from, with additional qualifications in literature, paediatrics, and kindergarten practice. The course of training might last three or four years and would guarantee a fair salary, of a minimum, perhaps, of £200 a year. The system

[116] *The Freewoman*, 14 December 1911, p. 70.
[117] Ibid., 8 February 1912, p. 221.

could begin as a voluntary undertaking, but might finally be incorporated into the system of state education. In this way women would be liberated from the daily round of domestic drudgery which currently inhibited them from productive work and the kind of personal development which would enable them to mature into true citizenship.[118]

Men in the household

It is worth noticing that at least one contributor to the debate in *The Freewoman* demanded to know why, if the work of the home was universally claimed to be of such social importance, the instigators of the King's College degree in Home Science who described their courses as 'open to both sexes' were not more actively seeking to recruit men as students. 'Why call it a degree for house-*wives?*' asked Coralie M. Boord: 'Why not house-*holders?* In a social transition stage like the present *words* need careful handling for the accepted meanings of yesterday may not be the accepted meanings of today or . . . to-morrow.'[119] This, of course, was a highly pertinent point. The idea that men should assume some share in child-care and the work of the home was sometimes voiced by feminists during the period with which this book is concerned. Even in the 1890s the feminist journal *Shafts* was featuring articles which mooted that women's entry into the public world of employment and citizenship needed to be counterbalanced by men's participation in the work of the home. In an article published in 1892 it was suggested that

Man is wont to shirk his share of the trouble and responsibility of bringing up the children on the plea of much business; women is wont to excuse her ignorance and want of interest in matters of importance to the community on the plea of much housework and of many stay-at-home cases.[120]

[118] Ibid., 8 February 1912, p. 223.
[119] Ibid., 14 December 1911, p. 70.
[120] *Shafts*, 31 December 1892, p. 135; and issues for March 1893.

On a number of occasions contributors voiced a demand that boys needed educating in domestic skills whilst at school and that they should be encouraged alongside their sisters to take responsibility for housework.

Similarly, in *The Morality of Marriage* (1897), Mona Caird argued that the fact that women *bore* children did not dictate that they alone should *rear* them; indeed simple considerations of equity might be held to indicate otherwise:

> Nature clearly has indicated fatherhood to man as much as she has indicated motherhood to woman, and it is really difficult to see why a father should not be expected to devote himself wholly to domestic cases; that is, if we are so very determined that one sex or the other shall be sacrificed *en masse*. As an aid, moreover, to the selection of the victim-sex, we must consider the fact that the actual production of the race is performed by women. Therefore, they have done at least half the work, even if every other burden connected with the children be taken off their shoulders. So that if nothing but a burnt-offering will satisfy our yearning to decide other people's duties for them, that burnt-offering should clearly be man. Even *then* his burden would be light compared with that which woman has borne for centuries.[121]

Members of the Fabian Women's Group, discussing the disabilities of mothers as workers in 1910, also commented on what they saw as a need to induce fathers to play a more active role in child-care. Marion Phillips, for instance, inquired whether 'many fathers were not far too little with their children, whilst many mothers were with them too much? The working father scarcely saw his children from Sunday night to Saturday afternoon. Economic arrangements keeping the mother always in and the father always out were hard on both and on their children.'[122]

B. L. Hutchins suggested that the time had come to try to educate *both* parents to look upon parenthood as a social duty.[123]

[121] Mona Caird, *The Morality of Marriage, and Other Essays on the Status and Destiny of Women* (Redway, London, 1897), p. 7.
[122] Fabian Women's Group, 'Summary of eight papers and discussions upon the disabilities of mothers as workers' (printed for private circulation, 1910), pp. 21–2.
[123] Ibid., p. 18.

Again, Wilma Meikle, like Mona Caird, emphasized that there was no physiological reason why a weaned child should always be tended by its mother. By no means all women were cut out for full-time child care.[124] Crèches staffed by trained professionals were an urgent necessity. In one memorable passage she conjured up a vision of a time when Girton, Newnham and other women's colleges would think nothing of instituting university crèches where the offspring of students in residence could play happily during the daytime whilst their mothers got on with their studies. Equally, she glimpsed at a future in which childcare might cease to be regarded as exclusively women's work. An 'enlightened society', she suggested, 'will find it desirable and possible very greatly to shorten the hours of wage-earning labour for both women and men, so that parental friendship for children may become far more complete and more nearly bisexual than it is today'.[125]

Quite apart from these more vexed issues of role-sharing in child-care and the greater flexibility in patterns of work which would facilitate such, feminists pointed out that the stereotyping of particular kinds of work as exclusively 'masculine' or 'feminine' often varied between cultures. Mrs Aldrich, addressing the National Union of Women Workers on the subject of domestic organization in Brighton, in 1900, pointed out that in France men were much more widely employed to do routine domestic work.[126] A few years later, Vera Brittain observed from Cornell that for all the continuing problems faced by business and professional women, American men regularly helped with domestic chores and at least the country had 'succeeded in abolishing the sacred immunity of the male from all forms of housework'.[127]

It has to be admitted though, that feminists who envisaged a radical restructuring of sex roles within the home as a necessary complement to the extension of women's role outside it were in

[124] Wilma Meikle, *Towards a Sane Feminism* (Grant Richards, London, 1916), pp. 111–13.
[125] Ibid., p. 113.
[126] *Women Workers: Papers Read at Conference Held at Brighton*, 1900 (P. S. King, Westminster, 1900), p. 175.
[127] Brittain, *Thrice a Stranger*, p. 55.

the minority. Margaret Cole, contemplating the problem of housework from a feminist point of view in 1939, put all her faith in rationalization, and movements in the direction of communalized and professionalized services. She had no enthusiasm, she confessed, for any solution that would 'Make the men share it.' Such demands were often made by Scots-women, she opined,

> who have their menfolk better under control than Englishwomen — there are fewer public school boys in Scotland; and I suppose that if there is to be drudgery it is fairer that all should share it. But two blacks do not make a white; nor do two people blacking a stove waste less time than one person blacking a stove.[128]

Problems of domestic organization and particularly child-care were certainly a central issue for feminists. But the force of demands for a more equitable division of labour between the sexes in this area remained latent whilst the middle classes could rely on paid labour to 'black their stoves' for them.

[128] Margaret Cole, *Marriage, Past and Present* (Dent, London, 1939), p. 221.

4

Marital Relationships

The feminist critique of Victorian marriage

Marital relationships were the subject of intense discussion amongst feminists between 1880 and 1939; indeed, the desire to re-shape the marriage relationship was a key theme in feminist ideology. There was a steady stream of literature dealing specifically with problems of marriage. Following the collapse of her marriage with Frank Besant in the early 1870s Annie Besant published *Marriage, As It Was, As It Is, and As It Should Be: A Plea for Reform*, in 1882.[1] In 1897 Mona Caird brought together the series of articles which she had originally published in the *Westminster Review* in a volume entitled *The Morality of Marriage, and Other Essays on the Status and Destiny of Woman*.[2] Cicely Hamilton's *Marriage as a Trade* appeared in 1909.[3] In the 1920s Edith Ellis's essays on marriage were collected for publication under the title of *The New Horizon in Love and Life* (1921),[4] and Vera Brittain published *Halcyon; or The Future of Monogamy* (1929).[5] Margaret Cole's *Marriage, Past and Present* appeared on

---

[1] Annie Besant, *Marriage As It Was, As It Is, and As It Should Be: A Plea for Reform* (Freethought Publishing Co., London, 1882). An earlier edition had appeared, edited by Asa K. Butts, in America in 1879.
[2] Mona Caird, *The Morality of Marriage, and Other Essays on the Status and Destiny of Woman* (Redway, London, 1897) (articles previously published in the *Westminster Review*, August 1888–February 1894).
[3] Cicely Hamilton, *Marriage as a Trade* (1909; The Women's Press, London, 1987).
[4] Edith Ellis, *The New Horizon in Love and Life* (A. & C. Black, London, 1921).
[5] Vera Brittain, *Halcyon; or The Future of Monogamy* (Kegan Paul, Trench, Trubner, London, 1929).

the eve of the Second World War in 1939.[6] These are only a few of the vast number of texts which could be cited as dealing directly with relationships in marriage, and if one were to include books with a wider focus which included discussion of such relationships the list would be extended still further.

The publication of Edward Carpenter's *Love's Coming of Age*, (subtitled 'A Series of Papers on the Relations of the Sexes'), in 1896, proved a highly important stimulus to feminist discussions of marriage.[7] The book was extremely widely read, going through seven editions between 1896 and 1911, and it was acknowledged by many as having represented something of a turning point. Edith Ellis submitted that Carpenter's text had produced almost as revolutionary an impact upon sexual ethics as Marx's *Capital* had had upon economic thinking,[8] and Irene Clephane, writing in the 1930s, echoed her opinion that the book's frankness about intimacy had heralded a new outlook upon personal relationships in late-Victorian England.[9]

Imaginative literature similarly fuelled discussion. The works of Tolstoy, Hardy and Meredith, Ibsen's plays, and an efflorescence of novels focussing upon 'The New Woman' in the 1890s all shared an obsession with the problems of relationships between the sexes both in and out of marriage, and the 'New Woman' literature in particular was distinguished from earlier forms by the frankness with which it approached problems of sexuality.[10] In an essay on *Jude the Obscure* Havelock Ellis emphasized that traditionally English novelists concluded their narratives at the altar; 'the convent gate of marriage' was 'not again opened to the intrusive novel-reader's eye': 'Your wholesome-minded novelist knows that the life of a pure-natured Englishwoman after marriage is, as Taine said, mainly that of a very broody hen, a series of merely physiological processes with

---

[6] Margaret Cole, *Marriage, Past and Present* (Dent, London, 1939).

[7] Edward Carpenter, *Love's Coming of Age: A Series of Papers on the Relations of the Sexes* (George Allen, London, 1896).

[8] E. Ellis, *The New Horizon*, p. 1.

[9] Irene Clephane, *Towards Sex Freedom* (John Lane, London, 1935), p. 183.

[10] See, among others, Gail Cunningham, *The New Woman and the Victorian Novel* (Macmillan, London, 1978); Elaine Showalter, *A Literature of Their Own: British Women Novelists from Brontë to Lessing* (Virago, London, 1978), esp. ch. VII.

which he, as a novelist, has no further concern'.[11] For Ellis, the value of Hardy and other modern writers lay in their willingness to explore relationships and the 'passions at play' *within* marriage, which they were no longer prepared to depict as 'a grave, or a convent gate, or a hen's nest'.[12] In *Modern Marriage and How to Bear It*, (1909), Maud Braby discussed the impact of Ibsen and Meredith on attitudes to marriage and quoted Tolstoy's contention that 'The relationships between the sexes are searching for a new form, the old one is falling to pieces.'[13]

Ibsen's heroines were a particular inspiration to feminists. In 1886, Eleanor Marx and George Bernard Shaw got together in a Bloomsbury lodgings house for a private reading of *A Doll's House*, Eleanor Marx taking the part of Nora, and Shaw, Krogstad.[14] This was three years before the first public performance of the play in England, which unleashed a storm of public controversy over the propriety of Nora's behaviour in walking out on her tyrannical husband and her children. Edith Lees recalled the first night of *A Doll's House*, privately staged at the Novelty Theatre in 1889, as the occasion of 'breathless' excitement and 'almost savage' argument amongst her friends in *avant-garde* London.[15] In the same year the feminist Maria Sharpe read a paper on 'Henrik Ibsen: His Men and Women' to her fellow members of the Men and Women's Club. In this paper (which was subsequently published in the *Westminster Review*), she contended that Ibsen's plays heralded a social revolution, his women characters 'standing out above the rest' as 'an aristocracy of character and will'.[16] Elizabeth Robins, who

[11] Havelock Ellis, 'Concerning Jude the Obscure', in *Savoy Magazine* (October 1896), p. 39.

[12] Ibid.

[13] Maud C. Braby, *Modern Marriage and How to Bear It* (T. Werner Laurie, London, 1909), p. 5.

[14] Michael Meyer, *Henrik Ibsen: The Top of a Cold Mountain 1883–1906* (Hart Davis, London, 1971), p. 112.

[15] Judith Walkowitz, 'Science, feminism and romance: the Men and Women's Club, 1885–1889', *History Workshop Journal*, no. 21 (Spring 1986), p. 54.

[16] See Papers relating to Men and Women's Club in Pearson Collection, University College, London, April Meeting, 1889. See also Maria Sharpe, 'Henrik Ibsen: His Men and Women', *Westminster Review* (June 1889), p. 633.

became an active suffragist in the 1900s, was the first to play *Hedda Gabler* in London, and her passion for Ibsen was explicitly linked with her feminism.[17]

Many of the 'New Women' novels were written by committed feminists such as Mona Caird, Sarah Grand and Emma Brooke, or by women with pronounced feminist leanings such as 'George Egerton' (Mary Chavelita Dunne).[18] Those novels of the *genre* which were written by men and considered to represent women's interests were much discussed and received short shrift from feminists in the critical literature of the day. In 1895, for instance, Millicent Garrett Fawcett demolished Grant Allen's notorious best-seller, *The Woman Who Did*, in the *Contemporary Review* as a work 'feeble and silly to the last degree', a product of 'the unregenerate male mind' and nothing to do with feminism.[19] Feminist involvement with imaginative literature as a vehicle for exploring relationships was probably at its height in the 1890s, although it continued into the present century, with something of a shift in emphasis being represented in an upsurge of novels and plays which addressed the suffrage question.[20] Elaine Showalter has noted that women writers constituted a conspicuous part of the suffrage campaign, and in the demonstration of June 1910 over a hundred of them marched behind the 'Scriveners' banner' with Olive Schreiner, Sarah Grand, Edith Ellis and May Sinclair.[21] The tradition of using the novel for feminist analysis of family relationships continued into the

[17] Elizabeth Robins, *Both Sides of the Curtain* (Heinemann, London, 1940); see also entry on Elizabeth Robins in Olive Banks, *The Biographical Dictionary of British Feminists*, vol. I, 1880—1930 (Wheatsheaf, Brighton, 1985), pp. 172—3.

[18] See, for instance Mona Caird, *The Daughters of Danaeus* (Bliss, Sands, London, 1894); Sarah Grand, *Ideala* (Heinemann, London, 1888), and *The Heavenly Twins* (Heinemann, London, 1893); Emma Brooke, *A Superfluous Woman* (Heinemann, London, 1894); George Egerton, *Keynotes* (Elkin Mathews & John Lane, London, 1893), and *Discords* (Elkin Mathews & John Lane, London, 1894).

[19] Millicent Garrett Fawcett, 'The Woman Who Did', *Contemporary Review*, 67 (1895), p. 629; see also Grant Allen, *The Woman Who Did* (John Lane, London, 1895).

[20] Showalter, *A Literature of Their Own*, chs. VII and VIII.

[21] Ibid., p. 220.

inter-war period and in the writing of Virginia Woolf, Rose Macaulay, Winifred Holtby and Vera Brittain.[22]

Feminist writings of the 1880s and 1890s were explicit in rejecting what they identified as the traditional middle-class concept of marriage which demanded strength in a husband and frailty and deference in a wife. Annie Besant approvingly quoted Harriet Taylor's defence of a more egalitarian ideal.[23] In the latter's article in the *Westminster Review* she had asked: 'Would it not, to begin with, be well to instruct girls that weakness, cowardice and ignorance, cannot constitute at once the perfection of womankind and the imperfection of mankind?'[24] 'It is time to do away with the oak and ivy ideal', concluded Mrs Besant, 'and to teach each plant to grow strong and self supporting.'[25] Dependence might be touching in an infant, she submitted, on account of its helplessness, but it was 'revolting' in a grown man or woman, because with maturity should come the 'dignity of self-support'.[26] In *Love's Coming of Age* Edward Carpenter made exactly the same point:

The long historic serfdom of women, creeping down into the moral and intellectual natures of the two sexes, has exaggerated the naturally complementary relation of the male and the female into an absurd caricature of strength on the one hand and dependence on the other. This is well seen in the ordinary marriage-relation of the common-prayer-book type. The frail and delicate female is supposed to cling round the sturdy husband's form, or to depend from his arm in graceful incapacity; and the spectator is called upon to admire the charming effect of the union — as of the ivy with the oak — forgetful of the terrible moral, namely, that (in the case of the trees at any rate) it is really a death-struggle which is going on, in which either the oak must perish suffocated in the

---

[22] See, among others, Virginia Woolf, *To The Lighthouse* (Dent, London, 1938); Rose Macaulay, *Dangerous Ages* (Collins, London, 1921); Winifred Holtby, *Anderby Wold* (John Lane, London, 1923), and *South Riding* (Collins, London, 1936); Vera Brittain, *Honourable Estate* (Gollancz, London, 1936).

[23] Besant, *Marriage As It Was*, p. 30.

[24] Harriet Taylor in *Westminster Review* (July 1874), quoted in Besant, *Marriage As It Was*, p. 30.

[25] Besant, *Marriage As It Was*, p. 30.

[26] Ibid.

embrace of its partner, or in order to free the former into anything
like healthy development the ivy must be sacrificed.[27]

This emphasis on the sentimentalized image of marital relationships beloved of Victorian painters and poets — the picture of
the oak wreathed by the tendrils of the ivy or clinging vine — as
essentially an image of *parasitism* was eagerly seized upon by
feminists who, as we have seen earlier in this book, were already
using the concept of parasitism to characterize the economic
dependence of women.

Women as property

Even more central to the feminist critique of marriage was the
revulsion against the notion of women as the *property* of the
male. Frances Power Cobbe had inveighed against this idea in
1878:

> The notion that a man's wife is his PROPERTY, in the sense in which
> a horse is his property (descended to us rather through the Roman
> law than through the customs of our Teuton ancestors), is the fatal
> root of incalculable evil and misery. Every brutal-minded man, and
> many a man who in other relations of life is not so brutal, entertains
> more or less vaguely the notion that his wife is his *thing*, and is
> ready to ask with indignation (as we read again and again in the
> police reports) of anyone who interferes with his treatment of her,
> 'May I not do what I will *with my own?*' It is even sometimes
> pleaded on behalf of poor men, that they possess *nothing else* but
> their wives, and that, consequently, it seems doubly hard to meddle
> with the exercise of their power in that narrow sphere![28]

Annie Besant and Mona Caird echoed Cobbe's sense of outrage
here, both emphasizing the view that a dominant evil of modern
society was this survival, in patriarchy, of the tradition of
marriage by capture or by purchase of the wife.[29] Besant, like

---

[27] Carpenter, *Love's Coming of Age*, p. 80.
[28] Frances Power Cobbe, 'Wife torture in England', *Contemporary Review*,
(1878), pp. 62–3.
[29] Besant, *Marriage as It Was*, p. 5; Caird, *The Morality of Marriage*, p. 36.

many feminists before and after her, saw the custom maintained in the very ritual of the Christian marriage service.[30]

Feminists saw clearly that the idea of women as the property of their husbands had complex roots. It was related in part to their legal status. In the nineteenth century, the legal doctrine of *couverture* involved the suspension of the legal personality of a wife and its incorporation into that of her husband.[31] Although the Married Women's Property legislation of 1870 and 1882 significantly modified this position, the idea of *couverture* continued to be defended into the twentieth century, and it was not until 1935 that married women obtained the same rights over their property as single women. However, the notion of wives as property was also bound up with conditions of economic dependence and the assumption that in return for a husband's protection and maintenance a wife would keep house and be sexually available to him. In law these obligations were defined as a husband's right to his wife's *consortium*. A famous legal case in 1891 (*Regina* v. *Jackson*) brought into question the right of a husband to detain his wife forcibly in order to secure services from her. The court ruled that Mr Jackson was not entitled to imprison his wife in order to obtain conjugal rights, although, as Jane Lewis and other feminist scholars have pointed out, this ruling did not challenge the legal position whereby a husband could not be found guilty of rape within marriage.[32] I shall return to a discussion of some of the legal changes affecting the position of women within marriage during the period in the next chapter, but it is worth emphasizing at this point that public opinion was much divided over the ruling in the Jackson case, and that however revolutionary its implications might have appeared to contemporaries, it could scarcely effect any major change whilst conditions of social and economic depen-

---

[30] Besant, *Marriage As It Was*, p. 7.

[31] See Jane Lewis, *Women in England, 1870–1950* (Wheatsheaf, Brighton, 1984), pp. 119–21. Much of what follows has been taken from this source. For detailed discussion of the legal position of married women in this period see also Erna Reiss, *The Rights and Duties of Englishwomen* (Sherratt & Hughes, Manchester, 1934); and Lee Holcombe, *Wives and Property: Reform of the Married Women's Property Law in Nineteenth Century England* (Martin Robertson, Oxford, 1983).

[32] Lewis, *Women in England*, p. 120.

dence for women persisted.[33] The Women's Co-operative Guild, collecting information on attitudes to divorce amongst its membership in the 1900s, found that the view, 'still sanctioned to some extent by law and custom', of a wife as the property of her husband, was deeply resented. 'We want to get rid of the idea that a man owns his wife just as he does a piece of furniture', wrote one member, speaking for many.[34]

Feminists who saw women's dependence within marriage as the root of personal and social impotence had little time for the idea of marriage as a 'protected' state, in which they might benefit from paternal benevolence or masculine chivalry. Cicely Hamilton, for instance, contended that her own experience led her to define chivalry, as commonly practised, 'as a form, not of respect for an equal, but of condescension to an inferior; a condescension which expresses itself in certain rules of behaviour where non-essentials are involved.'[35] In very few of the important areas of relationships between men and women, she submitted, 'is the chivalric principle allowed to get so much as a hearing; in practically all such matters it is . . . an understood thing that woman gets the worst of the bargain, does the unpleasant work in the common division of labour, and, when blame is in question, sits down under the lion's share of it.'[36] Hamilton argued that the time had come for women to reject small courtesies from men − 'the opening of a door and the lifting of a hat' − as only available at too high a price. Masculine courtesies were too often an expression of kindly contempt rather than reverence for women, and that women should assume an attitude 'of voluntary abasement . . . in order that man may know the pleasure of condescension − is the only thing that ever makes me ashamed of being a woman; since it is the outward & visible expression of an inward servility that has eaten and destroyed a soul'.[37]

Hamilton's spirited polemic against marriage was written in

[33] Ibid.
[34] Women's Co-operative Guild, *Working Women and Divorce* (Nutt, London, 1911), p. 32.
[35] Hamilton, *Marriage as a Trade*, p. 80.
[36] Ibid., pp. 80−1.
[37] Ibid., p. 83.

the context of the bitter struggle to obtain the suffrage on the
eve of the First World War, but similar sentiments were being
expressed by feminists in the 1890s. Mona Caird, for instance,
originally writing in the *Westminster Review*, had insisted that

> Some of the most mischievous elements of our present family life
> are created by the submissive attitude of the woman. It is impossible
> to describe, much more to overstate the far-reaching evil which it
> fosters. Disobedience, in the present crisis of affairs, is woman's
> first duty. 'That will lose her power,' someone exclaims, 'the power
> that she now possesses; the sceptre which, if cleverly wielded,
> might move the world.' That power, however, is but a power that
> is won by smiles and wiles and womanly devices; and, when won,
> is hers not by right but by favour. This is the power, not of a free
> being, but of a favourite slave.[38]

It was impossible for women to claim greater freedom, asserted
Caird, without 'the marriage-relation ... being called in question'. Feminism necessarily included − whether its adherents
so intended it or not − 'a claim for a modified marriage', away
from the present 'coercive' and inegalitarian system.[39]

The first step towards reform as envisaged by writers like
Caird, Hamilton, and may others was essentially based on
defiance. Like Nora in *A Doll's House*, women should refuse to
accept their confinement in the home as part of the *status quo*.
'Feminism led women away from the home,' asserted Dora
Russell in *Hypatia* (1925), 'that they might return armed and
unsubdued to make marriage tolerable.'[40] As we have seen
earlier, by no means all of those feminists who diagnosed path-
ology in patterns of contemporary marriage were bent on
'returning' to the family. Cicely Hamilton, for instance, believed
that the only way in which women would secure due appreciation
for the work which they did within the family would be through
'shirking the duties' and going on strike, as it were, against
marriage. She recognized full well the fact that marriage represented, for a majority of women at that time, their only

[38] Caird, *The Morality of Marriage*, p. 118.
[39] Ibid., p. 67.
[40] Dora Russell, *Hypatia, or Woman and Knowledge* (Kegan Paul, Trench,
Trubner, London, 1925), p. 37.

chance of a 'trade' or meal ticket, but considered that conditions would only be improved when sufficient women opted for celibacy, economic self-sufficiency and full personal autonomy, in order to raise expectations all round.[41]

Hamilton was at pains to emphasize that she was not against the *institution* of marriage in itself, but only its contemporary form:

My intention in writing ... has not been to inveigh against the institution of marriage, the life companionship of man and woman; all that I have inveighed against has been the largely compulsory character of that institution — as far as one-half of humanity is concerned — the sweated trade element in it, and the glorification of certain qualities and certain episodes and experiences of life at the expense of all the others. I believe — because I have seen it in the working — that the companionship in marriage of self-respecting man and self-respecting woman is a very perfect thing; but I also believe that, under present conditions, it is not easy for self-respecting woman to find a mate with whom she can live on the terms demanded by her self-respect. Hence a distinct tendency on her part to avoid marriage. Those women who look at the matter in this light are those who, while not denying that matrimony may be an excellent thing in itself, realise that there are some excellent things which may be bought too dear. That is the position of a good many of us in these latter days.[42]

Hamilton welcomed the loosening of family ties and the rise of feminism as heralding a new sense of fellowship amongst women. Mutual consciousness of social disadvantage fostered feminine 'class-consciousness', or sisterhood, which was a crucial source of strength. Together with the bringing out of private grievances for discussion in the public arena, she felt convinced that this represented enormous potential for change. Women of the 'silly angel class', she ventured, were 'well on the way to extinction'.[43]

Feminists were united in celebrating a new, stronger ideal of womanhood. The 'shopping doll', Carpenter's bourgeois lady, 'crucified 'twixt a smile and a whimper', would disappear.[44]

[41] Hamilton, *Marriage as a Trade*, pp. 137,145.
[42] Ibid., p. 141.
[43] Ibid., p. 129.
[44] Carpenter, *Love's Coming of Age*, p. 44.

Our upper and middle-class forefathers, Hamilton asserted, had admired fragility of health in women; hence our foremothers had appealed to the masculine sense of chivalry by 'habitual indulgence in complaints known as swoons and vapours'. But the attractions of well-paid employment for women had effected something of a decline in the prevalence of these complaints. Teachers, sanitary inspectors, journalists and typists had apparently repressed any tendency to such, and 'swooning' was 'practically a lost art'.[45] Olive Schreiner's 'New Woman' similarly acquires stature through her labour. Out of somewhat purple prose she emerges as Brünnhilde, the Valkyrie, a specimen of 'labouring and virile womanhood',[46] in opposition to previous effete forms of 'the parasite woman, on her couch, loaded with gewgaws, the plaything and amusement of man'.[47]

In these writers and many others the image of the economically dependent wife merges with that of the concubine, or the 'kept' woman. 'The relation of female parasitism generally, to the peculiar phenomenon of prostitution,' insisted Schreiner, 'is fundamental.'[48] 'Marriage as a trade' implied a debased ideal, commerce in relationships; marriage as prostitution. This was the light in which patterns of marriage in capitalist society were condemned by Eleanor Marx and Edward Aveling in an article in the *Westminster Review* in 1885.[49] For them, the only route towards securing marriage relationships based on the love and mutual respect of both partners untainted by commerce lay through the achievement of a socialism which would guarantee economic autonomy to all. Almost all feminists, throughout the period, coupled their desire for a reform in the relationship of marriage with the realization that this was only likely to be achieved alongside measures which would secure more economic autonomy for wives. Many identified this as the crux of the issue. Barbara Drake suggested to her colleagues in the Fabian Women's Group that the burden of breadwinning put strains

[45] Hamilton, *Marriage as a Trade*, p. 127.
[46] Olive Schreiner, *Woman and Labour* (1911; Virago, London, 1978), p. 145.
[47] Ibid., p. 132.
[48] Ibid., p. 82n.
[49] Eleanor Marx and Edward Aveling, 'The Woman Question, from a Socialist point of view', *Westminster Review*, 6, no. 25 (1885), p. 214ff.

on a husband's personality as much as the burden of dependence distorted a woman's, contending that 'Economic independence would remove from marriage that sense of living around one another's necks which made Stevenson condemn marriage as breaking men's courage.'[50] At the same time she added, 'If it was damning for a man to have something hanging round his neck, it was ten thousand times more damning for the woman to be the something that hung.'[51]

Alongside the emergence of new ideals of womanhood feminists hoped for a transformed ideal of masculinity. Men would be induced to yield their despotic power. 'A half-grown man is of course a tyrant', declared Carpenter in *Love's Coming of Age*.[52] Mona Caird similarly emphasized that the 'sons of bondswomen' could not be free, and quoted Hegel's dictum: 'The master does not become really free till he has liberated his slave.'[53] 'Tyranny in men, and parasitism in women, are foes to fine and clean sexuality', asserted Edith Ellis in her essay 'The Love of To-Morrow'.[54] In the reformed, companionate marriage of the future the enlightened, sympathetic male would seek intelligence and mutual interests in the female. In her preface to *Woman and Labour* Olive Schreiner tells us that the book emerged out of an earlier, more comprehensive work on 'the Women's Question' which had been destroyed when her house had been looted during the Boer War.[55] The last and longest chapter of the original book had 'dealt with the problems connected with marriage and the personal relations of men and women in the modern world'. In this chapter she tells us that she had argued that the emancipation of women would lead not towards 'a greater sexual laxity, or promiscuity' but towards 'a higher appreciation of the sacredness of all sex relations', and above

[50] Barbara Drake, Report of Annual Meeting of Fabian Women's Group, *Fabian News*, February 1920; as quoted in Linda Walker, 'The Women's Movement in England in the Late Nineteenth and Early Twentieth Centuries' (unpublished doctoral dissertation, University of Manchester, April 1984), p. 255.
[51] Ibid.
[52] Carpenter, *Love's Coming of Age*, p. 35.
[53] Caird, *The Morality of Marriage*, p. 191.
[54] E. Ellis, *The New Horizon*, p. 4.
[55] Schreiner, *Woman and Labour*, pp. 11−21.

all to 'a closer, more permanent, more emotionally complete and intimate relation between the individual man and woman'.[56] If, in 'the present disco-ordinate transitional stage of our social growth', divorce was to become more common, she emphasized that this should be regarded as merely a transitional phase in the adjustment of relationships towards a new ideal of harmonious monogamy.[57]

Ideals of monogamy and sexuality: the Men and Women's Club

This was a very common theme of feminist writing in the period, which constantly referred to the need for a period of readjustment and experiment in relationships but retained the conviction that out of such would emerge the condition for true monogamy. Edith Ellis submitted that

> To rid the world of prostitution, to have woman economically free and man spiritually free, and yet to realise passion as the flame of love, is no easy task in the great emancipation of the world. It cannot be carried through without personal suffering and social upheaval. Experiments, with both successes and failures in their train, must be tried.[58]

There was a strong vein of Utopianism in such literature. Olive Schreiner's writing moved away from realism into allegorical 'Dreams' and 'Visions'.[59] Some thirty years later Vera Brittain wrote *Halcyon; or The Future of Monogamy*, which she offers to her readers as the account of a dream she had had whilst planning to write a book on the future of marriage.[60] The text purports to recreate a section of a book about the history of monogamous marriage as a moral institution which appeared to her in her dream as written by 'Minerva Huxterwin', a professor writing in the middle of the twenty-first century. It documents a lengthy

---

[56] Ibid., pp. 25–6.
[57] Ibid., p. 26.
[58] E. Ellis, *The New Horizon*, p. 11.
[59] See discussion of Schreiner's writing in Showalter, *A Literature of Their Own*, pp. 195–204 and esp. p. 197.
[60] Brittain, *Halcyon*, pp. 5–7.

period of experimentation in marital and sexual relationships as
emerging out of the Victorian era of prudery and repression,
beginning with the World League for Sexual Reform's Conference
held in London in 1929 (a conference in which Vera Brittain
was actually a participant). This period of sexual freedom,
experimentation and scientific progress (a period depicted as
one in which important advances are made in hormone therapy
and ectogenesis) is followed by one in which a new, purified
form of 'voluntary monogamy' triumphs, somewhere between
the years 2000 and 2030.[61]

Vera Brittain might still have envisaged the 1880s and 1890s
as decades hallmarked by a crippling reticence over sexual
relationships in society, but as already indicated above, for
many of those who lived through them they were as much of a
watershed in terms of opening up the possibilities of new forms
of relationships as the next generation were to declare the 1920s
and 1930s. The late nineteenth century was not just the heyday
of what some literary critics dubbed 'The Anti-Marriage League'
(Mrs Oliphant's phrase) in fiction,[62] of 'Ibscenity' (*Punch*) or
'Erotomania' (a label coined by Hugh Stutfield) in drama and
the novel.[63] It was a period in which many feminists and
'freethinkers' saw themselves as actively forging new kinds of
personal relationships, as well as writing and discussing them.
There is a sense, of course, in which every generation can
be seen as living through experiments in personal and social
relationships, but there was undoubtedly a level of self-
consciousness and frankness about discussions of sexuality in
'advanced' circles at the end of the nineteenth century which
signified change. This was in the aftermath of the Bradlaugh–
Besant trial, in which Annie Besant and Charles Bradlaugh
were prosecuted for re-issuing Knowlton's pamphlet on birth

[61] Ibid., p. 79ff.
[62] M. Oliphant, 'The Anti-Marriage League', *Blackwood's Magazine* (January
1896), pp. 135–49.
[63] Hugh E. M. Stutfield, 'Tommyrotics', *Blackwood's Magazine* (June 1895),
and *'The psychology of feminism'*, *Blackwood's Magazine* (January 1897). See also
Carol Dyhouse, 'The role of women', in *The Victorians*, ed. Lawrence Lerner
(Methuen, London, 1978), pp. 187–92; and Cunningham, *The New Woman
and the Victorian Novel*.

control, *The Fruits of Philosophy*, which gave a 'jolt of publicity' to the birth control movement at a time when middle-class couples were indeed beginning to limit the size of their families.[64] These were the years of the Fellowship of the New Life, of the Legitimation League, the Proudhon Society, and the Men and Women's Club.[65] They were years, as Jeffrey Weeks as argued, which witnessed 'a new zeal in defining and categorising sexuality', so that indeed a new language of sexual variation 'began to seep into scientific discourse' by the end of the century.[66]

Feminists regularly protested against the conventions of contemporary morality which would keep women in ignorance about sexuality by identifying knowledge as contaminating and a threat to modesty or 'purity'. This protest was often voiced in imaginative literature: in George Egerton's short story, *Virgin Soil*, for instance, a young girl's innocence about male sexuality is shown as allowing her to become the victim of an exploitative and unhappy marriage. Having walked out on her husband she returns to remonstrate with her mother for having kept her in ignorance of the facts of life.[67] Similar themes recur in many of the novels of the 1890s and the demand for enlightened sex education was often registered in feminist literature throughout the period 1880−1939. In their article on 'The Woman Question, from a Socialist point of view' Eleanor Marx and Edward Aveling had condemned a society which silenced children's questions about reproduction and shrouded the whole subject of sex relationships in mystery and shame.[68] Edith Ellis called upon parents to teach young children about sex in an essay entitled 'Blossoming Time', which was published after her death, in 1921.[69] Similarly, Elizabeth Wollstenholme-Elmy insisted

[64] J. A. and Olive Banks, 'The Bradlaugh−Besant trial and the English newspapers', *Population Studies*, 8 (1954−5), p. 22ff.

[65] See, among others, Jeffrey Weeks, *Sex, Politics and Society: The Regulation of Sexuality Since 1800* (Longman, London, 1981), p. 180ff. Walkowitz, 'Science, feminism and romance'; and Preface (by Edward Carpenter) and Introduction (by Margaret Tracey) to Edith Ellis, *The New Horizon*.

[66] Weeks, *Sex, Politics and Society*, p. 21.

[67] George Egerton, 'Virgin Soil', in *Discords* (1894; Virago, London, 1983), p. 157.

[68] Marx and Aveling, 'The Woman Question', p. 216.

[69] Edith Ellis, 'Blossoming Time', in *The New Horizon*, p. 70ff.

that 'purity' depended upon open and honest discussions rather
than concealment, and (employing the same kind of flower-
imagery as Edith Ellis) herself compiled two books on the facts
of sexual life for children, *Baby Buds* for younger children, and
The Human Flower for older children.[70]

Feminists hoped, then, that more often discussion and greater
knowledge of sexuality would help transform relationships and
protect women from too easily becoming the victims of male
'lust' in or out of marriage. As Judith Walkowitz has emphasized,
the subject of prostitution was constantly in the public mind in
the last quarter of the nineteenth century.[71] In the 1870s, the
feminist moral crusade against 'male vice' crystallized around
opposition to the Contagious Diseases Act of 1864, the first of
three statutes providing for the sanitary inspection of prostitutes
in garrison towns in an attempt to curb the spread of venereal
disease amongst the military.[72] In the 1880s, the popular press
fed a scandalised (and titillated) public lurid details about an
allegedly widespread traffic in the sale of young virgins as child
prostitutes, following the publication of W. T. Stead's notorious
piece of journalism, 'The Maiden Tribute of modern Babylon'
in the *Pall Mall Gazette* in 1885.[73] Middle class women were
made uncomfortably aware of the links between marriage and
prostitution, and of the powerlessness which they shared with
their fallen 'sisters' in a society which licensed and legitimized
male sexuality as 'naturally' and 'uncontrollably' seeking regular
outlet. The unhappy wife in George Egerton's *Virgin Soil*, for
instance, laments bitterly to her mother that

[70] 'Ellis Ethelmer' (Elizabeth Wollstenholme-Elmy), *Baby Buds: On the
Physiology of Birth* (Women's Emancipation Union, Congleton, 1895); *The
Human Flower, Being A . . . Statement of the Physiology of Birth and the Relations of
the Sexes* (Women's Emancipation Union, Congleton, 1894). See discussion in
Sheila Jeffreys, '"Free From All Uninvited Touch of Man": women's cam-
paigns around sexuality, 1880–1914', *Women's Studies International Forum*, 5,
no. 6 (1982), p. 637.

[71] Judith Walkowitz, 'Male vice and feminist virtue: feminism and the
politics of Prostitution in nineteenth century Britain', *History Workshop Journal*,
no. 13 (Spring 1982).

[72] Ibid.; see also the same author's *Prostitution and Victorian Society*: Women,
Class and the State (Cambridge University Press, Cambridge, 1980), p. 74ff.
and *passim*.

[73] Walkowitz, 'Male vice and feminist virtue', p. 83ff.

'as long as marriage is based on such unequal terms, as long as man demands from a wife as a right, what he must sue from a mistress as a favour, ... marriage becomes for many women a legal prostitution, a nightly degradation, a hateful yoke under which they age, mere bearers of children conceived in a sense of duty, not love.'[74]

Again, as Walkowitz has emphasized, such perceptions reinforced the tendency among feminists to identify prostitution as something of a paradigm for the feminine condition.[75]

Discussions of prostitution in the press and elsewhere increased women's sense of sexual and social vulnerability, but at the same time made opportunities for them to examine their own sexuality and allowed them space to try to clarify their viewpoint. Judith Walkowitz and Lucy Bland, both of whom have studied the activities of the Men and Women's Club in the 1880s, similarly point out that the furore unleashed by the publication of Stead's 'Maiden Tribute' article facilitated Karl Pearson's task of finding enough potentially suitable women willing to join the Club, a task which he had previously found difficult.[76] In her 'Autobiographical history' of the Club, written in 1889, Maria Sharpe observed that 'everything is more open now, especially I think since the Pall Mall Gazette revelations, which however questionable did I believe break down a great barrier for women—after then no-one was supposed of necessity to be in ignorance.'[77]

Members of the Men and Women's Club were self-conscious about the pioneering nature of their discussions about sex and they were highly earnest about their purpose. Karl Pearson, particularly — the inaugurator of the group — was determined

---

[74] Egerton, 'Virgin Soil', p. 155. See also discussion in Lucy Bland, 'Marriage laid bare: middle-class women and marital sex, c.1880—1914', in *Women's Experience of Home and Family, 1850—1940*, ed. Jane Lewis (Blackwell, Oxford, 1986), p. 134.

[75] Walkowitz, 'Male vice and feminist virtue', p. 81.

[76] Walkowitz, 'Science, feminism and romance', pp. 42—3; Bland, 'Marriage laid bare', p. 126.

[77] Maria Sharpe, 'Autobiographical history of the Men and Women's Club', in Pearson Collection, University College, London. Quoted in Bland, 'Marriage laid bare', p. 126.

to preserve a high moral tone by repudiating associations with contemporaries whose lifestyles too easily gained them a reputation for irregularity or 'free love'.[78] He determinedly avoided any association with 'Hintonianism', for instance, a label which was coined by contemporaries to refer to the convictions and followers of the philosopher James Hinton (a man whom Phyllis Grosskurth has described as 'an obscure messiah with a small but fervid following'[79]), who had allegedly developed a messianic fervour for polygamous free unions in his later years. Maria Sharpe was equally anxious to safeguard the respectability of the Club, and her objection to admitting Eleanor Marx as a member seems to have been based upon the irregularity of the latter's lifestyle and in particular her openly living 'in sin' with Edward Aveling during this period.[80]

The attendance book which survives in the archives of the Men and Women's Club shows the involvement, at least as guests, of a number of contemporary feminist thinkers such as Mona Caird, Annie Besant, Jane Clapperton and Clementina Black.[81] The full-time members of the group were carefully selected: the intention at the outset was that numbers should not exceed twenty, and that as far as possible there should be equal numbers of men and women. The women who were originally chosen as members were almost all intelligent, articulate and feminist, and the intention was that members should take turns in presenting papers for discussion at monthly meetings. The archive shows that the subject matter of discussion ranged widely — from sexual physiology, through the ethics of contraception and marriage relationships in Victorian England, primitive society and Ancient Greece — during the four-year history of the Association's meetings.[82]

What becomes immediately clear from a study of this fascinating archive, as both Judith Walkowitz and Lucy Bland

---

[78] Walkowitz, 'Science, feminism and romance', pp. 40 and 57 n.22.

[79] Ibid.; see also Phyllis Grosskurth, *Havelock Ellis: A Biography* (Allen Lane, London, 1980), p. 42 and p. 93ff.

[80] Bland, 'Marriage laid bare', p. 128.

[81] Attendance Book, Men and Women's Club, in Pearson Collection, University College, London.

[82] Papers relating to Men and Women's Club, Pearson Collection, University College, London.

have emphasized, is that in spite of the Club's commitment to equality it was extremely difficult for women to explore ideas about sexuality in a mixed-sex milieu. The men were infinitely more confident in discussion than the women. As Walkowitz notes, they were mostly old friends of Karl Pearson:

> On the whole, the men were barristers and doctors, products of public schools, Oxbridge and the great European Universities, who extended and consolidated their old boy networks in London at the Saville, the Athenaeum and the National Liberal Club, and in their professional lives. They moved comfortably between the world of radical London and the institutions of the male ruling class.[83]

The women, on the other hand, lacked this social confidence, however 'advanced' some of their views; and only one of them (Henrietta Müller) had been educated at university. The men controlled discussions from the outset, always inclined to treat women as the *objects* of enquiry, and confidently representing their own stance as objective (the stance of the detached, rational observer), and accusing the women of emotionalism, subjectivity and bias. *Female* sexuality was defined as problematic, *male* sexuality was not.

This male dominance and essentially patronizing attitude did not go unchallenged, although it was characteristic of many of the earlier discussions that whilst the men indulged in rhetorical oratory the women often relapsed into embarrassed silences. Maria Sharpe recollected in 1889 that she had felt extremely nervous in these early sessions and could remember little of what had been talked about except Pearson's declaiming 'that if he had a young wife he should take her down to the Strand at night and tell her what things meant'.[84] To explore the women's real thoughts on, and reactions to, the issues discussed in formal meetings one needs to resort to the voluminous private correspondence which flourished amongst members around the edges of these meetings.

In July 1885, for instance, Pearson launched the Club's pro-

[83] Walkowitz, 'Science, feminism and romance', p. 41.
[84] Maria Sharpe, 'Autobiographical history of the Men and Women's Club', p. 7.

ceedings by delivering a longish paper on 'The Woman Question', in which he aimed to delineate some of the issues with which he felt they should be concerned. One of his main themes was that of motherhood and maternal feeling in women, which he defined as crucial in contemplating their position in marriage and in society generally.[85] The paper aroused the hackles of many of the women present. In correspondence after the meeting, Emma Brooke objected that the paper should really have been entitled 'Notes on a man's view of the Woman Question', and complained that Pearson could not see 'women as they are, because he looks at them through his own mental image of what he supposes them to be'.[86] She took issue, particularly, with Pearson's contention that in men, the sexual instinct represented desire for women, whilst in women sexual feeling was essentially a by-product of the desire to mother children. (Olive Schreiner agreed with her here, pencilling a note 'this is *very* true' against the passage in Brooke's letter in which she voiced this objection.) A desire for children could be found equally, in both sexes, argued Brooke; although it was common for women to dread the pains of childbirth and certainly they recoiled from any notion of unsolicited, debilitating annual pregnancies. At the same time the idea that women were lacking in sexual feeling was a male illusion, Brooke insisted; chastity was certainly as difficult for women as men, and the idea that 'a pure woman floats half asleep in a smooth pool of chastity all her life' unless some male awakened her passion was nonsense.[87] Pearson's obsession with maternal feelings, she concluded, stemmed from his primary concern with eugenics. He tended to sentimentalize motherhood, but real respect was lacking. Madonna and child imagery figured conspicuously in his writings, though she would 'not charge the writer with any act of worship'.[88]

This was only the beginning of a long series of disagreements

[85] Karl Pearson, 'The Woman Question', paper printed for private circulation, in archive of Men and Women's Club, Pearson Collection, University College, London.

[86] Emma Brooke, 'Notes on a man's views of the Woman's Question', Papers relating to Men and Women's Club, Pearson Collection, University College, London.

[87] Ibid.

[88] Ibid.

and difficulties which featured in the history of the group. Undercurrents of tension were undoubtedly generated by personal passions and entanglements. Olive Schreiner, for instance, nurtured an explosive and unrequited passion for the aloof Karl Pearson, who found himself increasingly attracted to Maria Sharpe (whom he eventually married).[89] But differences between the men and the women in the group were particularly pronounced over such issues as prostitution, contraception ('preventive checks'), and the double standard in sexual morality. Whilst the women were by no means always in agreement with each other over these issues, there was a general tendency amongst them to deplore the instrumental and frequently *de haut en bas* way in which the men discussed sex. Emma Brooke complained to Pearson about the 'distinctly dominant tone' he adopted in talking to women, and his 'inclination to lay down their duty for them'.[90] Shrewdly she observed that the somewhat arrogant, detached tone he adopted in questioning women directly about their experiences was ill-gauged to elicit confidence or intimacy: 'as a rule, upon being questioned, women draw about them the veil of conventionality, and speak out of *that*; to learn, you must listen to their words, observe their faces in the unconscious moments when nature and feelings speak for themselves.'[91] Henrietta Müller was similarly acutely aware of the difficulties women experienced in articulating their own views about sexuality. Angry with the men for not allowing women the space to speak, she eventually resigned, threatening to start a club for women only, and complaining in a letter to Pearson that it was

the same old story of the man laying down the law to the woman and not caring to recognize that she has a voice, and the women resenting in silence, and submitting in silence. Even when one who is bold opens her lips, they feebly admire her courage but do not venture to follow her example because the enemy is present.[92]

[89] Walkowitz, 'Science, feminism and romance'.

[90] Correspondence, Emma Brooke to Karl Pearson, 14 February 1886, Pearson Collection, University College, London (10/28).

[91] Brooke, 'Notes on a man's views', pp. 5–6.

[92] Correspondence, Henrietta Müller to Karl Pearson, 29 March 1888, Pearson Collection, University College, London (10/45), quoted in Bland, 'Marriage laid bare', p. 132.

Commenting on this resignation in a letter to Maria Sharpe in 1888, R. J. Parker, one of the leading male members of the Club, attributed it to the 'strong convictions' professed by Miss Müller, convictions which he regretted 'did not perfectly harmonise with the sceptical and enquiring spirit which rightly dominates our discussions'.[93]

The records of the Men and Women's Club provide us with ample evidence, then, of the difficulties feminists experienced in speaking their minds about sexuality even in liberal company where men were present. They also testify to the feelings of resentment, vulnerability and danger which these women frequently experienced when discussions were premised on assumptions about male sexuality which facilitated a distinction between sexual passion and emotional involvement, or 'love', and legitimized the former as 'normal'. The women felt debased by the idea of men seeking female company simply for 'sexual outlet' and the majority of them believed that men should learn self-restraint. Emma Brooke demanded that they stop acting like 'beasts of prey', and in one particularly bitter, emotional paragraph in her written response to Pearson's paper she accused men of 'having murdered love'.[94]

Sexuality, reproduction and birth control

A disgust for the brutality which might fuse with sexual feeling in men was fuelled by the dramatic accounts of child prostitution, and the grisly details of the 'Jack the Ripper' murders of five women in Whitechapel which filled the headlines of contemporary newspapers. As Judith Walkowitz has shown, these events and the media coverage which they occasioned left a deep and lasting impression on the public mind.[95] In particular, they massively increased women's sense of sexual and social vulnerability. In its turn, this sense of vulnerability fuelled 'social

[93] Correspondence, R. J. Parker to Maria Sharpe, 20 February 1888, Pearson Collection, University College, London (10/1).

[94] Brooke, 'Notes on a man's views', p. 38.

[95] Judith Walkowitz, 'Jack the Ripper and the myth of male violence', *Feminist Studies*, 8, no. 3 (Autumn 1982).

purity' movements amongst feminists and others, generating support for vigilance associations, the raising of the age of consent, the policing of prostitution, and 'rescue' work of all kinds.

Historians have for some time been aware of the undercurrent of fear and resentment of men which exists in some of the feminist texts on sexuality written in the 1890s and in the period before the First World War. Male historians such as George Dangerfield and David Mitchell have tended to dismiss some of these texts as wholly hysterical and the work of cranks.[96] The hypothesis – mooted by writers such as Elizabeth Wollstenholme-Elmy and Frances Swiney – that menstruation might be a pathological function allied to male abuse of women,[97] or Christabel Pankhurst's notorious contention that something like 75–80 per cent of men were infected with venereal disease,[98] represent the kind of ideas which have allowed some commentators to conclude that those who voiced them were deluded and fanatical in their resentment of men.[99] More recently, feminist historians such as Sheila Jeffreys have argued the need to look more carefully and sympathetically at these writings, and, above all, to see them in context.[100] Enough has been said already to indicate the depth of sexual antagonism and fear which existed through this period of feminist activity from the struggle against the Contagious Diseases Acts to the militancy of the suffrage campaign. Sexual tensions often reached a level where *both* sexes were liable to perceive and to castigate the other as 'contaminating' or 'polluting'. Frances Swiney's or

[96] See, for instance, George Dangerfield, *The Strange Death of Liberal England* 1935; Paladin, London, 1970), p. 182ff.; and David Mitchell, *Queen Christabel* (Macdonald & Janes, London, 1977).

[97] 'Ellis Ethelmer' (Elizabeth Wollstenholme-Elmy), *Woman Free* (Women's Emancipation Union, Congleton, 1893); Frances Swiney, *The Bar of Isis, or The Law of the Mother* (C. W. Daniel, London, 1919); see also Sheila Jeffreys, '"Free From All Uninvited Touch of Man"', p. 638, and Angus MacLaren, *Birth Control in Nineteenth Century England* (Croom Helm, London, 1978), p. 200.

[98] Christabel Pankhurst, *The Great Scourge and How to End It* (Women's Social and Political Union, London, 1913).

[99] Jeffreys, '"Free From All Uninvited Touch of Man"', p. 604.

[100] Ibid., pp. 629–45.

Christabel Pankhurst's revulsion against men as the carriers of
disease to 'innocent' women finds an easy parallel with the
insistence of some of the male defenders of the Contagious
Diseases Acts in the Men and Women's Club, for instance, who
refused to examine their conviction that such legislation was
needed because women were more dangerous to men than vice-
versa, 'from the hygiene point of view'.[101]

It is scarcely surprising, then, that some of the language of
social purity and the distortions of fear should have crept into
feminist writing on sexuality in these years. However, a more
dominant emphasis in both Wollstenholme-Elmy's and Swiney's
writings was simply the insistence on women's right to control
their own bodies and the call for more self-control in men. Both
of these writers rejected the idea that marriage licensed a husband
to make unlimited sexual demands on his wife, and argued that
the wife's inclinations and wishes should be accorded equal
respect. Elizabeth Elmy constantly emphasized what she described as the 'psychic' nature of the sexual relationship, maintaining that 'no true affection or love' would permit a husband
to engage in sexual activity with a reluctant partner, and that
to submit a woman to the risk of an unwanted pregnancy was
wholly 'unjustifiable and inhuman' to both the mother and to
any 'unwelcome child'.[102] Wollstenholme-Elmy's campaign to
secure legal recognition for women's right to refuse sexual intercourse within marriage was unsuccessful: as indicated earlier in
this chapter, even today a husband cannot be found guilty by
law of raping his wife.[103]

Frances Swiney's writings on sexuality similarly embodied a
protest against the sexual subjection of women in marriage, and
particularly their exposure to unwanted pregnancies. In *The
Bar of Isis* (which went through four editions between 1907 and
1919), she advocated an embargo on sexual intercourse during
pregnancy, and whilst a mother was involved in breast-feeding
her child, which she claimed was in accordance with 'Natural

[101] Correspondence, R. J. Parker to Maria Sharpe, 18 March 1888, Pearson
Collection, University College, London (10/1).
[102] 'Ellis Ethelmer', *Woman Free*, p. 43. Quoted in Jeffreys, '"Free From All
Uninvited Touch of Man"', p. 637.
[103] Ibid.

Law'.[104] The lengthy periods of continence which she recommended between pregnancies would, she envisaged, greatly
reduce the number of children any woman would expect to
bear and this would protect both her own health and that of
her children.[105]

Swiney spoke for many of those feminists who were reluctant
to separate the idea of sexual intercourse as a purely pleasurable
activity from its purpose in reproduction. Indeed, the ethics of
making such a distinction much exercised many of her contemporaries and surfaced particularly in arguments over the acceptability of contraceptive devices, or 'preventive checks', as
they were generally referred to at the time. Almost all feminists
believed that motherhood should be 'voluntary'.[106] The feminist
journal *Shafts* published an unambiguous manifesto to this effect
in the form of an editorial in 1892, claiming that

> when a woman marries a man, she and she alone should decide
> whether or not she will add another unit to the vast human popu-
> lation. She considers it nothing short of an impertinence for the
> man to have anything to say in the matter, considering that he has
> none of the pain and suffering, and very little of the trouble of
> training the child.[107]

Feminist writing abounds with denunciations of those men who
'inflicted' large families on their wives without consideration of
the cost in terms of the women's bodily sufferings. A few years
earlier, for instance, Emma Brooke commented acerbically on
the kind of questions currently posed by Karl Pearson about
the compatibility of childbearing with mental development in
women:

> In York Minister is a tablet put up by some church dignitary to the
> honour of his wife: she died at the age of 38 having borne him 24
> children. We need not dwell much on the question of this unfortu-
> nate human being's mental development; we might not unprofitably
> occupy ourselves, however, with the enquiry: what was the quality

[104] Swiney, *The Bar of Isis*, pp. 15–17.
[105] Ibid., p. 18.
[106] MacLaren, *Birth Control*, p. 197.
[107] *Shafts*, 31 December 1892, p. 135.

of the moral character and power of the husband who compelled such a state of things?[108]

However, there were undoubtedly many feminists who looked upon preventive checks as 'a sacrifice of womanhood to male passion' and feared that the widespread adoption of contraceptive devices would reduce a wife to what George Bernard Shaw described as 'a barren bodily slavery'.[109] A month after publishing the editorial quoted above, for instance, *Shafts* featured an article written by a man − Geoffrey Mortimer. Paying tribute to Charles Bradlaugh and protesting against 'Enforced Maternity', Mortimer contended that

> restraint of the family within the limits of adequate comforts, and subject to the wishes of the wife, will be the rule as we advance in knowledge and virtue. The remedy is already in the hands of women. It is useless to state that the increase in the number of marriages, and the decrease of the birth rate, has no significance. Conjugal prudence is spreading, and with the restriction of the family to reasonable limits will come health, leisure and higher happiness for women. Someone must risk the odium that attaches to an advocacy of the use of scientific checks to undue and immoral reproduction.[110]

This article stimulated some readers to write in support of Mortimer's arguments, but others took issue with him. In February 1892 for instance, an angry female correspondent protested that is was truly a *man's* remedy to look towards 'scientific checks' rather than the elimination of male lust to eliminate 'enforced maternity'. 'Restriction of the family', the writer agreed, was indeed 'a reform that women should strive for, for the sake of their children as well as for themselves; but it must be achieved by continence in marriage; so-called 'Scientific checks' are destructive to health, and often fail in their object, besides being morally degrading and leading to race deterioration.'[111]

---

[108] Brooke, 'Notes on a man's views', p. 10.
[109] G. B. Shaw, preface to *Three Plays by Eugene Brieux* (A. C. Fifield, London, 1911), p. xliii, quoted in MacLaren, *Birth Control*, p. 202 and n. 16.
[110] *Shafts*, 14 January 1893, p. 167.
[111] *Shafts*, 18 February 1892, p. 251.

The acceptability of contraception was much discussed by members of the Men and Women's Club. Karl Pearson suggested that sexual activity dissociated from reproduction 'may or may not be socially and physically harmful. It at any rate throws us into a sea of physiological and social questionings across which it is hard to discern any fixed beacon which might guide us.'[112] As we have already seen, some of the women in the group, such as Emma Brooke and Olive Schreiner, were prepared to suggest that 'the sexual passion' might be as strong in women as in men.[113] Although they frequently expressed distaste for the ease with which some of the men claimed to be able to separate sexual feelings from emotional involvement or friendship, they were also prepared to consider, at least, the argument that repression of sexual feeling could be physically harmful in both sexes. This undoubtedly led some feminists to look favourably upon the idea of contraception, even though they did not always find it easy to express this advocacy publicly, and in mixed company. On the question of 'scientific checks' within marriage, for instance, Emma Brooke confessed that

Upon this point, the subject being veiled to me, it is only possible to offer the opinions of others. But it may not be unfitting to record that I do not know a single woman, married or unmarried, of whatever shade of opinion orthodox or unorthodox, who has not accepted the preventative check system with joy and relief as *the only moral basis of marriage* — as we at present have it ... I can testify that every one of my married friends (of all shades as they are of exquisite and cultured womanliness) accept the checks system and speak of *marriage without them* as *the immoral* thing.[114]

There can be no doubt that some of the early historians of feminism underestimated the enthusiasm and relief with which some feminists greeted new techniques in birth control in the late nineteenth century. As Angus Maclaren has written, this has been one of the 'lost dimensions' of Victorian and Edwardian

[112] Karl Pearson, 'Note on the sexual feeling', 1885, Pearson Collection, University College, London (10/3).

[113] Brooke, 'Notes on a man's views', with marginal comments by Olive Schreiner.

[114] Ibid., pp. 13–14.

feminism.[115] However, it must be emphasized again that women found it difficult to speak openly on the subject. Even so bold a spirit as Emma Brooke's quailed at the risk of such self-revelation. In one of her many letters to Pearson, for instance, we see her getting cold feet about having already said too much on the subject:

> I want you not to mistake me about preventive checks ... (more especially I hope this, in that I *may* be saying something which, had I more knowledge, I should not say); I think women would prefer self-control and long seasons of abstinence; but on your own showing, this is not much to be hoped for. They (women) must help themselves as best they can.[116]

Her confusion is transparent here, and that it was related to anxiety about self-exposure becomes even more obvious when we find her begging Pearson, several times, not to let anyone else see her paper on the subject. Brooke explained that she was also a member of 'the Proudhon Society' and highly concerned lest 'any of the Proudhon men in the Wollstonecroft Society' should recognize her style.[117]

It is scarcely surprising, then, that it is difficult to collect evidence on feminist attitudes to birth control. Only a handful of the boldest and most radical women could countenance taking a public stand on such an issue, although their number was growing in the years approaching the First World War. Annie Besant, Jane Clapperton, Stella Browne, Dora Russell, Theresa Billington-Greig and Florence Fenwick Miller all did so.[118] Others, such as Anna Martin and Alice Vickery, actively involved themselves in a campaign to educate working-class women in the techniques of birth control (well before Marie Stopes's efforts in this sphere), establishing a private clinic for the purpose in South-West London as early as 1908.[119] Although

[115] MacLaren, *Birth Control*, p. 197.
[116] Correspondence, Emma Brooke to Karl Pearson, 14 February 1886, Pearson Collection, University College, London (10/28).
[117] Ibid.
[118] MacLaren, *Birth Control*, pp. 197–208, 211.
[119] Ibid., p. 211. See also M. Breed and Edith How-Martyn, *The Birth Control Movement in England* (John Bale, Sons, & Danielsson, London, 1930), p. 13ff.

some feminist doctors — most notably Elizabeth Blackwell — advocated continence as the best way of ensuring female control of fertility,[120] others did not. Barbara Strachey, in her portrait of the Pearsall Smith family, quotes a letter which Mary Costello (née Pearsall Smith) wrote to her mother, Hannah, in 1888, which clearly indicates that Elizabeth Garrett Anderson was disinclined to favour continence as a safeguard of health and virtue in marriage. Mary (whose husband, Frank, was a Roman Catholic) informed her mother that Dr Garrett Anderson had asked her whether she was pregnant again,

> and I said 'no', and then she asked me how I knew, so I told her that we had made up our minds not to have another child at once. Thee can hardly think what a lecture she gave me — I should think a woman would be ashamed to say such things. She said if I was *her* daughter she would warn me most seriously that such a way of life was wrong and wicked and all sorts of terrible things ... So I asked 'Isn't it very bad for a woman's health to have as many children as she possibly can?' 'Certainly it is,' she said, 'but there are plenty of other ways besides abstinence of avoiding that!' ... I do think it is *wicked* in physicians to give such advice to their patients. It is a fortunate thing I married a man who agreed with my principles — I think it would almost have turned me to *hating* my husband if he had wanted me to use any of Dr Garrett Anderson's 'other ways'.[121]

With the benefit of hindsight one may speculate about whether Mary's outrage on this occasion did indeed involve a clash of principle over the morality of 'checks', or whether as Garrett Anderson possibly divined, something more was at stake. Mary's feelings for Frank during that time were decidedly on the wane, and soon afterwards she began an illicit relationship with the young, attractive art historian Bernard Berenson, with whom she subsequently 'eloped' to Italy.[122]

Feminists were divided, then, in their attitudes to contraceptive techniques, but by no means in the main opposed. They were

---

[120] MacLaren, *Birth Control*, p. 128.

[121] Barbara Strachey, *Remarkable Relations: The Story of the Pearsall Smith Family* (Gollancz, London, 1980), p. 103.

[122] Ibid., p. 110ff.

united in their defence of 'voluntary motherhood'. As Emma
Brooke expressed it, 'Women put forth primarily a claim to the
possession of their own bodies.'[123] When Henrietta Müller spoke
on the subject of 'The Limitation of the Family' to the Men and
Women's Club she insisted that 'To be effectual a preventitive
check should be in the hands of the woman, she should be able
to apply it at her own will, without the knowledge of the man,
it should be certain in its effect and innocuous.'[124] 'The interests
of woman, child and society', she concluded, 'cannot be secured
until and unless the mother can regulate and control
conception.'[125] There is undoubtedly a sense in which both the
feminists who advocated continence and those who were prepared
to countenance the use of 'checks' were often in agreement, in
that both sought to guarantee the same basic principles of
feminine autonomy within marriage, and of mutual desire and
respect as preconditions of sexual union.

Reforming monogamy

In *Love, Morals and the Feminists*, written in 1970, Constance
Rover argued that the majority of feminists, at least until the
First World War, 'supported the rigid code of Victorian morality
rather than claiming for women emotional and sexual freedom
as well as civil rights.'[126] It is doubtful whether most contemporaries would have accepted this. After all, feminism was
generally recognized as representing a direct challenge to the
existence of 'the double standard' of sexual morality and indeed
to the whole pattern of contemporary family life. Rover's contention has purchase only in a limited sense: feminists who
focused their activities narrowly on the pursuit of the Suffrage
tended to avoid embroiling their cause with other, controversial

[123] Brooke, 'Notes on a Man's Views', p. 27.
[124] Men and Women's Club Papers, abstract of Henrietta Müller's Paper
on the Limitation of the Family (read on 9 May 1887) in Pearson Collection,
University College, London (10/11).
[125] Ibid.
[126] Constance Rover, *Love, Morals and the Feminists* (Routledge & Kegan
Paul, London, 1970), p. 145.

issues of sexual morality. This was sometimes seen as deliberate political strategy. At the same time it is quite clear that from the late nineteenth century onwards feminism projected many women into a wholesale revision of contemporary codes of sexual ethics.

What is striking, however, is the extent to which even those of the most 'advanced' views retained their faith in monogamy, at least as an ideal. But this by no means always implied adherence to a rigid code of sexual morality — sometimes, indeed, the reverse. Feminists such as Edith Ellis at the end of the nineteenth century, or Vera Brittain in the inter-war period, maintained that harmonious and stable monogamous relationships would probably only be arrived at after a period of experimentation and 'trial and error' in personal relationships. 'The lifelong faithful love of one man for one woman', contended Edith Ellis (in 'The Love of To-Morrow'), 'is the exception and not the rule.'[127] In order to achieve that 'rare meeting, when soul lies by soul ... many experiments may have to be tried, and apparent failure sometimes be an evidence of ultimate victory.'[128] 'It is more than probable', she conceded,

> that the evolved relationship of the future will be monogamy — but a monogamy as much wider and more beautiful than the present caricature of it as the sea is wider and more delicious than a frog-pond. ... The law of affinity being as subtle and as indefinable as the law of gravitation, we may, by and by, find it worthwhile to give it its complete opportunity in those realms where it can manifest itself most potently.[129]

In 'A Noviciate for Marriage' (1892), Ellis recommended that couples contemplating matrimony should consider a period of trial cohabitation for twelve months first. This would allow them to find out whether they were truly compatible and able to co-operate in ordering a household. It would help to reduce 'the gambling element in modern unions':[130]

---

[127] E. Ellis, *The New Horizon*, p. 5.
[128] Ibid., p. 3.
[129] Ibid., p. 5.
[130] Ibid., p. 13.

A noviciate for marriage, as open as any engagement, would surely minimise the gambling element in modern unions, and pave the way to a true monogamy, which to-day, with prostitution and secret temporary unions accepted as necessary evils, is simply a name Respectability and Idealism accept, but Life too frequently derides. If by monogamy we mean one man and one woman cleaving to each other for sexual love, we all know, if we are out of our teens, that the monogamic marriage in modern civilisation is either extinct or has never really evolved. The latter is surely the real state of affairs, and if, as the tendency of modern progress indicates, monogamy is the most complete form of human sexual relationship, it is certain that, in order to obtain it in reality, we must open the way, not only to free discussion on sexual matters, but to cautious experiment.[131]

Edith Ellis was adamant on one point: for her, no marriage could really succeed where the wife's position was one of dependency: the economic autonomy of both partners was the *sine qua non* of an equal partnership.[132] Honesty was also important. In other areas, flexibility was crucial. In an essay on 'Semi Detached Marriage', for instance (written in 1915), she contended that some marriages survived best where the partners decided (like Mary Wollstonecraft and William Godwin) to maintain separate households, or at least could resolve to live apart for some periods of their lives.[133] There is no doubt that Edith Ellis's theories both determined and evolved out of the experiences of her own life. The marriage which she alludes to as having survived according to these principles in this essay of 1915 is in fact her own union with Havelock Ellis. This highly unorthodox union — based on 'affectionate comradeship' and not physical passion, and guaranteeing considerable sexual and personal freedom to both parties, did indeed survive from 1891 until Edith died in 1916, full of vicissitudes, but ultimately judged as something of a successful achievement by both parties.[134]

[131] Ibid.
[132] Ibid., p. 5.
[133] Ibid., pp. 24–5.
[134] See Havelock Ellis, *My Life* (Heinemann, London, 1940), pp. 233–4, and *passim*; also Grosskurth, *Havelock Ellis*, ch. 9 and *passim*.

There were marked similarities between Edith Ellis's views on marriage and monogamy and those expressed after the First World War by Vera Brittain. Brittain's futuristic, Utopian treatise, *Halcyon; or The Future of Monogamy*, has already been mentioned. In a paper on 'The failure of monogamy', which she delivered at the third Congress of the World League for Sexual Reform (which was organized by Norman Haire and Dora Russell in London in 1929), she summarized her defence of the institution more prosaically.[135] Perceptions of the ideological climate had changed somewhat since the 1890s, and particularly with her audience of 'sexual reformers' in mind Vera felt obliged to be on the defensive. She would take it for granted, she said, that most of the people present in the room where she was speaking would be unfavourably disposed towards the idea of monogamy:

> Though this institution is still regarded by the State as an essential factor in the growth of the British Empire, and by the Churches as an indispensable passport to the Kingdom of Heaven, the hostility of sex reformers to both the name and the idea of monogamous marriage is only to be expected. Hitherto monogamy has resembled liberty in one respect only, that a large proportion of the crimes of society have been committed in its name.[136]

There were probably very few married couples, Vera ventured, for whom monogamy was either desirable or by whom it was obtainable. However, she herself remained convinced that 'when loyal and lasting friendship, arising from highly individualised selection and constantly cemented by mutual passion, does happen to be embodied in marriage, it constitutes one of the highest and rarest achievements of the human spirit.'[137] No more than any other 'difficult and worthwhile achievement', true monogamy could 'never be an ABC proposition'. It could only attained 'as a result of a trial-and-error method of experiments, investigations, innovations and mistakes'.[138] This true

---

[135] Vera Brittain, 'The failure of monogamy', *Proceedings of the Third Congress of the World League for Sexual Reform* held in London, 1929, ed. Norman Haire, (Kegan Paul, Trench, Trubner, London, 1930).
[136] Ibid., p. 40.
[137] Ibid., p. 41.
[138] Ibid., p. 42.

monogamy would not be brought about by prescription or repressiveness, but only through openness and freedom. Vera concluded her paper with a list of the conditions which she considered most conducive to successful monogamy. These included sex education (including 'instruction before marriage . . . in the detailed technique of intercourse and birth control'), the abolition of censorship, toleration of experimental unions, divorce by consent, and the economic independence of married women.[139]

Women and sexual pleasure

Possibly one of the areas in which there had been most change between the 1890s and the inter-war years was in the area of expectations about sexual pleasure for women. Some of the early, 'advanced' critiques of marital relationships had been relatively *un*advanced on the question of women's sexuality. In *Love's Coming of Age*, for instance, Edward Carpenter had submitted that monogamy was more easily obtainable by women than by men.

> Though it might be said, that the growing complexity of man's nature would be likely to lead him into more rather than fewer relationships, yet on the other hand it is obvious that as the depth and subtlety of any attachment that will really hold him increases, so does such attachment become more permanent and durable, and less likely to be realised in a number of persons. Woman, on the other hand, cannot be said to be by her physical nature polyandrous as man is polygynous. Though of course there are plenty of examples of women living in a state of polyandry both among savage and civilised peoples, yet her more limited sexual needs, and her long periods of gestation, render one mate physically sufficient for her; while her more clinging affectional nature perhaps accentuates her capacity of absorption in the one.[140]

This kind of pronouncement would have met with short shrift from many of those who attended the conference on Sexual

[139] Ibid., pp. 43–4.
[140] Carpenter, *Love's Coming of Age*, p. 97.

Reform in 1929, an occasion on which the authors of a number of papers addressed themselves to the task of establishing that women were 'by nature and instinct' no more inclined to monogamy than men.[141] By this time, and in this environment, Naomi Mitchison felt able to discuss nuances of passion and erotic impulse between married (and unmarried) partners in some detail, extending her discussion even to take into account the erotic and psychological advantages and disadvantages of different kinds of birth control, including abortion.[142]

This growing interest in, and more publicly discussed awareness of, women's sexual response owed something to the work of 'sexologists' like Havelock Ellis and much to feminism; it was also clearly linked to advances in both the technique and knowledge of birth control.[143] Self-publicist though she was, Marie Stopes's own description of her book, *Married Love*, as having 'crashed English Society like a bombshell' in 1918 is probably not too much of an exaggeration.[144] Two thousand copies were sold within a fortnight, and the book was into its sixth edition by the end of the year. The list of individuals who have testified to its impact is endless. Naomi Mitchison's account is only one of the most eloquent. She describes how when she and Dick married in 1916, they were both virgins, and their early experiences of lovemaking (when he came back on leave from the war in Flanders) were disappointing to her.

> I got little or no pleasure, except for the touch of a loved body and the knowledge that for a time he was out of the front line. The final act left me on edge and uncomfortable. Why was it so unlike

[141] See, for instance, V. F. Calverton, 'Are women monogamous?', and Naomi Mitchison, 'Some comment on the use of contraceptives by intelligent persons', papers included in *Proceedings of the Third Congress of the World League for Sexual Reform*, 1929.

[142] Mitchison, 'Some comment', pp. 182–7. See also Stella Browne's paper, 'The right to abortion', in the same volume.

[143] See Barbara Brookes, 'Women and reproduction, 1860–1939', in *Labour and Love: Women's Experience of Home and Family, 1880–1940*, ed. Jane Lewis (Blackwell, Oxford, 1986).

[144] Quoted by Ellen Holtzman, 'The pursuit of married love: women's attitudes toward sexuality and marriage in Great Britain, 1918–1939', *Journal of Social History*, no. 16 (Winter 1982), p. 39. See also Marie C. Stopes, *Married Love* (Putnam, London, 1918).

180 *Marital Relationships*

Swinburne? Where were the raptures and roses? Was it going to be like this all my life? I began to run a temperature.

Dick went back, now on the staff. I had my baby. Then I heard about and bought Marie Stopes's *Married Love*, rushed out, bought a second copy and sent it off to Dick. It seems incredible now that this book was such an eye-opener. Why had none of these elementary techniques occurred to either of us before? Well, they hadn't. It was not the kind of thing young people talked about or, in spite of the poets, thought about.[145]

Like many others Naomi Mitchison contended that the availability of effective contraception was probably the main reason why 'the accepted ideas and practice of marriage and of extramarital relationships altered so much between 1920 and 1940.'[146] Together with increased opportunities for economic independence, she believed these changes significantly altered the lifestyle of many women, particularly in the professional middle class. She is open about the fact that an increased awareness of the possibilities of sexual pleasure coupled with the diminished risk of unwanted pregnancies enabled both Dick and herself to take lovers at various points in their married life, whilst preserving their family relationships as a secure environment in which to raise their children.[147] This pattern, she suggests, was not uncommon amongst her contemporaries: 'Several of our friends were, like us, behaving in ways which I think would have been utterly unacceptable even twenty years before.'[148] She is equally frank in her discussion of the problems of divided loyalty and sexual jealousy which so often accompanied extramarital affairs, and how she and Dick attempted to cope with these tensions, through trust and honesty, and the determinedly rational stance that jealousy was a 'degrading emotion which should not be allowed to take possession'.[149]

In a paper on 'Marriage and freedom' which she presented

[145] Naomi Mitchison, *You May Well Ask: A Memoir, 1920–1940* (Fontana, London, 1986), pp. 69–70.
[146] Ibid., p. 69.
[147] Ibid., p. 70ff.
[148] Ibid., p. 71.
[149] Ibid.

to the Sexual Reform conference in 1929 Dora Russell similarly put forward the case for marriages founded on trust, 'psychological loyalty' and the responsibilities of shared parenting rather than the rigid adherence to a code of sexual fidelity.[150] Like Naomi Mitchison she saw possessive affection and jealousy as destructive forces in a partnership. She remained convinced, however, that

> the stable and non-possessive love of two parents is the best emotional background for young children. The dangers of sexual starvation in the parents, or the too-small family, both leading to over concentration of emotion on the child, must be met by mutual tolerance of freedom between the father and mother, and allowing the child at an early age the wider companionship of the nursery school.[151]

Margaret Cole (who was a close friend of the Mitchisons) attempted to grapple with the same problems in her analysis of *Marriage, Past and Present*, in 1939. Like Dora Russell and Naomi Mitchison, she sought to reconcile her recognition of an adult's need for sexual fulfilment with her equally strong conviction that young children flourished best in the context of a stable family environment. On this latter issue she was prepared to move towards prescription:

> Where children are born, there they are born into families. And this, I feel, is right. I do not agree either with the Freudian view of family as a seething pond of sex inhibitions or with the Victorian revolt against it as a stifling institution — which was derived partly from the quite unnecessary stuffiness of the Victorian family. I think that children need a family, at least, need fathers and mothers, and that for this reason . . . the fathers and mothers should wherever possible remain with the children and with one another.[152]

At the same time, Cole insisted, one had to recognize the fact that individuals exhibited marked differences in sexual temperament and in their degree of sexual desire. Arguably much less

[150] Dora Russell, 'Marriage and freedom', *Proceedings of the Third Congress of the World League for Sexual Reform*, 1929, pp. 25–9.
[151] Ibid., p. 29.
[152] Cole, *Marriage, Past and Present*, p. 173.

was known about women's sexuality than men's. It was possible, she submitted, that women tended 'to run to extremes' more than men: some of them might be 'colder than almost any man', whilst there were others 'whose sexuality runs so high that no ordinary man is likely to satisfy it'.[153] Following Marie Stopes, she suggested further that women were more likely to experience 'fluctuations', or 'periodicity' in desire than were men.[154] In the last analysis, she contended, sex was not the only thing that was important in married life; nor the only way of showing love. If progress could be made in controlling jealousy and possessiveness in marriage, it was quite possible that in some relationships, extra-marital liaisons could exert a stabilizing influence.[155]

Feminists who put forward arguments of this kind were well aware of the 'advanced' nature of their views, and none of them would have underestimated the difficulties of translating some of these ideals into practice. Indeed, all three of the women whose ideas have been discussed here – Naomi Mitchison, Margaret Cole and Dora Russell – learned a good deal about problems of divided loyalties, sexual possessiveness and jealousy in difficult attempts to balance individual fulfilment with family responsibilities in their own lives.[156] Nor did these women deceive themselves into underestimating the advantages with which the economic and social securities of their class position supplied them, and which immeasurably facilitated experiments in personal relationships and new ways of living. Reviewing Winifred Holtby's book on *Women and a Changing Civilisation* in *Left Review* in 1934, Naomi Mitchison observed that many intelligent feminists were being forced to re-examine 'the Woman Question' more narrowly in the context of 'the general economics of possessors and possessed'.[157] Capitalism might not much

[153] Ibid., p. 229.
[154] Ibid., p. 230.
[155] Ibid., pp. 226, 252–3, 258–9.
[156] Betty Vernon, *Margaret Cole, 1893–1980: A Political Biography* (Croom Helm, London, 1986), see esp. pp. 51–3, 67–77; Dora Russell, *The Tamarisk Tree: My Quest for Liberty and Love*, vols I and II (Virago, London, 1975 and 1980).
[157] Naomi Mitchison, 'The reluctant feminists', *Left Review*, 1, no. 3 (December 1934), p. 93.

longer 'afford itself the pleasant amusement of a class of un-owned women'.[158] As Barbara Brookes has emphasized, for most women during this period 'sexual expression and maternity continued to take place in a relationship of economic dependence with a man'.[159]

At the same time there is evidence that the discussions about women's capacity for sexual pleasure that were linked with the impact of feminism and expertise in controlling conception did begin to make their impact on a variety of social groups. At the Sexual Reform Conference in 1929, for instance, Janet Chance presented a paper describing her work for a 'Marriage Education Centre' in the East End of London.[160] A primary aim of the Centre was to advise on birth control, but, she argued, 'No one can work for long at a Birth Control Centre without realising the scope there is for further sex-instruction among the women who come there to learn methods of contraception ...' [161] 'There is a widespread lack of the experience of orgasm amongst the women', she lamented; 'By many it is not even expected that the marriage relationship should be enjoyed by the wife.'[162] 'Marriage education' was needed amongst all classes of the community, she concluded, now that birth control had become 'the foundation of respectable sex life for women'.[163]

Ellen Holtzman, who has made a detailed analysis of some two hundred of the enormous number of letters written to Marie Stopes in the years between 1918 and 1939, has pointed out that Stopes's middle-class women correspondents confessed to a marked dissatisfaction with their sexual experiences within marriage.[164] As Holtzman suggests, Stopes's rhetorical descriptions of female sexual pleasure ('the wonderful tides', and 'flower-wreathed' transports) in *Married Love* and elsewhere probably helped to shape these women's own expectations about sex. The very resemblances between Stopes's sexual vocabulary and

[158] Ibid.
[159] Brookes, 'Women and reproduction', p. 166.
[160] Janet Chance, 'A Marriage Education Centre in London', *Proceedings of the Third Congress of the World League for Sexual Reform*, 1929, pp. 37–9.
[161] Ibid., p. 38.
[162] Ibid.
[163] Ibid., p. 39.
[164] Holtzman, 'The pursuit of married love', p. 40.

that of her correspondent would seem to indicate this.[165] Stopes's insistence on the importance of men acquiring sexual skills and technique better calculated to give women pleasure may have had important implications for relationships within marriage. Stopes herself remained convinced that lack of sexual harmony implied an unhappy marriage — something which was obviously true of her own experience.[166] Holtzman points out, however, that many of her correspondents would have parted company with her on this point, often insisting that in spite of their sexual disappointment, their marriages remained contented and stable.[167] She comments on what she sees as 'the transitional nature' of this generation of women, arguing that 'While the women's assumption that a good marriage need not be based upon female sexual pleasure links them to the nineteenth-century, if not earlier, their efforts to better their sexual relationship with their husbands link them to the modern age.'[168] New expectations, a willingness to speak more openly on these issues, and the self-confessed longing of many women for greater possibilities of sexual expression were undoubtedly indications of change.

---

[165] Ibid., pp. 40–1.
[166] Ibid.; see also Ruth Hall, *Marie Stopes: A Biography* (Deutsch, London, 1977).
[167] Holtzman, 'The pursuit of married love', p. 47.
[168] Ibid., p. 48.

5

Conclusions: Feminism and Social Class

It has been the aim of this book to explore some of the ways in which feminists challenged the family, on both the personal and political level, during the period 1880–1939. Almost all feminists wanted to see change in certain areas, and their criticism of existing patterns of family life was particularly likely to focus around issues of economic and domestic organization, and in the area of marital and sexual relationships. It would be misleading to suggest that there was always unity in this critique.

Even the attitudes of individual feminists could encompass contradictions. On the personal level, we must always remind ourselves, as was argued in the first chapter, that it is common for individuals to discover both their greatest sources of emotional strength, and yet also the root of their deepest frustrations, in the experience of family life. In a society such as that of late-Victorian England, characterized not least by the strength of its demarcations between the spheres of private and public life, this was especially so for women, and feminists were no exception. The personal satisfactions and happiness associated with good marriages and stable family relationships gave meaning to the lives of many feminists, as autobiographical accounts clearly indicate, even where these contentments were alloyed by the frustrations of unremitting domestic routines. Novels by feminists are probably even more revealing than direct personal testimonies, or feminist polemics on this score. The latter, particularly, will aim towards coherence and consistency in analysis, whereas a novel can arguably encompass more complexity, nuance, and ambiguity in stance. Thus it is that May Sinclair's *Mary Olivier* (1919) can 'speak volumes' about the psychological complexity of a mother-daughter relationship,[1] or Virginia Woolf's novel, *To The Lighthouse* (1927), can reveal so much about the author's ambivalence towards the family and particularly the maternal role of Mrs Ramsay, the central figure in the novel, based in part upon Virginia Woolf's memories of her own mother.[2]

Again, in the context of a society such as that of late-Victorian and early-Edwardian England, riven through with inequalities in wealth and income, it was inevitable that personal experiences of family life should be shaped by social class. These class differences explain in part the different priorities feminists envisaged in contemplating the agenda and direction of family change. Different priorities were clearly apparent, for instance, in discussions of household organization and domestic reform. We have touched upon Virginia Woolf's impatience with those working-class women in the Co-operative Movement whom she saw as setting their sights on 'ovens and bathtubs' rather than nurturing spiritual or intellectual aspirations.[3] It is scarcely surprising that working-class women who were struggling to keep families together in single rooms or dilapidated tenements should find it difficult to identify with the plight of those middle-class women seething with frustration over their confinement in elaborate bourgeois households. Schemes for cooperative housekeeping and communal urban dwellings often held out little appeal to those working-class women who dreamed of living in small modern houses of their own. This was an issue which worried Naomi Mitchison, who was involved during the 1930s with housing issues whilst canvassing for Labour in a provincial municipal election, a great deal. 'We have been going all out on housing' she reported,

Schemes for clearing up slums and building decent homes. These are always envisaged as nice little home-nests, brick houses with

---

[1] May Sinclair, *Mary Olivier: A Life* (1919; Virago, London, 1980).

[2] Virginia Woolf, *To The Lighthouse* (J. M. Dent, London, 1927); see discussion in Carol Dyhouse, *Girls Growing Up in Late Victorian and Edwardian England* (Routledge & Kegan Paul, London, 1981), pp. 38—9.

[3] Virginia Woolf, introductory letter to Margaret Llewelyn Davies (ed.), *Life As We Have Known It, by Co-operative Working Women* (1931; Virago, London, 1977), pp. xvii—xxxxi.

every convenience for the housewife and home-lover, all separated
so that no one need know what her neighbour is doing or saying,
each with a little garden. These are the kind of houses which
are going to encourage the feeling of the close family group, the
comfortable feeling of male ownership, the house-pride in the
women, all the things which those of us who hate ownership in all
forms must be up against. But these are the houses which as a
matter of fact almost all working men and women do want. The
exceptions are rare, and usually unpopular at least, most workers
have a thorough dislike of flats, of anything except the conventional
home in the conventional architecture.[4]

Class differences were often equally apparent in attitudes to
women's work outside the home. For the middle-class feminists
this had come to be seen as a right or a privilege, whereas for
the working-class woman such work was often experienced as
yet another source of oppression, an onerous obligation to be
given up as soon as economic circumstance permitted. Chapter
2 has described how a gulf had developed, around the turn of
the century, between the economic individualism of one group
of feminists, and others, particularly those involved in the
Labour Movement, who chose to defend the ideal of 'the family
wage' and sought to extend legislative 'protection' for women in
the labour market.[5]

Feminists who remained convinced that women's real interests
could never be served by a 'family wage' which involved economic dependence on a male provider, and who lamented what
they saw as the essential 'conservatism' of many working-class
housewives, sometimes consoled themselves by arguing that it
was simply a question of time; as standards of living rose
working-class women would come to share some of the discontents of their middle-class sisters. In *Woman and Labour*, Olive
Schreiner predicted that the debilitating effects of female
'parasitism' could be expected to percolate down the social
scale as a community grew in wealth, but that ultimately this
would seed support for feminists who insisted upon women's

[4] Naomi Mitchison, 'The reluctant feminists', *Left Review*, 1, no. 3
(December 1934), pp. 93–4.
[5] See Hilary Land, 'The family wage', *Feminist Review*, no. 6 (1980),
pp. 55–77.

right to work.[6] Naomi Mitchison ruefully conceded that the small family houses which exerted such popular appeal 'must go up, and the workers must wear through that particular stage of aesthetic development, and must wear through the idea of the close family group and ownership by the father'.[7] 'This will hold things up for a generation,' she admitted, 'perhaps more, unless it can be short-circuited . . . there are plenty of problems for the feminist just now!'[8]

Writing on the eve of the First World War, Mabel Atkinson had allowed herself a more optimistic vision. She had conceded that there were, undeniably, 'two sections of the women's movement' and that the division was based upon social class.[9] Middle-class women were in revolt against parasitism, and rebelling against the sex-exclusiveness of men. Working-class women were primarily oppressed by capitalism, and 'the un-ending burden of toil' which had been laid upon them by such a system. 'The working class woman feels her solidarity with the men of her class', she submitted, 'rather than their antag-onism to her.'[10] Atkinson, like Schreiner, thought that

> one of the possible dangers of the future was that the working class women in their right and natural desire to be protected against that exploitation which the first development of machinery brought with it, should allow themselves to drift without observing it into the parasitism which was the lot of middle class women.[11]

Atkinson was confident, however, that there were signs of a growing unity between feminists across the cleavage of social class. In particular she drew attention to the increasing sense of injustice felt by working-class women who had had of necessity to learn that their economic interests were 'not altogether safe in the hands of men'.[12] The all-male Parliament which had

[6] Olive Schreiner, *Woman and Labour* (1911; Virago, London, 1978), p. 118ff.
[7] Mitchison, 'The reluctant feminists', p. 94.
[8] Ibid.
[9] M. Atkinson, 'The economic foundations of the Women's Movement', Fabian Tract, no. 175 (London, 1914), pp. 6–7, 14–15.
[10] Ibid., p. 15.
[11] Ibid.
[12] Ibid., p. 16.

introduced social security legislation in the form of National Insurance in 1911, for instance, had notably failed to secure the position of widows and orphans. Practically no provision was made for the health of married women who were not themselves employed.[13] Working-class women were becoming more aware of the pitfalls involved in depending upon a male breadwinner at the same time, she believed, that middle-class feminists were beginning to comprehend the fact that the right to work was no panacea, and to experience something of the exploitativeness of the labour market.[14]

As described in chapter 3, Atkinson remained convinced that state provision for motherhood should be recognized as one of the primary aims of feminism.[15] Acutely aware of the dangers of any scheme for the endowment of motherhood which might be envisaged by conservative thinkers or eugenists bent on securing women's dependence in the family, she insisted repeatedly upon the need for feminist vigilance in this context. It was essential that feminists should work to secure a system of provision which guaranteed economic autonomy to the mother, and at the same time legitimized and strengthened her position in the labour market, through, for instance, a system of maternity leaves.[16]

Atkinson confessed that she held little hope of seeing such a system implemented in an economy dominated by private enterprise.

Such a system could be deliberately and consciously introduced into the public services; it could be imposed on private enterprise by factory legislation, though with much greater difficulty. But it is the development of Socialism, and that alone, which can make it possible throughout the whole fabric of society for the normal woman to attain her twin demands, independent work and motherhood. It is only Socialism which can make the endowment of women during the maternal years a possibility, that endowment being one of the first charges on the surplus value or economic rent

[13] Ibid.
[14] Ibid., pp. 16−17.
[15] See ch. 2 above, and Atkinson, 'Economic foundations of the Women's Movement', p. 23.
[16] Ibid., pp. 23−4.

which the State will absorb; and until the State has made itself
master of the land and the capital of this country, it will not have
an income big enough to enable it to provide adequate endowments
for the childbearing women.[17]

It was this which underlay her conviction that feminism had to
work through Socialism: 'Therefore it becomes clear that the
only path to the ultimate and most deep lying ends of the
feminist movement is through Socialism, and every wise feminist
will find herself more and more compelled to adopt the principles
of Socialism . . .'.[18] In the meantime, however, 'the wise Socialists
must also be feminists', and women in the Fabian Society and
elsewhere must work to this end.

In an essay on 'The family in contemporary feminist thought'
(1982),[19] Jane Flax has emphasized that a central focus
of debate amongst Marxist and other feminists has been 'the
issue of the relative importance of capitalism and patriarchy in
shaping the character of the family and women's status within
it.[20] Feminists in England during the period with which this
book is concerned rarely defined the sexual division of labour
within the family as such a central issue as did their successors
in the 1970s and 1980s, and this may in part be attributed to
the fact that most middle-class feminists at least were still able
to rely on the services of working-class women in the house.
Neither did the majority of feminists in the late-nineteenth and
early-twentieth century use Marxist terminology in their analysis of the family in relation to production. However, the question
of the relative importance of capitalism and patriarchy in struc-
turing family forms and shaping women's oppression did afford
considerable scope for disagreement. In the essay which they
contributed to the *Westminster Review* in 1885, on 'The Woman
Question, from a Socialist point of view', Eleanor Marx and
Edward Aveling argued forcefully that economic relationships
lay at the root of women's predicament: 'The woman question

[17] Ibid., p. 23.
[18] Ibid., pp. 23–4.
[19] Jane Flax, 'The family in contemporary feminist thought: a critical
review', in *The Family in Political Thought*, ed. J. B. Elshtain (Harvester,
Brighton, 1982), pp. 223–339.
[20] Ibid., p. 236.

is one of the organization of society as a whole.'[21] Feminists had
to learn from economic history, and master the techniques of
political economy, they insisted, in order to get to 'the bed-rock
of the economic basis'; the current obsession with the franchise
was only a superficial issue.[22] The ideas discussed in chapter 2
above suggest that many feminists − perhaps more than
Eleanor Marx and Edward Aveling indicate − would have
sympathized with this viewpoint. Certainly the members of the
Fabian Women's Group were moving towards a highly coherent
and comprehensive analysis of the economic status of women in
the first decade of this century.[23] Some aspects of the *Westminster
Review* article were however, rather more contentious. For Marx
and Aveling, for instance, Socialism was the panacea which
would remove *all* traces of sexual oppression. Prostitution, for
instance − which they defined wholly in terms of economic
necessity − would, they claimed, disappear altogether alongside
changes in the relationships of production.[24]

One of those who felt constrained to challenge this viewpoint
most directly was Alys Russell, whose essay on 'Social Democracy and the Woman Question in Germany' was appended
to the 1896 edition of Bertrand Russell's book on *German
Social Democracy*.[25] Alys Russell (like Eleanor Marx and Edward
Aveling), had made a careful study of the writings of August
Bebel, but found herself less impressed than they were by his
arguments. Bebel's insistence on the impossibility of women
achieving equality with men under existing social conditions,
Russell contended, was belied by the fact that his vision of what
women needed contained nothing that was theoretically incompatible with the continued existence of private property.

He really asks for no more than is demanded in other countries by
those advanced women who are not followers of Marx, and whose

---

[21] Eleanor Marx and Edward Aveling, 'The Woman Question, from a
socialist point of view', *Westminster Review*, 6, no. 25 (1885), p. 209.
[22] Ibid., p. 210.
[23] See ch. 2 above.
[24] Marx and Aveling, 'The Woman Question', p. 219.
[25] Alys Russell, 'On Social Democracy and the Woman Question in
Germany', *Appendix* to B. Russell, *German Social Democracy* (Longman, Green,
London, 1896).

suggestions are more practical than Bebel's. There is no reason why women should not attain to a very fair degree of economic independence, for instance, through Trade Unions for the unmarried, and through payment of motherhood for the married. This latter, though a Socialistic measure, is theoretically compatible with private property. And the equal mental and physical training of the sexes, one of Bebel's chief demands, is certainly possible in an individualistic state of society while equal laws for men and women are more and more taking the place of the old unjust laws.[26]

Alys Russell maintained that Bebel had failed fully to appreciate both the predicament of individual women as mothers, and the social importance of motherhood: 'As is natural to a person who views the world entirely from the standpoint of the wage-earner, he regards woman much more as an industrial worker than as a child-bearer, and treats the 'woman question' as only one side of the labour question.'[27] She contended further that it was naive to believe that Socialism would automatically 'solve' the problem of unhappy marriages (by facilitating divorce without loss of income for women) and that a Socialist society would 'naturally' eliminate prostitution. The oft-repeated statement that prostitution was simply an economic phenomenon she dismissed as mere dogma. Women's oppression was *not* wholly reducible to economics. These two aims — the abolition of prostitution, and the economic possibility of divorce without loss of subsistence — she concluded, 'may also be said to be two of the principal aims of thoughtful women in other countries, but they do not think, as the Social Democrats do, that the subjection of women is entirely due to a single cause, or that the removal of this one cause is a sufficient condition of the solution of the woman question.'[28]

With hindsight we have to conclude that Mabel Atkinson's vision, in 1914, of a growing unity amongst feminists, traversing the divisions of social class and political allegiance, was somewhat over-sanguine. As historians have often observed, the

[26] Ibid., p. 183.
[27] Ibid., p. 187.
[28] Ibid., p. 194.

struggle to secure the franchise served, temporarily, to cement allegiances. Once the vote was obtained (by women over thirty years of age in 1918, and by all women on the same basis as men in 1928), feminism as a political movement lost focus and direction. Pro-natalist and eugenist tendencies flourished in the context of the slump, as did the public pressure on married women to relinquish their jobs and return to the home. Some of the anxieties entertained by Atkinson in 1914 were to prove justified. There was an ever-present danger that the tendencies of what the historian Jane Lewis has described as the 'new feminism' of Eleanor Rathbone and others, emphasizing as it did the different needs of men and women, and the special needs of women as mothers, would find itself in uneasy alliance with more conservative forces — as in the campaign, for instance, for family endowment.[29] The social and political climate, already hostile to feminism, did not improve during the 1930s, a decade in which deepening resentments and antagonisms of social class in England were experienced in the context of increasingly ominous tendencies in world politics.

During these years, feminists were ever more prone to attack each other on account of their class allegiances, real or otherwise. In the critical journal *Scrutiny*, Q. D. Leavis mounted a blistering and contemptuous attack on Virginia Woolf's feminist essay *Three Guineas* (1938), which she dismissed as a 'preposterous' piece of self-indulgence.[30] Mrs Woolf's concept of the 'art of living', Mrs Leavis sneered, was 'the art of living as conceived by a social parasite'.[31] Naomi Mitchison, as we have seen, objected to Winifred Holtby's book on women for not paying enough attention to the plight of the working class.[32] And an even more hostile review of Holtby's book, by Philippa Polson, appeared in the *Left Review* in 1935, accusing Holtby of 'dangerous and fallacious' complacency in chronicling the successes of feminism and in slurring over the fact that the predicament of

[29] Jane Lewis, 'Beyond suffrage: English feminism in the 1920s', *Maryland Historian*, (1973).
[30] Q. D. Leavis, '"Caterpillars of the Commonwealth Unite": A review of Virginia Woolf's *Three Guineas*', *Scrutiny*, 7, no. 2 (1938–9), pp. 203–14.
[31] Ibid., p. 204.
[32] Mitchison, 'The reluctant feminists', p. 93.

working-class women remained much the same.[33] 'The family as an economic remained unassailed', insisted Polson, 'and the double exploitation of working women continued unchanged.'[34] There was much truth in this allegation of Polson's, but it was not, as we have seen, the whole story.

Changes in the legal status of married women and in law affecting the family have been touched upon in the foregoing pages, but since they have been described reasonably fully elsewhere they have not constituted a major theme of this book.[35] However, it should be remembered that feminism played a crucial part in bringing about such legislative changes from the mid-nineteenth century onwards. As Mary Stanley has argued, the 1857 Divorce Act, which made civil divorce possible, 'constituted the opening wedge in the effort to obtain legal recognition of the independent personality of married women'.[36] This initiated a reform movement of enormous significance, and 'a reconsideration of marriage which was central to the development of feminist thought in the later nineteenth century'.[37] The campaign to secure property rights began soon afterwards. The Married Women's Property Acts of 1870 and 1882 conceded the recognition of a married woman's independent legal personality, secured her right to her own earnings and gave her control over property acquired by inheritance or gift.

Significantly, demands for further reform in divorce and matrimonial property laws as well as in legislation governing custody and the guardianship of infants reappeared soon after

---

[33] Philippa Polson, 'Feminists and the Woman Question', *Left Review*, no. 12, (December 1935), p. 500.

[34] Ibid.

[35] See, for instance, Erna Reiss, *The Rights and Duties of Englishwomen: A Study in Law and Public Opinion* (Sherratt & Hughes, Manchester, 1934); Lee Holcombe, *Wives and Property: Reform of the Married Women's Property Law in Nineteenth-Century England* (Martin Robertson, Oxford, 1983); R. L. Travers, *Husband and Wife in English Law* (Duckworth, London, 1956); O. R. McGregor, *Divorce in England: A Centenary Study* (Heinemann, London, 1957); D. Stetson, *A Woman's Issue: The Politics of Family Law Reform in England* (Greenwood Pres, Conn., 1982).

[36] Mary Lyndon Stanley, '"One Must Ride Behind": married women's rights and the Divorce Act of 1857', *Victoria Studies* (Spring 1982), p. 348.

[37] Ibid.

women gained the vote. Almost all feminists wanted to see a liberalization of the divorce law which would eliminate the double standard and allow women to sue for divorce on the same grounds as men. There was considerable unanimity amongst the members of the Women's Co-operative Guild, for instance, on this issue, even though many recognized full well that economic insecurity bound 'the mother of children to her husband far more strongly than the law'[38] and that legislative reforms, without changes in the economic position of women, would be 'of little use to many whose lives [were] being ruined by marriage'.[39] Partly in response to these pressures, the Matrimonial Causes Act of 1923 allowed women, like men, to sue for divorce on the grounds of simple adultery and a further Act of 1937 extended the grounds for divorce to include insanity, cruelty and desertion. In 1935 married women gained the same rights and responsibilities in respect of contracts and property as single women and men.[40] The Guardianship of Infants Act (1925) gave mothers rights equal to the father to appoint guardians for the children after death and to bring disputes into court for settlement, although some feminists argued that this did not go far enough in the direction of guaranteeing equal rights and responsibilities to mothers and fathers in respect to their children.[41] As Dorothy Stetson has pointed out, in spite of these movements towards equality of legal status, the assumption of separate responsibilities for husband and wife in marriage remained embedded in English Law during this period, and only effectively began to be challenged in the 1960s and 1970s.[42] Feminists such as Muriel Pierotti (writing for the Women's Freedom League in the 1920s),[43] Vera Brittain and Margaret

---

[38] Women's Co-operative Guild, *Working Women and Divorce* (Nutt, London, 1911), p. 35.

[39] Ibid., p. 36.

[40] Stetson, *A Woman's Issue*, p. 9.

[41] See, for instance, Muriel Pierotti, *What We Have and What We Want* (Women's Freedom League, London, n.d. [1925?]) pp. 8, 15.

[42] Stetson, *A Woman's Issue*, pp. 9–10.

[43] Pierotti, *What We Have and What We Want*. Muriel Pierotti later served as General Secretary of the National Union of Women Teachers, 1940–61, subsequently publishing a history of the union (*The Story of the National Union of Women Teachers*, London, 1963).

Cole were eloquent about the changes they wanted to see and regarded as crucial,[44] but this should not lead us to underestimate the scale of those changes which had undoubtedly been effected.

The 1930s were inauspicious in many ways for feminism. Writing in 1935, Winifred Holtby attempted to 'take stock' of progress, concluding that this was no easy matter.[45] 'The march of the women', she ventured, 'is never regular, consistent nor universal'; 'It advances in one place while it retreats in others. One individual looks forward, another backward, and the notions of which is "forward" and which is "backward" differ as widely as the directions followed.'[46] The social policies and ideas about the family being experimented with in Russia, Holtby suggested, might be of vital interest to feminists everywhere, although it was as yet too early to predict their outcome. On the other hand the rise of Fascism in Italy and Germany with its denial of individual liberties was full of portent, its 'cult of the cradle' particularly ominous for women.[47] Writing a few years later, in 1939, Margaret Cole made similar observations about politics and family policies in the Soviet Union and in Germany, observations which were by then infused with an even greater sense of insecurity. 'The position of women in England today can best be described as uncertain', she wrote, and 'No-one knows quite what is likely to happen next.'[48]

The family remains a crucial and yet a highly controversial issue for feminists. Fifty years have passed since Holtby and Cole published their accounts, yet there are disconcerting parallels between the situation they diagnosed and that which we are experiencing today. Many — if not most — of the problems with which earlier generations of feminists attempted to grapple remain with us still.

[44] Margaret Cole, *Marriage, Past and Present* (J. M. Dent, London, 1938), Vera Brittain, *Women's Work in Modern England* (Noel Douglas, London, 1928).

[45] W. Holtby, *Women, and a Changing Civilisation* (1935; Academy Press, Chicago, 1978), p. 182.

[46] Ibid.

[47] Ibid., pp. 182–8; 166–9.

[48] Cole, *Marriage Past and Present*, p. 141.

Index

Index by Isobel McLean